*"Nothing in the past
is dead to the man who would
learn how the present came
to be what it is"*

MAGNA CARTA: THE BIRTH OF ENGLISH LIBERTY

(*See page* 88)

THE STORY
OF THE
BRITISH PEOPLE
IN PICTURES

Edited by
HARLEY V. USILL, B.A.

LONDON
ODHAMS PRESS LIMITED
LONG ACRE, W.C.2

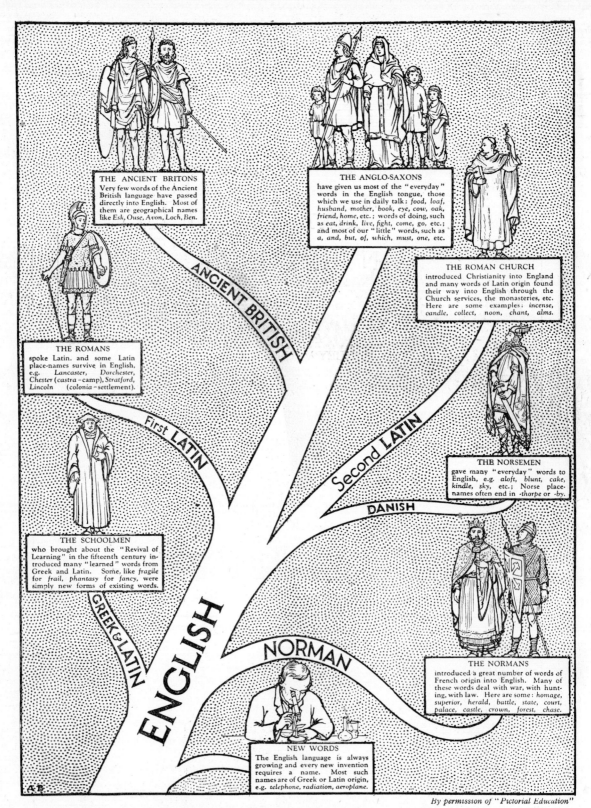

THE ANCIENT BRITONS
Very few words of the Ancient British language have passed directly into English. Most of them are geographical names like *Esk, Ouse, Avon, Loch, Ben*.

THE ANGLO-SAXONS
have given us most of the "everyday" words in the English tongue, those which we use in daily talk: *food, loaf, husband, mother, book, eye, cow, oak, friend, home*, etc.; words of doing, such as *eat, drink, live, fight, come, go*, etc.; and most of our "little" words, such as *a, and, but, of, which, must, one*, etc.

THE ROMAN CHURCH
introduced Christianity into England and many words of Latin origin found their way into English through the Church services, the monasteries, etc. Here are some examples: *incense, candle, collect, noon, chant, alms*.

THE ROMANS
spoke Latin. and some Latin place-names survive in English, e.g. *Lancaster, Dorchester, Chester* (castra = camp), *Stratford, Lincoln* (colonia = settlement).

THE NORSEMEN
gave many "everyday" words to English, e.g. *aloft, blunt, cake, kindle, sky*, etc.; Norse place-names often end in *-thorpe* or *-by*.

THE SCHOOLMEN
who brought about the "Revival of Learning" in the fifteenth century introduced many "learned" words from Greek and Latin. Some, like *fragile* for *frail, phantasy* for *fancy*, were simply new forms of existing words.

THE NORMANS
introduced a great number of words of French origin into English. Many of these words deal with war, with hunting, with law. Here are some: *homage, superior, herald, battle, state, court, palace, castle, crown, forest, chase*.

NEW WORDS
The English language is always growing and every new invention requires a name. Most such names are of Greek or Latin origin, e.g. *telephone, radiation, aeroplane*.

ANCIENT BRITISH

First LATIN

Second LATIN

DANISH

GREEK & LATIN

NORMAN

ENGLISH

By permission of "Pictorial Education"

THE MAKING OF THE ENGLISH LANGUAGE

The above diagram shows some of the sources from which we have obtained many words in daily use.

CONTENTS

GREAT FIGURES OF THE REFORMATION
Here is a symbolic picture of the development of learning, art and science during the Reformation.

BEFORE WE BEGIN

THE world of to-day would be impossible but for the acts, good or evil, of our ancestors. The past is our heritage and our country, our character, our life itself is a gift that we have been compelled to accept and to pass on, with our additions and alterations, to successive generations.

The past is like a never-ending tapestry, begun so long ago that the colours of the earlier parts have faded and the figures grown dim and a little unreal. As it unfolds, however, we begin to recognise more: the knights and the ladies, the kings and the commoners seem less strange, and their clothes and general appearance not so angular and fantastic.

But these outstanding figures are not the only ones in our tapestry. Behind them are thousands of others, of men and animals, of ships and houses, of farms and cities—a living, pulsating background: the very texture of existence.

We ought to feel warmly towards those less prominent people, busy at their tasks, for they are our ancestors, our great-grandfathers. They were flesh and blood. They lived and died and had their cares and pleasures as we do to-day. For we, no less than they, are part of history, and their lives, like ours, were not always concerned with the conflicts of kings or the decisions of parliaments, but more often with the lesser events that go to make up existence—the household bills, a removal, or the effect of the weather on the newly-sown fields.

The past is teeming with human interest of every description. There is love and laughter, sadness and cruelty, high ideals and the lowest forms of human degradation, and withal, the endless struggle of the mass of the people to free themselves from servitude.

Out of that struggle, out of those tangled myriads of lives, we have emerged as we are to-day, and only by looking backwards can we understand our position in regard to the world in which we live. It is as if the threads that link our personalities with the past stretch back unbroken to the very beginning of time—the warp of our tapestry, without which no brightly coloured histories could ever have been woven.

This book has been made to emphasise the pageantry of the past. We have tried to enable you to see history rather than to read it. Therefore, in this book, the text has been reduced to the minimum necessary to make the picture story intelligible. For the rest, the pictures with their accompanying captions, unfold one of the most wonderful stories in the world.

It opens long ago, before the time of recorded history when man was living in caves and had only the crudest implements with which to combat the attacks of beasts and enemies, and it traces the slow growth development of our race through the vicissitudes that have threatened, from time to time, to thrust us backwards into savagery again.

Here are the Romans, who came to conquer and to civilise, but who had to return home to fight the enemies at their own gates, leaving behind a country exposed to the ravages of the plundering pirates of the north. Christianity comes to Britain—a feebly flickering flame, in constant danger of extinction—and here is another conquest, by William of Normandy, that reorganised our country and represents, with the birth of the feudal system, a vital turning point in our history.

Now starts a procession of kings, weak or strong, wise or foolish; and we can see the violent contrasts in the happiness of their people : now an age of wars, disease and desolation, now a glorious period of romance and discovery. Onwards they pass and ever the development, though gradual, is sure.

Tudor, Stuart, Hanoverian—dynasties rise and fall—and now we are nearly at modern times. Here is the coming of machinery—with all the accompanying horrors of its infancy, that make the social history of the nineteenth century one of the blackest pages of all in our story. Victoria has ascended the throne, and, faster and faster, the speed of life increases, onward and upward, until we catch up with our own age and can stop to look back again at the mistakes, the achievements, the retrogressions and the advances that have all played their part in our present civilisation.

There is a tendency among some of us to-day to despise this civilisation of ours. If anyone is tempted to do so, let him or her consider what advantages we possess over other peoples; let him think for a moment what might have been if men and women of the past had not sacrificed their lives to give us what we have to-day. It is only by seeing how things came about that we may appreciate them—how much, indeed, there is to appreciate! Freedom, not from laws, because, living as we do in a society of people that would be impossible, but, far more important, freedom to *think!*

Let us see the good and the bad things of the past, let us compare them with what is happening to-day and remember, in turning over these pages that each one of us is now making history.

THE EDITOR

From the picture by A. Forestier   *By permission of "The Illustrated London News"*

A CAVE-MAN OF HALF-A-MILLION YEARS AGO

Here in his lonely cave sits one of man's earliest ancestors, who lived about half-a-million years ago. He is a hunter, and around him are scattered the relics of many successful hunts. The man, himself, dressed only in an animal's skin, is busy making a stone weapon by chipping the edges of one stone with another.

IN THE BEGINNING

" If we go back far enough in the story of man, we reach a time when he possessed nothing whatever but his hands with which to protect himself, satisfy his hunger, and meet all his other needs. He must have been without speech and unable even to build a fire. There was no one to teach him anything."—PROFESSOR J. H. BREASTED.

WHEN we look at the wonders of modern civilisation—aeroplanes, telephones, wireless, motor-cars, and numberless other miracles of our mechanical age—we feel a natural pride, but how many of us stop to think of the achievements of people who lived many thousands of years before civilisation, as we know it to-day, began ?

WHAT IS TIME ?

Have you ever stopped to consider what is meant by TIME ? No human being can possibly fully understand its meaning, but Dr. H. W. Van Loon has attempted to explain it in the following graphic manner :—

" High up in the north in the land called Svithjod, there stands a rock. It is a hundred miles high and a hundred miles wide. Once every thousand years a little bird comes to this rock to sharpen its beak. When the rock has thus been worn away, then a single day of eternity will have gone by."

What a magnificent conception of time, and yet what a staggering thought. The mind reels at such a picture of eternity, especially when we remember that man's occupation of the earth is probably only about 500,000 years, that recorded history extends for not more than 7,000-8,000 years, and that the known history of Great Britain is little more than 2,000 years.

AN ETERNAL QUESTION

From time immemorial man has asked the question, " How did the whole thing start ? " Gazing at the heavens on a glorious starlit night he has been struck with awe and has sought for an explanation of countless universes, each complete in itself. In other words, he has sought a First Cause. Fortunately, the historian is not required to answer this eternal question ; he must leave a solution to each man's selection of the theory which makes the most appeal. The historian is only concerned with man on his arrival, and in the absence of definite records, not the manner of his creation.

Whether there was a separate creation of man according to the story given in the Book of Genesis, or whether, as Darwin maintains, man has evolved from a lower form of life, are questions which do not concern us here—we start where we first find human beings, and by collecting available evidence, attempt to portray the probable mode of life of early man and the stages by which he attained what we are pleased (or conceited) to call civilisation.

LIFE IN THE STONE AGES

Most of our knowledge to-day is the result of building upon what we already know : one discovery is made, and this leads naturally to a further development or improvement. But when we go back to the people of the Stone Age, we discover that they could have possessed little experience upon which to draw. Every advance which they made was as the result of personal experience, and once they had made a discovery, and only then, were they able to pass this knowledge on to their successors. If we thoroughly appreciate this, it will help us to obtain a clearer idea of what the Stone Ages have contributed to human progress. It is a story of man's struggle to survive, the triumph of the human mind over the lesser intelligence of the animal world, and of his finding means by which he could defeat the rigours of early climatic conditions. For man in his early stages, and before he had learned to cultivate or to domesticate animals, was a hunter, and if he failed to kill, he and his family died of starvation.

MAN'S FRIEND—FIRE

Human progress may be said to have really begun with the discovery of fire, of which the uses increased in the same ratio as human culture itself. Lightning was probably man's first experience of fire, and we can imagine him seated fearful as he watches the spectacle of streaks of flame playing on the thick forest tree tops, and often, maybe, setting fire to large tracts of dry wood. Terror stricken he would flee from that which in due time was to prove one of his greatest friends—fire. But comparatively early in man's history he must have discovered how to kindle fire for himself, or he could never have survived. Doubtless this discovery was due to the accidental rubbing together of pieces of stone—the sparks therefrom setting fire to the dry undergrowth of the forest. This probably occurred many times before early man appreciated the law of cause and effect and realised that he had discovered the secret of kindling fire for himself. Had he but known, he had also discovered the secret of electricity—friction—but mankind had to wait many thousands of years before this secret was appreciated and put to practical use.

THE FIRST CAVE-MAN

Towards the end of the Early Stone Age, the ice round the North Pole and the Alps crept farther and farther southward until the greater part of Europe was covered. As the climate became colder and the conditions of living an open and exposed life more acutely uncomfortable, the people were compelled to seek new homes, and these they found in caves which gave them protection from the cold and from wild beasts. The Late Stone Men, with their improved tools, learned by repeated experiment how to build houses, and traces have been found of lake dwellings. The growth of civilisation begets a demand for comforts, and dishes, bowls and jars belonging to this period have been unearthed.

MAN SETTLES DOWN

As men began to settle down in their lake villages or land homes, they showed less inclination to travel on long and dangerous hunting expeditions. Thus in course of time they learned the use of various seeds and wild grasses. These seeds the women crushed between two stones and made into cakes. Afterwards they learned to plant seeds, and this marks the beginning of agriculture. Further, they tamed some of the wild animals—the dog, the goat, the sheep, cattle, and finally the horse. The roving savage had now become a farmer or shepherd. Instead of ceaselessly roving in search of food with no fixed abode, " home," however rude according to our modern conceptions, became the centre of family life.

Much progress as we have seen has been made since man first appeared on the world's surface, but with all this, these Stone Age people still lacked three essentials for further advance

towards a state of civilisation as we understand it to-day. These were :

(a) *Writing*.—Although the Stone Age man had learned to talk, he had not yet discovered any means by which he could give permanent expression to his speech and thought, although he did paint scenes in his caves, some of which, as shown in the picture on the opposite page, have been discovered during excavations.

(b) *Metals*.—Here again he was very seriously handicapped. Rough stone weapons were good enough in a savage state of development, but until the discovery of metals he was unable to undertake such a task as the building of the Pyramids, which could have been made possible only by the use of more durable tools than those employed by the Stone Age men.

(c) *Sailing Ships*.—Even if the Stone Age men had discovered writing and metals, trade would still have been restricted to the requirements of the people in their own immediate neighbourhood, since they had not yet invented ships which would take them to other lands to carry on a more extensive trade.

These three great discoveries were made by the Egyptians, Babylonians and Assyrians, who lived on the fertile banks of the Nile or in the plains between the rivers Tigris and Euphrates. Here, for thousands of years before any recorded incident in British history, these people were living civilised lives, while the inhabitants of Britain were still savages. Then arose Greece and Rome, and it is to the influence of the latter that the subsequent history of Britain belongs.

In viewing the history of the past, a word of warning is necessary. Too often, our view is distorted by conditions as they exist to-day. To understand properly we must attempt to place ourselves in the position of those we are trying to understand—to view events as *they* saw them. Finally, history is the story of the law of cause and effect. Great events are recorded and assigned a date, but he who would obtain the greatest pleasure out of the most fascinating of all studies—the Story of Man—will look for the causes. Why did the Romans come to Britain ? Why did Henry II murder Becket ? What caused Henry VIII to seek six wives ? Why did the Great War commence on that fateful day in 1914 ? Look for the cause and history becomes as fascinating as the greatest novel ever written.

From the picture by A. Forestier   *By permission of "The Illustrated London News"*

SKIN-CLOTHED ARTISTS DECORATING THEIR CAVES

Hunting was the only life they knew and, therefore, it was natural that all their pictures should be of animals which not only provided them with food, but if they were not wary, threatened their very existence.

From the picture by A. Forestier   *By permission of "The Illustrated London News"*

AN ARTIST'S WORK IN BONE 15,000 YEARS AGO.

He is much better clothed than his predecessor on page 8.   He has learnt to carve in bone, and the example in his hand is worthy of the most skilful craftsman.   Note the picture of the horse in the background.

From the drawing by Paul Hardy   *By permission of "Pictorial Education"*

AN INVENTION WHICH HAS CHANGED THE WORLD

How did man first think of wheels ? Many of man's inventions were shown to him by Nature. But the wheel was his own idea. The wheel began as a slice of tree-trunk pulled along an unmade track. Much later he conceived the idea of adding spokes. To-day it is important on the ground, in the sea, and in the air. The existence of the wheel, like the law of gravity in its simplest form, is one of those things which we take for granted; but the invention or discovery of which has changed the whole course of human life.

From the painting by F. Cormon *Rischgitz*

HUNTING FOR FOOD IN THE LATER ICE AGE

Imagine the semi-tropical climate which our early ancestors enjoyed. Imagine forests with nimble monkeys playing in the trees, great lumbering elephants and prowling bears, in fact, every kind of wild animal or beautiful bird. Then an extraordinary thing happened. Immense masses of ice began pushing their way southwards from the Polar regions. When this period was at its height, the greater part of England was smothered by ice. The burden of the ice was so heavy that the British Isles began to sink and the valley connecting England with the Continent became flooded—thus forming the English Channel. Here we see a family, with bow and arrow, hunting for food during the Later Ice Age. Food, under such adverse conditions, is scarce and a poor shot may mean many days of hunger. The bow and arrow is a definite advance on stone weapons. The artist has portrayed well the anxiety of husband and wife who must kill before they eat.

From the drawing by Paul Hardy   *By permission of "Pictorial Education"*

A BUSY FOUNDRY IN THE BRONZE AGE

These men of the Bronze Age are busily at work making spear heads, daggers and swords. We have mentioned on page 13 the importance of the discovery of the wheel. The discovery of metal and the introduction of smelting were no less important. Without metal and the knowledge of smelting, we should have no sharp knives, no strong fine tools such as chisels, axes, pins and needles. Imagine a world without metal. There would be no railways, ships or aeroplanes—telephones and wireless would be unknown. Great engineering feats, such as the Sydney Bridge in Australia or the great Aswan Dam would have been impossible of achievement. Wood and stone would have remained our only materials. Modern man owes a deep debt of gratitude to the first men who eventually arrived at epoch-making discoveries, many of which they did not understand, or the necessity for adjusting to our modern usages had not arisen in these far-off days.

From the painting by F. Cormon   *Rischgitz*

FISHING IN THE BRONZE AGE

Most of the early inventions and discoveries came from the East, where civilisation developed much faster than in Western Europe. Somewhere in the near East it had been discovered that copper mixed with tin in the appropriate proportion of ten per cent. tin to ninety per cent. copper, produced a substance which we call bronze. This was much harder than copper and its discovery enabled very much better weapons and tools to be made. The earliest bronze articles came into Britain from the Continent, but in time, and with the help of continental teachers, bronze was manufactured in Britain. Life is now becoming very much more civilised, and we see the beginning of the desire for luxuries which distinguishes the civilised man from the savage. Pottery, as can be seen in the picture on page 17, advanced considerably. Here we see the sort of people who lived in those days. They are hauling in their catch of fish.

From the painting by F. Cormon   *Rischgitz*

A PROUD POTTER OF THE BRONZE AGE

This proud husband is examining the pottery produced by his wife.   The busy scene illustrates the fact that
life is now becoming more settled.   Note the hand-made axe in the man's belt.   Since man, even in these
early days, could not live peaceably with his neighbours, he found it necessary to invent means whereby he
could protect himself from the weapons of his enemies.   The invention of bronze enabled him to construct a
shield, which, with deft handling, was a better protection against arrows to the type made of wood and hide.

From the painting by F. Corman   *Rischgitz*

HUNTING IN THE IRON AGE

The Iron Age began in Europe about 500 B.C., thus opening the dawn of a new era. The discovery of how to work iron was made somewhere in Western Asia, and reached Britain when the Celts invaded our shores. The Celts were a tall, fair people who had become numerous and powerful in Central Europe, and owing to their contact with Mediterranean peoples had advanced to a higher form of civilisation than the Germans or Scandinavians. Large bands of them moved into France, Spain and Northern Italy, while others crossed the Channel to settle in Britain. They brought with them their chariots and cavalry, a fact which was to cause Julius Cæsar considerable trouble when he came about five hundred years later. Iron mines were worked in the Wealde Forest, in the Forest of Dean and in Northamptonshire. Considerable trading was carried on with the Continent, and Greek merchants from as far away as Marseilles visited our shores.

From the picture by A. Forestier   *By permission of "The Illustrated London News"*

A PRE-HISTORIC LAKE VILLAGE NEAR GLASTONBURY

The above picture of a lake village, built during the Iron Age, was probably occupied as late as 100 B.C. The high palisade surrounding it served to keep off any unwelcome visitors, whether man or beast.

From the painting by Hippolyte Coutou   Rischgitz

LAKE DWELLERS RETURNING FROM THE HUNT
The first boat that man ever used was probably a fallen tree trunk floating down a river or stream. In course of time he thought of the idea of hollowing out this tree trunk and of propelling himself with a pole.

From the picture by A. Forestier
By permission of "The Illustrated London News"

INTERIOR OF A HUT IN GLASTONBURY LAKE VILLAGE
The discovery of fire made possible such a comfortable domestic scene as that depicted in the picture.

THE ANCIENT BRITON—NOT MERELY A WOAD-PAINTED SAVAGE

Here are some typical scenes in the daily life of the ancient Britons. Note the cock-fighting and dice-playing.

From the painting by Sir Frederick Leighton   *Rischgitz*

PHŒNICIANS TRADING WITH EARLY BRITONS

Here in this famous picture we see Phœnician traders bartering their wares for the valuable skin which the Briton is holding up for admiration.   The women folk are obviously interested in the richly-coloured clothes which these merchants have brought with them from the East.   Trade was carried on by means of barter, and the Phœnician is probably indicating that his cloth is worth at least two such British skins.   These early Britons were skilful traders, however, so maybe one skin will suffice to procure the new dress material for their women.   The first recorded date in British history, 325 B.C., marks the visit of a Greek merchant, Pytheas. Pytheas is said by another Greek writer named Polybius to have personally explored a large part of Britain.

THE ROMANS IN BRITAIN

" When Britain became a Roman province, it became a member of civilised society. It entered 'history' in the full and complete sense of the word."

MANKIND lived in Britain for thousands of years before any contemporary records of history were made, but while mighty empires were rising and falling in the East, and a standard of culture reached which, even to-day, we look back upon with admiration, the peoples of the West were still living in a state of comparative barbarism. The absence of written records makes it extremely difficult to obtain any exact information about our early ancestors, but science comes to our aid with a few facts (not dates) which enable us to piece together something of a story.

BRITAIN BECOMES AN ISLAND

Far away back in the distant past, the distribution of land and water over the earth's surface was very different from what it is now. Yet such is the nature of things, that even during that remote period, the Industrial Revolution which occurred in Britain a mere hundred and fifty years ago was being prepared. Vegetation was gradually being fossilised into that coal which thousands of years later was to make Britain the first of the great industrial nations of the modern world. Again, for hundreds of thousands of years, Britain was a part of what we call the continent of Europe, and the Thames was actually a tributary of the Rhine. Then some great cataclysm of nature took place, and the Channel was formed which ever since has separated these islands from Europe—an event which in due time necessitated the building of a mighty navy to defend the liberties of an island people.

THE YEARS BEFORE CÆSAR

Then followed thousands of years occupied by the successive Stone and Bronze Ages, during which time Stonehenge was built—probably about 1,000 B.C. Then came the Celts (about 600 B.C.) who, with improved iron weapons, conquered the bronze-using tribes whom they found in possession. It was these people who introduced the mysterious priesthood, the Druids, an account of which is given on page 26.

About 325 B.C. a Greek merchant called Pytheas came to our shores and has left behind the earliest written account of the existence of these islands. He visited Cornwall and Kent, and was particularly impressed by the abundance of wheat. The tin mines of Cornwall had also become famous and attracted foreigners in search of trade. As early as 150 B.C. some of the southern British tribes had a gold coinage which they had copied from the kings of Macedon, and during the fifty or sixty years before the coming of Cæsar they were in close contact with their neighbours of Northern Gaul. Thus we see that —on the southern coast, at any rate—the early Britons had reached a stage of civilisation which does not merit the term " painted savages " which is too often applied, although in other parts of Briton the term could be more justly used. But the earliest period must have been occupied by tribal warfare, and apart from the occasional rising of a strong chief who would temporarily hold together several tribes, there was no element of unity—the first requisite of nationhood.

JULIUS CÆSAR COMES TO BRITAIN

Why Cæsar came to Britain is not quite certain. Two reasons have been suggested, either of which may be true. It has been suggested that he intended to punish the Britons for the help which they had been giving to the Gauls—an assistance which considerably impeded his military campaign. The Gauls were undoubtedly receiving grain and weapons from Britain, and it is probable that Cæsar felt that such help would undermine a final conquest of the Gauls, who had already appeared more stubborn in their resistance than had been anticipated. Or, with the Imperator's laurels as a prize ever before his eyes, he may have considered the effect on the Roman populace of adding yet another territory to the mighty Roman Republic when he should return in triumph to Rome. The truth is probably a combination of the two suggestions, but Cæsar himself is silent on the point. Of Gaul he was able to say, " Veni-vide-vice " (" I came, I saw, I conquered "), but in the case of Britain he came and saw but he did not conquer. In fact, he found the resistance of the Britons on his two visits in 55 B.C. and 54 B.C. rather more than he had expected, and he soon realised that a mere punitive expedition would not suffice to conquer permanently these islands.

As a military undertaking, Cæsar's first visit to Britain was a failure, since he took too small a force, and scarcely moved inland more than ten miles from the Straits of Dover. Also, his fleet was badly damaged when it had been beached, and fearful lest he might be cut off from his base in Gaul, he hurriedly withdrew his forces. In the following year, having spent the winter months in equipping a bigger force and fleet, he returned, and after winning several battles he forded the Thames and penetrated the territory of Hertfordshire. An interesting feature of this campaign is the use of the chariot by the Britons. Although not permanently effective against the trained cavalry of the Roman legions, it occasioned some considerable havoc. It is not quite certain at what date the wheeled chariot was introduced in Britain, but since the invention of the wheel represents an advanced step of civilisation, it is probable that the Britons

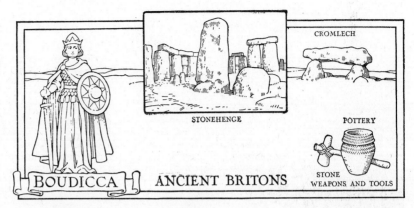

BOUDICCA   ANCIENT BRITONS

STONEHENGE

CROMLECH

POTTERY

STONE WEAPONS AND TOOLS

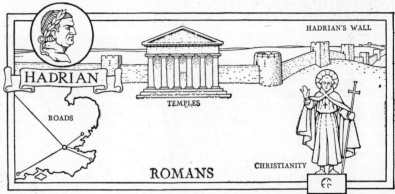

HADRIAN   ROMANS

ROADS

TEMPLES

HADRIAN'S WALL

CHRISTIANITY

ÆLFRED   ANGLES, SAXONS AND NORSEMEN

SHIPS

CHURCHES

AGRICULTURE

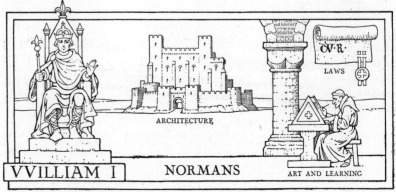

VVILLIAM I   NORMANS

ARCHITECTURE

LAWS

ART AND LEARNING

A FESTIVAL OF THE DRUIDS

The Druids were a highly organised caste of priests who, both in Gaul and Britain, held unchallenged power over the people. Cæsar tells us that they were judges in all disputes, whether between tribes or individuals, and that they practised human sacrifice and held the mistletoe to be sacred. Cæsar had no time to deal with them, but when the Romans returned in A.D. 43, these religious practices were abolished.

acquired it from early trading relations with the people bordering the Mediterranean.

CÆSAR RETURNS HOME

In the midst of this campaign, Cæsar learned of the political troubles which were arising in Rome and which, if he were to take advantage of them, necessitated his immediate return. The withdrawal of the legions marked the end of this attempt at military conquest, but the beginning of peaceful penetration of Roman culture which definitely brought Britain into the sphere of continental society.

Britain was to profit in no small degree by the next hundred years—probably the most important in the history of the world. G. M. Trevelyan writes of this as follows :—

"While Cæsar was being murdered and avenged, while the loves of Antony and Cleopatra were raising the question of the relations of east and west inside the Roman world, while Augustus was cannily constructing the empire, while Christ was preaching and while Paul was being converted, far in the north Roman traders and colonists, working from the base of the Latinised province of Gaul, were establishing settlements in the interior of Britain and gaining influence at the courts of its tribal kings."

One of these tribal kings, Cumobelin, whom Shakespeare has immortalised as Cymbeline, had reached such power between A.D. 5 to 40 that he had himself styled on his gold coinage " Rex Brittonum." This proud boast, and the use of the Roman language, clearly indicated the subtle influence of Roman culture, and it was probably during his reign that London began to exist, serving as an ideal centre for ever-increasing trade with Europe. The principal exports of Roman Britain were tin, skins, slaves, pearls, and grain.

THE ROMANS RETURN TO CONQUER

Such was the condition of Britain until the Romans returned to conquer under the Emperor Claudius in A.D. 43. He organised an army of four legions, and in the summer the army set sail and landed in Britain, where the Emperor joined his forces a little later. A series of small battles was fought in the country along the River Thames till the camp of the most powerful of the British chieftains at Colchester was captured. This broke the back of the resistance of the tribes of the south-east, but it was not until A.D. 82 that the country was completely conquered. Caractacus was one of the most famous of the tribal leaders who stubbornly fought against the advance of the Romans. During this long period of resistance—thirty-nine years—many tribes revolted against the Roman rule, and the most serious of these occurred in A.D. 61 when the Iceni, a warlike tribe, rose under the leadership of their queen, Boudicca (Boadicea).

During times of warfare, little can be done in the way of building up a country. But when the Britons had been pacified the real work of making Britain a Roman province began. Julius Agricola, a great Roman governor, during the period A.D. 78 to 85 established permanent military garrisons in well-chosen localities. He en-couraged the use of the Latin language, the adoption of the Roman dress, the building of temples, public baths and private dwelling houses, and the adoption by the people of the civilised Roman ways. Soldiers, when they had finished their military service, often settled in Britain with their families, and many Romans who visited the new province for purposes of trade decided to remain. This all led to a big increase in trade, and towns began to be built, remains of which have been found in many parts of the country. The cities and camps were connected by excellent roads extending over the length and breadth of the island.

THE POWER OF ROME DECAYS

In spite of this great advance in civilisation, there were forces at work which suggested that the Roman system was decaying. Two main causes contributed to the decline of Roman Britain. Firstly, and this was common to the whole Roman Empire, the Romans were becoming very wealthy, and with this increase of wealth they became less efficient in the arts of government. And secondly, they were called

After Armitage   *Rischgitz*

CÆSAR'S FIRST INVASION OF BRITAIN

Much to his surprise, Cæsar met with stern opposition from the Britons on the two occasions when he attempted to conquer the country. If he had not been compelled to return hurriedly to Rome, the Roman conquest of Britain might have gone to his credit, instead of which, it was nearly one hundred years later that the real conquest of the Britons by the Romans began. Note the Roman standard in the background.

upon to defend the frontiers of the Empire against the barbarian races outside the borders. In Britain, as early as about A.D. 140, Hadrian was compelled to build his famous wall from the Solway to the Tyne, in order to keep back the turbulent northern tribes. Later, the Franks and the Saxons ravaged the south-east coast from the sea ; the Scots from the north of Ireland made frequent descents upon the north-west coast ; and the Picts and Caledonians still invaded the province as they had in the time of Hadrian. In 368 we hear of marauders capturing slaves and cattle within a few miles of London. Obviously, the might of Rome was beginning to weaken. But affairs were even more serious in Italy, where the Empire was fighting a life-and-death struggle against the Goths. All available troops were required and more and more troops were withdrawn from Britain, until in 410 the Emperor Honorius wrote from Italy urging the cities of Britain to provide for their own defence. Deprived of its military garrisons and deserted by its Emperor, Britain ceased to be a Roman province.

THE GROANS OF THE BRITONS

For a period of about 200 years after the abandonment of Britain by the Romans, there is an almost complete blank in British history. Practically nothing is known about the state of the country during this period, although it appears obvious that the Britons relapsed into a state of barbarism. This is easily explained by

After Prell   Rischgitz

DRUIDS RECEIVING SPOILS TAKEN FROM THE ROMANS

From the picture by K. von Piloty

Rischgitz

THE MURDER OF JULIUS CÆSAR

Brutus had been persuaded by Cassius and his fellow-plotters that Cæsar must be put to death to make Rome free. The conspirators seized an opportunity when Cæsar went to the capital to the meeting of the Senate. They presented a petition which Cæsar refused. Whereupon he is murdered—Cassius striking the first and Brutus, his dearest friend, the last blows. Thus ended the life of a man who planned to rule the world.

the fact that while the Romans governed their provinces efficiently, they did not teach the natives how to govern themselves, or even how to defend themselves. Thus, when the Romans departed, the Britons were left helpless. The following two extracts from a description of Gildas, who lived in Britain and wrote about A.D. 550, are the nearest we have to the history of these times :—

"After this, Britain is left deprived of all her soldiery and armed bands, of her cruel governors, and of the flower of her youth who went with Mariunus, but never again returned ; and utterly ignorant as she was of the art of war, she groaned in amazement for many years under the cruelty of two foreign nations—the Scots from the north-west and the Picts from the north.

"Again, therefore, the wretches' remnant, sending to Actius, a powerful Roman citizen, address him as follows : ' To Actius, now consul for the third time : the groans of the Britons,' and again a little further, thus : ' The barbarians drive us to the sea ; the sea throws us back on the

barbarians ; thus two modes of death await us : we are either slain or drowned."

A BRITISH REVOLUTION

Another historian, Zosimus the Greek, tells us that the Britons, when the Roman military forces withdrew, deposed the magistrates and proclaimed their own independence. They obviously felt that it was useless to remain under the governance of a power that was no longer able to protect them. They split up into a series of individual domestic governments, each controlling a separate state. When the news of this reached the emperor Honorius, he is said to have written to the governors of these states with directions 'to provide for their own defence'—thus shelving all responsibility and in a sense releasing them from their allegiance.

The might of Rome had vanished and no help was forthcoming to the Britons in their dire need. "The Roman," says Haverfield, " has passed from Britain as though he had never been. He has left us no name on hill or river ; he has not even bequeathed a few drops of Roman blood."

By courtesy Messrs. Metro-Goldwyn-Mayer

ROMAN GALLEYS ROWING IN LINE AHEAD

The first is a great trireme with three " banks " of oars, the second a bireme with only two.   At the prow
and on the water-line is the ram or beak. Ships were rowed by slaves, and carried more soldiers than sailors.

From the picture by D. MacPherson　　　　　　　　　　　　　　*By permission of "Pictorial Education"*

QUEEN BOUDICCA INCITING THE BRITONS TO REVOLT

The Romans did not have things all their own way when they landed in Britain in A.D. 43. There were many uprisings throughout the country, but the most important, and one which nearly succeeded, was that of Boudicca, whose statue is on the Thames Embankment. Some of the Roman soldiery committed acts of extreme cruelty, and the British womenfolk had suffered many indignities, the queen herself being scourged and her two daughters dishonoured. The whole tribe of the Iceni (modern Norfolk and Suffolk) rose in arms, and were joined by the neighbouring tribes of Essex (A.D. 60). But the superior military genius of Rome prevailed against the wild fury of the Britons; Boudicca, who escaped from the battlefield, died soon after.

From the drawing by Ernest Board   *By permission of "Pictorial Education"*

CARACTACUS—ANOTHER BRAVE BRITISH CHIEF

When a Roman emperor had won a victory his captives were shown to the people. Here we see Caratacus, a British chief, in a triumphal procession. When he was brought before the Emperor he said, "If my punishment is death, I shall be forgotten. But if you spare my life, I shall be a lasting memorial to your mercy." The Emperor saw the wisdom of this and pardoned him and his family. The Romans were cruel, either killing their prisoners outright, or offering them to wild beasts in the presence of the multitude.

From the fresco by W. Bell-Scott   *Rischgitz*

BUILDING A ROMAN WALL

Not only were the Romans fully occupied during the early stages of the conquest of the turbulent British, but they met a considerable amount of trouble from the raids of the Picts and the Scots in the north. These people crossed the border from Scotland to steal cattle and plunder generally. Such was the nature of the country, that the Romans soon realised that the conquest and settlement of Scotland was likely to be too lengthy a business to make it worth while. They therefore built a wall from the Clyde to the Forth to keep back these fierce tribesmen. Another wall was built from the Solway to the mouth of the Tyne. Forts were placed at intervals of about a mile throughout its length of eighty-two miles. The Scots were held back, but not conquered. When the Romans left England they swarmed over the border, fighting and plundering throughout the neighbourhood.

Donald McLeish

THE REMAINS OF A ROMAN WALL
This picture shows one of the most perfect parts of the wall near Housesteads, Northumberland, as it is to-day.

From the drawing by Paul Hardy

By permission of " Pictorial Education "

"ALL ROADS LEAD TO ROME"
The Romans were among the greatest road-makers that the world has ever known. The picture shows a Roman legion and some of the conquered Britons at work on a new road. A road of this kind, with its irregularly-shaped paving stones, is very different from those of the present day, yet many such roads form the foundation upon which modern ones have been built. The remains of several Roman roads are still in use.

THE FIRST PREACHING OF CHRISTIANITY IN BRITAIN

Christianity came to England some time in the first century, but at first made little headway against the religion of the Druids. Augustine's mission, landing on the Isle of Thanet in 597 was the first organised effort at conversion. In the top picture we see the first baptism; in the bottom a priest is seeking refuge with a Christian family. .

A CONVERTED FAMILY SHELTERING A PRIEST FROM THE DRUIDS

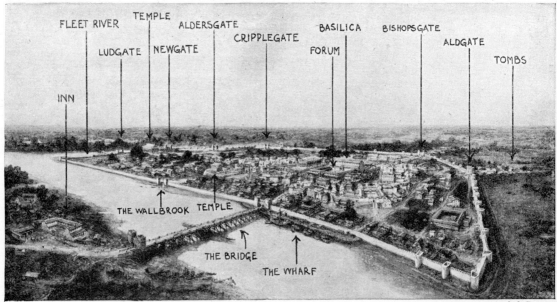

From a drawing by A. Forestier   *By permission of M. Forestier*

WHAT LONDON MAY HAVE LOOKED LIKE BEFORE THE ROMANS LEFT

Although London became finally the greatest city in Britain under the Romans, it was a very tiny place compared with the London of to-day, as can be seen if the area shown in the above picture be compared with a map of present-day London. The city was surrounded largely by woods and marshes, crossed here and there by the great military roads. The city itself was defended by a wall the thickness and height of which made it difficult for an enemy to attack it successfully. Notice the position of the gates whose names are still in use to-day.

Courtesy: Great Western Railway

ROMAN BATHS BUILT IN THE FIRST CENTURY A.D.

These old Roman baths are still fed by hot springs that well up from the limestone rocks beneath the city of Bath at a temperature of 120°F. Near the bath shown here were hot air baths and cooling rooms where the Romans could take their ease. The hot springs are famous for their curative powers and are still visited by invalids.

From the Dresden Museum   *Rischgitz*

A ROMAN PORK BUTCHER'S SHOP

From the British Museum   *Rischgitz*

ROMAN KITCHEN UTENSILS

With the landing of the Romans, England was linked with the civilisation of the continent. Art, commerce and a code of laws were firmly established and a permanent influence left on English culture.

From the picture by A. Forestier

By permission of M. Forestier

A MARKET IN ROMAN LONDON

London had its busy market in Roman times, whither came merchants from Gaul and Rome, and even from distant Tyre and Carthage. In the foreground we see a British girl being sold as a slave. Perhaps, like the English slaves shown in the picture on page 44, she is destined to be sold again in the slave market at Rome. A Roman slave was owned completely by his master, who had powers of life and death over him; but " it was not such a slavery as we have known in modern times for stripes and bonds were rare."

From the picture by J. L. Gerome   *Rischgitz*

ROME—THE MIGHTY

The gladiators who appeared in the Roman amphitheatres for the entertainment of the people were professional fighters. When a gladiator was at the mercy of his rival the crowd waved handkerchiefs if they wanted his life to be spared, or, as in the picture, turned down their thumbs if they desired his death. Here the fatal sign is being given by the Priestesses of the Temple of Vesta. Rome was now at the height of her power.

From the painting by Checa   *Mansell*

ROME—THE FALLEN

The power of Rome began to wane as luxurious living at the centre increased. Wealth and licentiousness were poor weapons to fight the fearless bands on the borders of the Empire. Here we see the Huns, led by the famous Attila, pouring into Italy to ravage and pillage. It was necessary to recall the British legions to help against the invaders. Rome as a world power was soon to be no more, but her culture has survived through the ages.

THE DARK AGES

" In the fifth and sixth centuries—that is, between the year 401 and the year 600—South Britain came to be so completely changed that the Romans, if they could have returned, would have been unable to recognise it."

WHEN the Romans withdrew from Britain, the full failure of their system of civilisation was soon realised. While they remained, the ever-increasing petty raids of continental tribes were suppressed by the Roman soldiery, but once they had departed the whole system of government and protection left with them. In other words, the Roman system of civilisation did not take into account the possibility of circumstances which the structure could not control. The Romans, indeed, were so certain of the permanence of the power of the great empire which they had created, that the possibility that mighty foes would arise to wrest their spoils from them never entered their minds ; therefore, no attempts were made to teach a conquered people the arts of self-government—it was, indeed, a superior civilisation transplanted wholesale to a new home. Such a conquered race was enslaved and took no part in the government of the country. So long as they did not rebel, and performed the tasks, such as building roads, walls and bridges, they were treated with justice and a reasonable measure of kindness. Indeed, after a brief period of persecution, even Christianity was tolerated. Not only as far as Britain was concerned was it a military occupation, but such was the climate of southern Britain that it was considered a most desirable place for permanent residence, and hosts of retired Roman civil servants remained in the towns built by the Romans which were models of luxury and comfort. The early Britons, however, were no part of this life, and when the Romans departed they left behind roads, temples and towns, but the usefulness of these passed with them.

The news of the withdrawal of the Roman legions soon spread, and almost immediately pagan tribes of Angles, Saxons and Jutes began

From the picture by Louis Ginnett

PILLAGING A ROMAN CITY

After the departure of the Roman Legions, Saxon hordes devastated Britain. Here we see them pillaging Anderida, a Roman fort built as part of a scheme of defence against Saxon pirates. These heathen tribes were attracted by the riches of the church. They murdered the monks and stole the gold ornaments and sacred vessels.

to land on the shores of Britain. They came at first, not to settle, but to plunder and ravage. They, too, had no use for towns except to pillage, and with the neglect of the Britons and the depredations of invaders, the civilisation of Rome was soon no more—all that remained was a memory, roads that could not be pillaged and the ruins of cities. For nearly two hundred years nothing is known definitely about Britain, but it can be safely assumed that it was a period of almost continual warfare between the numerous British tribes, and also between British tribes and invaders.

THE REAL GIFT OF ROME

Are we to assume then that the Roman occupation of Britain meant nothing ; that it was literally a mere incident, having no permanent affect upon our subsequent history ? Not altogether, for although the Romans had departed, a certain loose contact was maintained with the Britons. The Romans still demanded taxes, which were rarely paid, and it is fairly certain that some trade was still carried on. But what is really important is that the name of Britain, in spite of the terrible troubles which were afflicting Rome, was never forgotten, and nearly two centuries later (A.D. 597), the civilisation of Rome was to return in the person of St. Augustine. The greatest gift of Rome was to be not the military occupation which left nothing of value behind, but the re-introduction of Christianity, an event which was to have a permanent affect upon the whole subsequent history of our race. Christianity had been introduced into Britain during the Roman occupation, but the pagan invaders swept this aside and drove the remnants into Wales, where alone it survived. Before dealing with St. Augustine, however, we must pause to see what had been happening to the Angles, Saxons and Jutes.

PILLAGERS BECOME SETTLERS

Before the year 600, fully one-half of the island had been more or less completely occupied and conquered by the tribes from the Continent, and a number of petty kingdoms had been founded, each under its own ruler. One group of Angles settled in the north-east from the Firth of Forth to the River Humber, forming two kingdoms, Bernicia and Deira, and these were frequently combined into one which was then spoken of as the Kingdom of the Northumbrians. Another group of Angles occupied the district between the Humber and the Wash, forming the Kingdom of Mercia, while still further from the east coast were the North Folk and South Folk, who were together known as the East Angles.

The country to the south of this was occupied by Saxons, except two small districts which were settled by Jutes. The land just north of the Thames was settled by the East Saxons and a branch of these which had gone westward and captured London were known as the Middle Saxons. The land on the extreme south-east had been occupied by Jutes, who became known as Kentishmen. This kingdom extended to the Thames on the north and to the Great Forest on the west. The narrow strip of land between this forest and the Channel on the south was the Kingdom of the South Saxons. The Isle of Wight and the mainland just north of it were early settled by a body of Jutes.

The most important conquerors, however, were the West Saxons, who landed in Southampton Water about A.D. 500, under their leader Cedric, and, in time, they became the strongest and most compact race of the Anglo-Saxon invaders. The seven kingdoms formed by the Northumbrians, Mercians, East Anglians, East Saxons, Kentishmen, South Saxons and West Saxons are often referred to as the Heptarchy, i.e. seven kingdoms, though there was actually no permanent grouping into this number. Sometimes a strong chief would conquer his neighbours and temporarily compel them to acknowledge his rule ; at other times, local rebellions or other causes made the number of independent kingdoms greater.

WHAT WERE OUR ANCESTORS LIKE ?

What were these invaders like ? The early English were as superstitious as other barbarians and their minds were full of mythical heroes, of giants, witches, monsters, and other strange beings belonging to a world not of reality, but of imagination based largely upon fear. They worshipped many gods, the most important of which were Thor and Woden, from the names of whom we get Thursday and Wednesday. In the matter of government, the family or class was important, and the heads of families had much influence. There was no conception of equality among the people, the earls or nobles being clearly distinguished from the Cearls or common people. Slavery was common, and such law as existed was merely an appeal to custom, but on occasions of more than ordinary importance the people gathered themselves into general meetings of the tribe. Trade was almost at a standstill, since tribes living in a natural agricultural state have little need of luxuries and therefore no incentive to exchange any but the bare necessities of life. The great body of the population lived in small villages and the great Roman cities, such as London, York and Canterbury were almost deserted. In fact, England had gone back to much the same state of barbarism as existed before the Roman Conquest, and the work of civilisation had to be begun almost anew.

THE COMING OF CHRISTIANITY

In the spring of the year A.D. 597 there landed on the shores of Kent a Roman priest named Augustine. There is an old story which tells that Pope Gregory when he was a deacon, visited the market place in Rome and there saw some fair-haired slaves for sale. On enquiring who they were he was told that they were Angles from a heathen land. He replied that they looked more like Angels and ought to be rescued from paganism. The sending of Augustine with a small band of missionaries was one of his first tasks when he became Pope. The wife of Ethelbert, king of Kent, was the daughter of the Frankish king who reigned in Paris, and she was a Christian, and had been accompanied to England by a Christian bishop. She therefore welcomed Augustine and persuaded her heathen husband to meet him. Ethelbert received him well and allowed him to make his headquarters at Canterbury.

But for the stubborn survival of paganism in London, this city would have taken the place of Canterbury as the centre of English Christianity. While Ethelbert lived Christianity spread in Kent, but on his death progress was retarded. In Northumbria, however, circumstances were more favourable, for about thirty years after, Edwin obtained the crown of Northumbria and married a Kentish princess who brought with her Pauline, a Kentish priest. After a long struggle he persuaded the Northumbrians to forsake their heathen gods for Christianity, and a church was built at York, which afterwards became York Minster. In spite of relapses into paganism, by A.D. 650 all England except Sussex had become Christian.

THE TRIUMPH OF ROMAN CULTURE

But as the various missionary bodies established themselves in the land, dissensions began to arise. There was a definite clash between the missionaries who came from the Continent and those who came from Wales and Ireland, the remnants of Britons who had escaped successive invasions. Differences existed in the calculation of the date of Easter, in the forms used in baptism, and in the ceremonial cutting of the hair of churchmen. There was a clash, too, between the orderly government of Roman Christianity and the looser system of the early British. The king of Northumbria realised the disadvantages arising out of this lack of unity, and in the year A.D. 664 he invited both parties to a conference at Whitby, when the arguments for the two points of view were stated. After a lengthy discussion, the culture of Rome prevailed against the cruder British Christianity, a result which was to have a tremendous effect upon the future of Britain. It meant that once again Britain was brought into contact with continental culture, and the superior organisation of the Roman Church established a system of bishoprics, parishes and monasteries which served as a pattern to subsequent kings of England for the building of a state organisation of government on similar lines.

THE WORK OF THE CHURCH

The reintroduction of Christianity had another effect which had tremendous influence throughout the Middle Ages, and explains the great power which the Church possessed. Christianity taught that man possessed a soul, and by going a stage further and claiming that the Church possessed the keys of heaven or hell, the priests were able to make even kings and princes obey her will. It was not until the Reformation, which will be discussed in a later chapter, that some of these claims were disputed. Whatever may be thought about the claims of the Church, it cannot be denied that the Church organised the lives of men and women in a reasonable state of society before the State was ready to play its part. The whole of the Poor Law, for instance, was centred round the monasteries, and it was not until the year 1601, during the reign of Queen Elizabeth, that the first secular Poor Law Act was passed. Education, too, was in the hands of the Church, and here a much longer time was to pass before the State introduced the first Education Act in 1870. The most famous early Saxon writer was the Venerable Bede, a monk who lived his whole life writing and thinking in the monastery at Jarrow.

From the drawing by Paul Hardy

By permission of " Pictoria Education "

THE LANDING OF HENGIST AND HORSA

The Anglo-Saxon Chronicle, which is the oldest English history book, tells us about the warriors in this picture. They are Jutes, brothers called Hengist and Horsa, who landed in Britain in the fifth century at the invitation of Vortigern after the Romans had returned to their own country to fight against other barbarian tribes. The Chronicle says : '' Hengist and Horsa invited by Vortigern, king of the Britons, landed in Britain . . . at first in aid of the Britons, but afterwards they fought against them. King Vortigern gave them land in the south-east of this country on condition that they should fight against the Picts. Then they fought against the Picts and had the victory wheresoever they came. They then sent to the Angles ; desired a larger force to be sent, and caused them to be told the worthlessness of the Britons and the excellencies of the land. Then they soon sent thither a larger force in aid of the others.'' Six years later they fought with Vortigern at Aylesford where Horsa was slain.

From the drawing by D. Macpherson   *By permission of "Pictorial Education"*

ST. GREGORY AND THE ENGLISH SLAVES

When St. Gregory visited the market place at Rome he saw some fair haired slaves for sale. He asked who they were, and when told that they were Angles, he replied, " They should be called Angels.   And what is the name of their king ? " " Ælla." " Alleluia shall be sung in Ælla's land," he cried.   When he became Pope he sent St. Augustine to Britain as first Christian missionary with his band of holy " strangers from Rome."

From the drawing by Paul Hardy   *By permission of "Pictorial Education"*

THE LANDING OF ST. AUGUSTINE, A.D. 597

Ethelbert received the monks on the chalk-down above Minster (at approximately the same spot where Hengist landed 150 years before), and though he refused the new religion he promised shelter and protection.

From the painting by Stephen B. Cartill   *Rischgitz*

ST. AUGUSTINE PREACHING TO ETHELBERT AND BERTHA

Seated on an improvised throne, and surrounded by their devoted subjects, Ethelbert, King of Kent, and his beloved wife, are here seen listening to the words of Augustine, who had been sent by St. Gregory to convert Britain to Christianity.   The king had refused to hear them indoors lest they should cast a spell on him.

THE MISSION OF ST. COLUMBA TO THE PICTS :
A.D. 563-592

St. Columba was the Irish missionary who brought Christianity to Scotland. He founded a church and a monastery on the island of Iona (563), and then crossed to the mainland.   Here he is shown preaching to the Pictish king, surrounded by his courtiers. St. Columba died in 597. For some months, during which he had been engaged upon a transcription of the Psalter, he had known that his end was approaching; but he continued his work as usual.   Death came peacefully upon him at the altar of his church.

From the painting by William Hole, R.S.A.   *Mansell*

From the picture by M. Yardley   *By permission of "Pictorial Education"*

THE VENERABLE BEDE FINISHES HIS TASK

Bede lived in the monastery at Jarrow in Anglo-Saxon days. When he was very old he decided to translate the Gospel of St. John into Anglo-Saxon, the language of that time, so that the people could understand it when the monks read it to them. Before the book was finished, Bede became very ill, but he was determined to complete his task. At last the final sentence was written, and the young scribe looked up thankfully. "Now it is finished," said he. "Well, thou hast spoken truth; it is finished," replied the old man, and, praising God with his last breath, he died. He was buried at Jarrow, but his bones were afterwards removed to Durham.

ALFRED VERSUS THE DANES

WE read in the last chapter that the early Britons were unable to withstand the onslaughts of the Angles, Saxons and Jutes, and that these peoples, who at first came merely to pillage, eventually decided to conquer and settle down in Britain. If organised Christianity had not returned, it is impossible to say what would have been the eventual history of this island. Probably, after many centuries of bitter internal warfare, a strong man would have arisen and welded all the tribes into one nation. This, as we shall see, actually occurred, but it was considerably accelerated by the presence of a well-organised Church system of government which served as a pattern for the more enlightened kings to follow.

After Ethelbert's death in 616, there was a brief reaction against Christianity, even in Kent and Essex, but about ten years later, Edwin, king of Northumbria, adopted Christianity, and not long after Wessex did likewise. But the mighty King Penda of Mercia was a determined heathen, and it was not until he died in 655 that Christianity finally triumphed. The Synod of Whitby in 664, as we have already seen, at last decided the form which Christianity was to take.

THE END OF THE SEVEN KINGDOMS

Meanwhile, the kingdoms continued to fight for supremacy. In 685, Egfrith, king of Northumbria, was defeated and killed by the Picts in the disastrous battle of Nectan's Mere, near the Tay, and with him ended the supremacy of Northumbria. Mercia then came to the front. This great kingdom, which originally included all the lands of middle England, was increased by the capture of the West Saxon settlements in the Severn valley. The most famous of her kings were Penda (mentioned above) and Offa. Offa ruled his kingdom with a strong hand—he made war on the Welsh, and took from them Shrewsbury and the surrounding district. To protect these conquests he built an enormous dyke which extended from Chester to Chepstow. But the

Rischgitz

AN EARLY SAXON CHURCH AT ST. ALBAN'S HEAD, DORSET

From the drawing by H. W. Koekkoek   *By permission of "The Illustrated London News"*

MAKERS OF BRITAIN: A NORSE INVADER
A fine portrait of a leader of the savage raiders who nearly extinguished the newly kindled flame of Christianity.

From the picture by W. Bell-Scott   *Rischgitz*

THE DANES DESCEND UPON THE COAST OF NORTHUMBRIA : A.D. 867-870

In the picture on the previous page we see a typical Viking invader. The Vikings first came as bands of marauders, descending upon the coast of Northumbria and plundering churches, firing homesteads, and slaying all who resisted them. In the picture above, we see them in sight of the shores of Britain, and can imagine the terror which their coming struck into the hearts of the Britons who were ill prepared to resist them. As yet, the Britons did not possess a navy which could set out and meet the enemy at sea, a lesson in strategy which they were to learn from King Alfred, who built the first British navy. Once the Vikings, dressed in their mail shirts and armed with two-handed battle-axes, had landed, the Saxon peasants, with no weapons but shield and spear, proved no match against the Danes who were also skilful with the bow. It was as if the whole history of the civilisation of England had to be started from the beginning again. Art, letters, government—all were swept away. The whole of the east coast shuddered under repeated invasions that penetrated further and further inland. For five terrible years, from A.D. 866-871, the invaders rode through the length and breadth of England destroying everything that came in their path. Amateur soldiers availed little to stem the progress of rape and desolation, and until Alfred reorganised the militia, the invaders met with no effective resistance. This great king set about the task of organising a well organised army, and although he was unable to drive the Danes from the shores of Britain, the stout resistance of the South under his leadership finally led to a lasting peace.

power of Mercia depended upon the strength of the king, and soon after his death in 786, Egbert became king of Wessex. He soon set about an attempt to make his kingdom supreme, and in 826, Kent, Sussex, Essex and East Anglia submitted, and in the next year Mercia was conquered, and the Northumbrians received him as their overlord. Egbert was now king over his own kingdom of Wessex and overlord of the whole English-speaking race from the Channel to the Firth of Forth. The seven kingdoms were no more.

THE COMING OF THE DANES

Before Egbert's death in 839, a new danger to England began to appear. For two hundred years no invader had landed on the shores of Britain, and although, as we have seen, it was a period of almost continual internal warfare, the original invaders had settled down to a mainly agricultural life, and had left their seafaring prowess far behind. But there were hardy men across the sea who were seeking adventure, and while Egbert's predecessor was ruling in Wessex, the first galleys of the Danes or Vikings made their appearance on the east coast. These first sea-rovers were pirates, who sailed in their " long-ships " from Denmark or the fjords of Norway, to carry off spoils and captives, and leave behind them desolation. So troublesome did they become that in the churches a new petition was added to the Litanies—" From the fury of the Northmen, Good Lord deliver us." Had King Alfred lived when they first began to arrive, the future history of England might have been different, for as we shall see later this wise king built a navy to protect our shores, but no one in Egbert's time thought of leaving our shores to fight the Danes at sea and before they had an opportunity to land. By the time of Alfred it was too late, for the original pirates had now given place to equally determined men, but with a different motive—they came to conquer and make England their home.

ALFRED BECOMES KING

When Alfred became king he was faced with the fact that the Danes had already established themselves in England, and had especially a tight grip on the Midlands and the North. In 876 they began to pour into Wessex, and in the following year took Alfred so much by surprise that he only escaped with difficulty. Then the tide turned ; a victory in Devon enabled him to collect his forces against the main Danish

army, and at Ethandune (Eddington) in Wiltshire, he gained a great victory. Both sides, however, were exhausted, and it was realised that a decisive battle which would leave Alfred or the Danes in sole sway over the whole of England was unlikely. Therefore, both sides met and signed the Treaty of Wedmore, or Chippenham (878), by which it was agreed that the Danes should return north to a line which extended roughly from Chester to London, and that Alfred should govern the rest of England. Fourteen years of peace followed this arrangement.

In times of war, all that makes human life worth living and raises mankind above the animals is likely to be forgotten, or sadly neglected.

ALFRED THE GREAT

Alfred was by nature a scholar, but until he finally made peace with Guthrum, the Danish leader, in 886, his time was too occupied with warfare to allow of attention being paid to education and culture. Where the Danes had gained their greatest influence, and especially in Northumbria, learning had almost been wiped out, and even in Alfred's domains very little remained. He was now, however, able to concentrate upon repairing the ravages of the past, and he set about reorganising his kingdom in no uncertain manner. Then he conceived the glorious plan of having a national Chronicle, which was to be a record of the public life of the nation. He probably began this himself, but at any rate he handed it over to the monks of certain monasteries, especially of Winchester and Peterborough, and it was continued year by year until the reign of Stephen. He built schools for boys, and set the monks to teach in them. Alfred's ideal is expressed in his instruction that every free-born youth " should abide at his book till he can well understand English writing." He could not find the teaching material which he required in Wessex and so he had to seek teachers from abroad. This is what he says, " So clean was learning decayed among English folk that very few there on this side of the Humber that could understand their service books in English or translate aught out of Latin into English, and I think there were not many beyond the Humber. So few of them were there that I cannot bethink me of even one when I came to the kingdom." He says again, " In olden times men came hither from foreign lands to seek for instruction, and now if we are to have it, we can only get it from abroad."

From the drawing by Ernest Board   *By permission of " Pictorial Education'*

ALFRED AND THE CAKES

The story which the picture tells is a very famous one, but historians say that it is probably quite untrue. Alfred, fleeing from his enemies the Danes, took shelter in a herdsman's hut where he remained for some weeks. One day the herdsman's wife left him to watch some loaves that she had made. The king sitting near the hearth was making ready his bow and arrows when the ill-tempered woman beheld the loaves burning. She ran hastily and removed them, scolding the king: " You, fellow! You will not turn the bread which you see burning, but you will be glad enough to eat it when it is done." She little thought that she was addressing Alfred.

From the picture by Herbert A. Bone   *Rischgitz*

THE WRECKING OF THE DANISH FLEET

In 877 a Danish fleet set out to invade Britain. Between Poole Harbour and the Channel, this Viking "Armada" was attacked by Alfred's ships, and it is reported, although probably greatly exaggerated, that the Danes lost about 120 ships. Their army entered Exeter from Wareham and made a temporary truce.

In law Alfred has left his mark upon history, not because he made new laws, but rather by reason of the fact that he collected together into what are called the "Dooms of Alfred," customs established by long usage and the judgments of preceding rulers, and the old Mosaic law. A good deal of this he modified in consultation with his Witan or Council of State. The law of "An eye for an eye and a tooth for a tooth" is the basic principle of Anglo-Saxon law, but although punishments are set out for various crimes, in most cases the payment of a fine was accepted instead.

Slavery was universal, and as yet the Church had not condemned it. The laws, as the following shows, were very strict :—

"If a slave worked on Sunday by his lord's command, he shall become free. If, however, a freeman works on that day, except by his lord's command, he shall be reduced to slavery."

It will thus be seen that the lord had control of the lives of those over whom he ruled. But it was a period of great transition, and law and government, although cruel as judged by modern standards, served their purpose well, that of maintaining a semblance of order in otherwise barbarous times.

Summing up Alfred's reign it may be said that he was one of the most high-minded of men, and that nothing to the detriment of his character and no mean or unworthy act has been recorded against his name. It is at his court, says the historian Green, that English history begins.

From the picture by D. Macpherson

By permission of " Pictorial Education "

KING ALFRED AT THE DANISH CAMP

Many stories have grown up round the name of Alfred the Great, England's darling. Legend tells us that while hiding from the Danes he dreamt that St. Cuthbert promised to look after him. Encouraged by this, he visited the Danish camp disguised as a minstrel, and overheard their secrets. In A.D. 878 the important battle of Ethandune (probably Eddington) was fought, which resulted in a great victory for Alfred over the Danish leader Guthrum. In the picture on page 55 we see Guthrum submitting to Alfred, and at the Treaty of Wedmore which followed, the Danish leader agreed that he and his followers should be baptised and retire into the "Danelaw." There the Danes became acknowledged masters of north-eastern England, while Alfred retained the South, including Wessex, the upper part of the Thames Valley, the valleys of the Severn, Mersey and Dee, and London. Alfred settled down to govern his kingdom and there was peace for the rest of his reign.

From the tapestry by Herbert A. Bone   *Rischgitz*

GUTHRUM'S SUBMISSION TO ALFRED AFTER THE BATTLE OF EDDINGTON, 878
Guthrum surrendered not only his sword but his religion, for he became a Christian at Alfred's command.

ALFRED'S CANDLES

An old writer called Asser, who is said to have lived in the reign of Alfred the Great, tells us that the king wanted to spend a certain number of hours by day and by night in prayer.   But by night it was dark, so he could not tell how the hours were passing and by day clouds often hid the sun, so Alfred made a plan.   He ordered wax to be brought and he had candles made, each of the same weight and each twelve inches high.   Some of them he had marked in six equal divisions, some in twelve, to show the time of burning.   These candles were put in different places and burnt brightly for twenty-four hours.   But sometimes they did not burn evenly, " for," says Asser, " the violence of the winds blew too much upon them and they finished their course before the right hour," like clocks that are fast.   So Alfred sent for some workers and ordered them to make lanterns of wood and ox-horn, for ox-horn, when planed down to a fine sheet, is almost as clear as glass.   When the lanterns were ready, the candles were put inside them and the horn door was closed.   The wind could no longer blow the flames and so the candles burned evenly.   In this way Alfred knew how the hours were passing.

From the picture by Bridge   *Rischgitz*

ALFRED SUBMITTING HIS LAWS TO THE WITAN

There was no Parliament as we understand it in Alfred's day. Kings then ruled in consultation with a council of wise men called the Witan. Here we see Alfred consulting with his Witan regarding the laws which he proposed to make. The members of the Witan were chosen by the king himself and not selected by the people.

From the picture by E. Armitage, R.A.   *Rischgitz*

AN ANGLO-SAXON NOBLE FREEING HIS SLAVES

Slavery was common in Anglo-Saxon times, but gradually disappeared with the growing influence of the Church. Here we see a lord carried into the courtyard to free his slaves before he dies. His son witnesses the deed which is being recorded by the steward, while the wondering serfs express their gratitude. Usually the slave was freed in a church or at a cross-road and a record of the ceremony made in the margin of the Gospel-book.

FROM ALFRED TO THE NORMAN CONQUEST

" The customs that became established at this time, notwithstanding many later changes and influences, became some of the fundamental permanent institutions of the English race."

WHEN Alfred died in 901, more than half of England was still under Danish rule. Alfred had wisely realised that with his kingdom in the state which he found it when he became king, it would be impossible to defeat the Danes and turn them out of the country. Therefore, as we saw in the last chapter, he spent the fourteen years of peace in the task of repairing the ravages of constant warfare. His son, Edward the " Elder," and then Athelstan, took

the Danes who had settled on the east coast of Ireland, together with the Welsh who lived along the west coast of England, were not content to give in so easily, and they joined forces in an attempt to overthrow the West Saxon power in the north. Athelstan met them at Brunanburgh (somewhere in Cumberland) and gained a great victory.

A PERIOD OF QUIET

After the death of Athelstan in 940, there

From the Bayeux Tapestry

A SAXON HAWKING PARTY

full advantage of Alfred's great work, and succeeded in the re-conquest of Danish territory. Edward's sister, Ethelfreda, married the king of the Mercians, and such a strong personality did she possess that she was able to withdraw her adopted kingdom from the influence of the Danes. We have now seen the work of three great women—Boudicca, who fought the Romans, Bertha, who persuaded her husband, the king of Kent, to receive St. Augustine, and now Ethelfreda, whose influence recaptured Mercia. Edward himself reconquered East Anglia, and later his son Athelstan won Northumbria. But

followed three short reigns before Edgar, called the Peaceful, was acknowledged king of all England, even by the turbulent Welsh. The memory of the bitter wars between Anglo-Saxons and Danes was now becoming dimmed by the passage of time, and Angles, Saxons and Danes were learning to live peaceably together. Edgar, with the assistance of that great man, Dunstan, whom he had appointed Archbishop, set about improving the kingdom. The Church, which had become slack during the period of warfare, was reorganised, schools were built, and generally, law and order re-established. Indeed,

From the picture by A. Forestier   *By permission of the Waverley Book Co.*

THE BATTLE OF BRUNANBURGH, 937

After the death of Alfred, Edward the Elder and his son, Athelstan, succeeded in the re-conquest of the Danish territory. Some of the Danes who settled on the east coast of Ireland, however, resisted, and were joined by the Welsh, who, at this time, were always ready to seize an opportunity to cross the border. At the Battle of Brunanburgh, Athelstan defeated these combined forces and thus for the first time, although only temporarily, the whole kingdom was under one ruler. Athelstan was succeeded by his brother Edmund, a brilliant leader.

it was said that a man could fare across England with his bosom full of gold and meet no harm.

THE DANES COME AGAIN

But this peaceful state of affairs was not to last for long. The Danes across the sea had not forgotten the days when their ancestors ruled more than half of England. In times of peace the warlike qualities of a nation tend to weaken, and when there is added to this natural tendency a corresponding weakness in leadership, there is no available resisting force to stem the inroads of an invader. Government then was so much a matter of the personality of individual leaders. The king and the Church governed together, and the success of the system depended upon the ability of the combination to put down disorder. The successors of Alfred and Athelstan were a strange mixture, but perhaps the most futile of them all was Ethelred, called the " Unready,"

who reigned from 979-1016. He proved no match for Sweyn, king of Denmark and Norway, a powerful monarch who was bent upon conquering England. Ethelred was defeated at the first battle fought between them, and realising that warfare was not one of his strong points, he attempted to buy off the Danes by a money payment. He, therefore, in 991 called together his Witan to levy a tax upon the country, and this marked the beginning of Parliamentary taxation. The policy failed, since the Danes took the money willingly, but invariably returned to make increasingly greater demands. Weak men, however, often have occasional periods of misapplied strength, and when Ethelred discovered that some of the original Danes living in England were showing sympathy to their cousins across the sea, he ordered a general massacre on St. Bride's Day, November 12th, 1002. Sweyn was naturally angry, and he returned to England

From the picture by G. Merry

LIFE IN AN ANGLO-SAXON VILLAGE

Nearly everything that was needed for daily life was to be found in the Saxon village. The dwellers there had only to go to market to buy salt for salting meat and tar to cure sheep when they became ill from standing in boggy fields. There were beehives and honey was precious, for it was the only kind of sugar that could be got. In autumn everyone went to the woods to gather fallen branches and to cut logs for fuel, and to the hillside for bracken and heather. This made a warm bed and a soft pillow, and the cattle liked it, too. There were two open fields in every village. One was used for growing wheat or rye, while the other remained fallow.

By permission of " Pictorial Education"

BEFORE THE NORMAN CONQUEST

When the wheat-field was left fallow in the following year, the other field was sown with barley or beans. Each freeman had one strip, and sometimes more, in each field. A strip was large enough for eight oxen to plough in a day. The largest house in the village belonged to the chief or lord of that place. The hall was large enough to hold all the freemen in the village who gathered there in the winter. In this hall the lord and freemen would mete out justice to evil-doers and settle quarrels among neighbours and kinsmen. Everyone went to the wooden church on Sundays and often on weekdays, and the priest was a friend to all.

From the picture by A. Forestier

By permission of the Waverley Book Co.

THE MURDER OF EDMUND, 946

As the king was feasting at Pucklechurch a robber named Leofa entered and attacked the cupbearer who tried to turn him out. Edmund seized him by the hair to prevent him wounding his servant and was stabbed before anyone could interfere. Thus did the brief but energetic reign of King Edmund come to a tragic conclusion.

After R. E. Pine   *Rischgitz*

CANUTE REBUKES HIS COURTIERS

The story of King Canute sitting on the seashore, ordering the waves to recede is probably merely a myth, but it serves to illustrate the sterling character of this Danish king of Britain. He had his throne set by the seaside and commanded the waves to retire. When they would not he said : " Confess how frivolous and vain is the might of an earthly king compared to that great Power who rules the elements." He wished to show that idle flattery was no effective substitute for deeds, and that it was only with co-operation of his followers that he could weld Britain into a nation. It is said that after this incident he is supposed to have taken off his crown and deposited it in Winchester Cathedral, never wearing it again. Canute met his death in 1035.

From the picture by Lorentz Frolich   *Rischgitz*

THE LAST PHASE OF THE BATTLE OF ASSUNDUN : 1016

The South of England had always shown stronger resistance to the Danes than the North. During the reign of Edmund (called Ironside), London was besieged by Canute, but the citizens defended their homes with the same bravery as they had shown on two previous occasions in 994 and 1009. Edmund came to their rescue and defeated the Danes at Brentford and raised the siege. But Edmund had to fight in many districts with inadequate forces, and he was defeated at the Battle of Assundun in 1016. But he was still strong enough to secure good terms, and England was again divided between Edmund and Canute, as it had been between Alfred and Guthrum. Unfortunately Edmund who might have proved a great leader of the English died (see page 62), leaving his people without an effective leader to resist Canute who became king of all England. Under his rule England was peaceful until his death in 1035, when civil war immediately broke out under his sons Harold and Harthacnut.

From an old manuscript   *Rischgitz*

ST. DUNSTAN, THE GREAT ARCHBISHOP

St. Dunstan was one of the great archbishops who taught kings how to govern. Although he was not Prime Minister in our modern sense, he was a minister and adviser to Edmund and his successors of such importance that, without his influence and guidance, kingship would never have risen above the status of a mere tribal warrior. He was born at Glastonbury.

possessing an unusual amount of sound commonsense, as instanced by the story of his demonstration to his flattering followers that even a king could not compel the waves on the seashore to recede at his command. One of his acts, however, was to prove very unwise. He divided the kingdom into four earldoms—Northumbria and East Anglia had Danes, while Mercia and Wessex had Englishmen. These earls, especially Godwin, who was given Wessex, were to cause a good deal of trouble, since their subjects owed immediate loyalty to them rather than to the king direct. Thus, before the king could depend upon the loyalty of his subjects, he had to be quite sure of the loyalty of the four earls. Then, too, the earls became jealous of each other, and especially of the ever-increasing power of the House of Godwin. In the reign of Edward the Confessor (1042-1066) matters came to a head, and the northern earls combined with the king to force Godwin to flee the country. But Edward, although a very saintly man, was a weak ruler, and soon Godwin and his son Harold returned to England, and on the death of his father, Harold became virtual ruler of England.

determined to revenge this crime. Ethelred was forced to flee the country, and Sweyn became king instead. He died in 1014 and was succeeded by Canute, who, having put down several rebellions in Wessex, eventually ruled over England, Norway, Denmark and Sweden.

A DANISH KING

This re-association with the Continent was a very good thing for England, since it brought her once again into contact with superior culture and learning. Canute proved a very good king,

HAROLD BECOMES KING

When Edward died in 1066, the Witan unanimously elected Harold as king. Immediately there was an invasion of the Danes in the North, and although Harold knew that William was preparing to land in the South, he rushed his forces northwards and defeated his enemies at the battle of Stamford Bridge on September 25th. Three days later, William landed on the unguarded coast at Pevensey Harold, on hearing the news, rushed back from

After Donald Maclise, R.A.   *Rischgitz*

HAROLD DEPARTS FOR NORMANDY

Harold was the son of Earl Godwin, who had become the strongest man in the kingdom next to the king. Here we see Harold taking leave of King Edward the Confessor before departing on a visit to Duke William of Normandy. The Duke was a personal friend of Edward who, it was later asserted, had promised him the throne on his death. Edward had no right to do this, since kings at this period were still elected by the Witan, or Council of Wise Men, but no doubt his youthful exile in the Norman Court had influenced his mind.

After Donald Maclise, R.A.   *Rischgitz*

THE STRANDING OF HAROLD'S SHIP

This journey was to prove of great importance, not only for Harold, but, as we shall see later, for the future history of England. By an unfortunate mishap Harold's ship was stranded on the Norman coast, in the territory of a man called Guy, Count of Ponthieu, who promptly took him prisoner. The Count, realising the importance of his prisoner, sent a message to Duke William of Normandy demanding a ransom for Harold's release. At first William ordered that Harold be sent to his court without ransom but the Count merely pressed his claims.

After Donald Maclise, R.A.   *Rischgitz*

A DEMAND FOR RANSOM

William could not offer a refusal to this demand and after the ransom had been paid, Harold was allowed to proceed on his journey, and eventually arrived at his destination without further mishap. Duke William, too, saw in the arrival of Harold an opportunity to further his own ends, since the only possible rival to his own claim to the English throne was Harold, and here he was an apparent guest but actually a valuable prisoner.

From the picture by Ernest Board   *By permission of " Pictorial Education "*

HAROLD'S FAMOUS OATH

This picture shows the famous scene of Harold kneeling before William, Duke of Normandy, and swearing upon the relics of saints that he would support William in his claim to the English throne. This oath exacted under compulsion he eventually repudiated, and at the death of Edward was immediately proclaimed king.

After Donald Maclise, R.A.   *Rischgitz*

HAROLD KNIGHTED BY WILLIAM

Duke William, wishing to cement the friendship with Harold, confers upon him the dignity of a Norman knight. Doubtless he felt that the friendship of Harold would be useful to him when he came to claim the throne of England on the death of Edward. He could hardly have anticipated the trouble in store for him before he became king of England owing to Harold repudiating his oath and claiming the crown after Edward's death

After Donald Maclise, R.A.   *Rischgitz*

HAROLD'S RETURN FROM NORMANDY

Here we see Harold on his return from Normandy kneeling before Edward the Confessor. Doubtless he told the king about his capture by Guy, but it is unlikely that he mentioned the oath, which he had no intention of keeping, or that Edward told him that he had already promised the crown to William, assuming William's statement to have been true that such a promise had been made him by the gentle king.

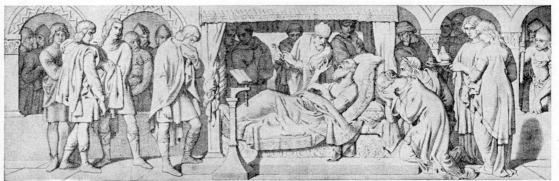

After Donald Maclise, R.A.   *Rischgitz*

THE DEATH OF EDWARD THE CONFESSOR

The death of Edward the Confessor was to bring about a crisis in our history : Harold was determined to seize the throne, while Duke William, on the Continent, was waiting his chance to assume the crown, either by peaceful means or, if this failed, military measures. He was able to summon to his aid a powerful army of followers well trained in the art of warfare and only too eager to seize land and riches from the Saxon nobles.

After Donald Maclise, R.A.   *Rischgitz*

THE LANDING OF WILLIAM THE CONQUEROR

When William realised that Harold did not mean to keep his oath he gathered together his army and set sail for England. As William lands he stumbles, but grasping the earth with his hand, calls out that he thus takes possession of the English soil and so reassures his superstitious followers who might have regarded his fall as an ill omen despite the blessings of the Church of Rome and the support of many continental princes.

After Donald Maclise, R.A.   *Rischgitz*

ANNOUNCING THE INVASION TO HAROLD

When William landed, Harold was in the North fighting against the Norwegians who had landed in the Humber and invaded England. After Harold's great conquest over his enemies at the Battle of Stamford he retired to York wounded. Here we see him at a banquet, which was interrupted by the arrival of a herald who announced the landing of Duke William at Bulverhithe, a deserted spot between Pevensey and Hastings.

After Donald Maclise, R.A.   *Rischgitz*

THE DAY BEFORE THE BATTLE OF HASTINGS

On hearing the news, Harold rushed out with such of his forces as he could gather together, having given instructions that the remainder of his forces were to follow him without delay. William, meanwhile, had sent a knight with monks to negotiate a peace, but Harold refused to consider the proposals and decided instead to fight.

the north in the belief that the other earls would follow to assist him in repelling the invader. But the northern earls, either through jealousy or incompetency, failed to follow, and Harold was left alone to meet William.

THE DEFEAT OF HAROLD AT HASTINGS

At the famous Battle of Hastings, Harold fought with the greatest bravery, but his comparatively untrained bands were no match for the disciplined troops of the Duke. Actually, he was in a better strategical position, situated as he was on a hill, but William gave orders for his troops to retreat, and although Harold saw through the strategy and gave orders to stand firm, his enthusiastic followers thinking that a glorious victory was in sight left their strong position in pursuit of the Normans. The retreat was a feint, and the Normans turned and slaughtered the English before they could regain their stronghold. Harold was killed by an arrow through his eye and died in battle the last of the Anglo-Saxon kings.

Whereas, here and there, the Anglo-Saxons had shown strength, it is doubtful whether they could ever have succeeded in making England really strong. Thus, the last invader to land successfully on English soil was to prove the factor which made possible the next thousand years of English history, for whereas the Anglo-Saxons had seen many visions, especially of the creation of a united nation under one king, it was the Normans who made this dream an actuality.

THE DEATH OF HAROLD

Through jealousy, the earls, who should have followed Harold failed to do so, and he was left alone to meet William at the Battle of Hastings. He was fatally wounded in the eye. Thus ended an epoch in English history.

THE NORMAN CONQUEST

" So the Castles looked over the land and kept order, and the Saxons dug and sowed and reaped till in time Norman and Saxon mixed as one people."

THE Norman Conquest, unlike those of the Angles, Saxons, Jutes and Danes, was not a migration of peoples. Duke William was a powerful landowner in Normandy, and he came as a personal conqueror with an army of lesser nobles and mercenary soldiers. It will be remembered that he claimed that the Crown had been promised to him by Edward the Confessor, and that this promise had been confirmed by Harold when, as a captive, he was forced to swear an oath to assist William. But William was far too astute to embark upon an unprovoked attack upon England. It would be better for him if he could turn his exploit into a religious crusade. He therefore appealed to the Pope to bless his expedition on the ground that Stigand, the Archbishop of Canterbury, had had dealings with an anti-Pope, and that Harold was a wilfully perjured individual. The Pope willingly gave his blessing in exchange for promises to bring England back to full Communion with Rome. To his own followers he promised gifts of land.

HOW WILLIAM CURBED THE BARONS

We have already seen the result of the Battle of Hastings at which Harold was killed. The Witan elected Edgar Atheling as king in his stead, but after a few weeks they faced up to the inevitable and invited William to assume the Crown. Thus an act of brigandage was legalised by the election of William by the Witan, and then his subsequent coronation.

We must now pause to consider the type of government which prevailed on the Continent, with the strength and weaknesses of which William was only too well aware. The continental form of feudalism, that is, a system based

From the picture by A. Maignan

THE FAREWELL TO DUKE WILLIAM FROM NORMANDY

From the picture by Gibbert   *Rischgitz*

CORONATION OF WILLIAM THE CONQUEROR

After the Conquest, William was anxious to legalise his position, and although he could have taken the crown by force, he preferred to be crowned in London, after having been elected by the Witan. It was not, however, to be a peaceful coronation, since the shouts of acclamation by the English were mistaken by William's Norman followers as a sign of insurrection. They rushed out and massacred a number of the cheering crowd. Much blood was to flow before William conquered England and brought the country to more prosperous times.

From the picture by Seymour Lucas   *Rischgitz*

WILLIAM I GRANTING A CHARTER

William was anxious from the first to secure, where possible, the allegiance of his new subjects. Here we see him granting a charter of liberties, based upon the laws of Edward the Confessor, to the citizens of London. In fact, it was William's policy to maintain all that was good in the Anglo-Saxon system of government, and only to graft on to this such Norman customs as would bind a number of turbulent elements under one king.

upon the holding of land, rested upon obedience to an immediate overlord. That is to say, for instance, that William's vassals owed allegiance to him alone, and if he were to engage in warfare with his overlord, in this case the King of France, then they must follow William and not the king. This system worked all right so long as the nobles remained loyal to the king, but since they were constantly quarrelling with each other or attempting to increase the size of their territories, or in open rebellion against the king, the head of the State could never depend at any given time upon the support of the

FROM A PAGE OF THE DOMESDAY BOOK

nobles or their armies. William, when he became king of England, was determined to prevent any of his nobles from becoming too powerful. To this end he did two very interesting things. Firstly, when he was making good his promise to reward his followers, he split up the land which he gave to any individual into estates scattered in various parts of the country. Thus it would be extremely difficult for a noble who had land, let us say, in Norfolk, Cornwall and Cheshire, to gather all his forces against the king. Secondly, at Salisbury in 1086 he made all landowners swear an oath of allegiance to him in exchange for their land. From thenceforward, any landowner who took up arms against the king would be guilty of treason, together with his followers, and would, by forfeiture, be deprived of power to create dissension.

For six years after the Conquest, William was busy organising his kingdom against the possibility of a successful revolt. Indeed, these years portray the ruthless character of the Conqueror, and his cruelty can only be excused by accepting the dictum that the end justifies the means. Fire and sword went through the land, and the Saxons of the northern counties wept amidst their burned homes and crops. When peace was secured, however, the organising genius of the king to desirable ends began to assert itself.

THE MAKING OF DOMESDAY BOOK

His first big task was the compilation of the Domesday Book. From Winchester he sent out skilled lawyers to make a complete inventory of all land in England. They went the length and breadth of the country, with the exception of Northumberland, Cumberland, Westmorland, Durham, and Lancashire, which at that time were presumably too sparsely populated to bother about, since they are not mentioned in the book. These men did their task well, for they obtained a complete record of every estate— the buildings and the construction of them, the grounds and how they were being farmed and tended, the lakes and waterways and their stock of fish, the kind and amount of timber in the woods, and the amount and kind of livestock. Altogether over 5,000 manors are recorded, and the information gained served as the first great Income Tax assessment in our history.

WILLIAM QUARRELS WITH THE POPE

When Hildebrand became Pope, he put forward a theory of government which, if it had been accepted, would have changed the history of Western civilisation. He maintained that the Church had been founded by God and entrusted with the task of embracing all mankind in a single society ; that the Pope as head of this Divine institution was the vice-regent of God on earth, and that disobedience to the Pope implied disobedience to God. This theory led to the Pope's claim to dictate to kings and princes, and in his attempt to interfere in the internal affairs of states, kings often found themselves faced with a strong opposition to their own plans to build a

From the picture by Paul Hardy   *By permission of " Pictorial Education "*

WILLIAM THE CONQUEROR BUILDS THE TOWER OF LONDON

Twelve years have passed since William the Conqueror seized the English crown and here he stands protected by his Norman bodyguard, watching his workmen at the task which he has set them.   He has ordered them to build a great stone tower to guard the river gate at London, and the picture shows some of them at work on the walls and a mason, kneeling on the ground, busy with hammer and chisel, putting the finishing touches to the stone capital of a pillar for the chapel.   Is William remembering that he has insolently pulled down a length of defensive wall which the people have known all their lives, since it existed in Roman times ?   Or is he thinking that this tower will prevent any enemy from venturing up the Thames ?   He is certain to overawe Londoners.

strong state with themselves as heads. William experienced his first difficulty with the Papacy when Hildebrand commanded him to take an oath of submission to him. William refused, and made his position quite clear by ordering that no Pope should be recognised without his permission, that no Papal Bull should be published, that no royal official should be excommunicated, and that no Church councils were to be held or laws enacted without his consent. In other words, William would not tolerate a state within a state recognising an exterior power superior to his own authority. Here is, indeed, a clash of ideals—the universality of the Church as expressed by Hildebrand versus the growing feeling of nationality as represented by William. For good or evil, the Hildebrand theory failed, but it is interesting to speculate what might have been the state of

Europe to-day, if one thousand years ago Hildebrand had prevailed.

WILLIAM THE REFORMER

We have already seen that the Church was civilised when the majority of kings were little better than successful warriors; in fact, almost all educated men were to be found in the Church. William's secretaries, judges and most of his civil servants were Churchmen. But reforms were needed, and William set about the task in no uncertain manner. All law, for instance, whether ecclesiastical or lay, had been dispensed in the same court. Now this led to considerable confusion of thought, since the Church was not only interested in crimes, but also in sin. A sin may be an offence in the eyes of the Church, but as our modern judges are constantly pointing out, a court of law is not a court of morals.

From the picture by Arnold

PETER THE HERMIT PREACHING THE CRUSADE

The Holy Land had been conquered, first by the Arabs and then by the Turks. In 1096, Peter the Hermit collected together, in France and along the Rhine, an army consisting of peasants, workmen, vagabonds, and even women and children to recapture Jerusalem from the infidels. Here we see him preaching his crusade.

From the picture by C. Verlat   *Rischgitz*

THE CRUSADERS CAPTURING JERUSALEM, 1099

The Holy Sepulchre had fallen into the hands of the Mahommedan Saracens and here we see Godfrey de Bouillon capturing Jerusalem at the point of the sword. His triumph, however, was short-lived. He was left with some 2,000 men to maintain order but political troubles caused him to become the vassal of Dagobert who had been elected to the patriarchate, and he died in 1100, hardly a year after his momentous victory.

From the picture by J. Pettie, R.A.   *Rischgitz*

THE PALMER'S TALE

The Palmer, who has come from the pilgrimage to the Holy Lands, has found rest and food in a great house. He is telling to the master and mistress and their young son the story of his many adventures.

William therefore separated the courts, and by doing so laid the foundation of that great system of English law which has developed independently of Church law. He then reorganised the Shires to become part of local government, thus cementing that localisation of government, as distinct from the central authority, which to-day is so peculiarly English. Such reform, however, could only be carried out by able men, and these he obtained from the Continent. Lanfranc, whom he made Archbishop of Canterbury, transferred many bishoprics from obscure villages to important towns, and also reorganised the whole system of parishes, which for centuries has proved a useful medium for local government.

THE CHARACTER OF WILLIAM

William's character is summed up in the *Anglo-Saxon Chronicle* : " He was mild to the good man who loved God : and over all measure severe to the men who gainsayed his will." When he died, he was succeeded by his son, William Rufus, who proved too weak to maintain his father's system. While Lanfranc lived, the king's weakness was less noticeable, since this great bishop managed to keep him in order. But with the passing of Lanfranc, William is shown up in his true colours. As bishoprics became vacant he refused to fill them but took instead the revenues to his own purse. He was cruel and crafty and quite incapable of keeping in order the barons who, as we shall see later, in spite of William the Conqueror's safeguards, were always waiting a chance to rebel against organised society. As yet, national interests were little understood, each baron, with few exceptions, was out to serve his own ends, and the slightest weakening of the central authority was used to their advantage. Rufus was " accidentally " killed at a hunting party in the New Forest, and died unmourned in 1100. His " evil customs " had entirely alienated his people's sympathy, and they looked forward to some improvement in the government of the new king, Henry, when he came to the throne.

THE FIRST CRUSADE

The first Crusade in 1096 was set in motion through the preaching of Peter the Hermit and the enthusiasm of Pope Urban II. The Holy Sepulchre at Jerusalem had fallen into the hands of the Mohammedan Saracens, and the whole of Christendom was roused in an attempt to wrest it back again. This campaign affected England in a peculiar and quite indirect manner. William

the Conqueror had left England to William Rufus, his Dukedom of Normandy to his son, Robert, and no territory to this third son, Henry. Now Robert very badly wanted to go on the Crusade, so he offered to sell his Dukedom to William. The offer was accepted and Normandy became a possession of the English king. The Crusades, generally, served a useful purpose in that they were an outlet for the energies of men who, if they had remained at home, might have directed their warlike tendencies against the government. England, in fact, was fortunate, for when William Rufus died Robert was on the Crusade and his brother Henry immediately claimed the throne. The Witan hurriedly assembled and elected Henry as king. It should be noted that the king is still elected by the Witan, and it was not until considerably later that the principle of succession by right of birth was accepted.

HENRY I—" THE LION OF JUSTICE "

Henry was at the hunting party at which Rufus was killed, and immediately he rushed off to Winchester to seize the royal treasury. There was no banking system in these days, money being literally kept in chests. Money is power, and having secured it, there only remained one more thing—to be elected king by the Witan. When this was done, he issued a charter promising to redress all grievances, to abolish evil customs introduced by Rufus, and to enforce the laws of Edward the Confessor with such additions as were made by William the Conqueror. Henry had been born in England, and this appeal to laws which existed before the Norman Conquest was an attempt to show the English that the conquest was ended, and that thenceforth Englishmen would receive equal treatment with the Normans. His marriage to Matilda, sister of Edgar Atheling, brought an English queen to the throne, and thus Norman and English were united in kingship. He dismissed the worst of the advisers of Rufus, and Archbishop Anselm returned to Canterbury.

But it is in the realm of justice by which Henry is chiefly remembered. The king's justice had become highly organised under the Normans, but since it was administered by the king's personal ministers, whose duty it was to follow him wherever he went, considerable confusion and delay was found to arise. A person who sought justice, let us say, in Kent, might have to wait many months before he could present his petition

From the picture by F. Burney　　　　　　　　　　　　　　　　　　　　　　　　*Rischgitz*

THE DEATH OF WILLIAM RUFUS

While hunting in the New Forest, William (called Rufus) was hit by an arrow and died of his wounds. He had so many enemies that it has often been suggested that this was not an accident, but there is no proof of this.

From the picture by H. Tresham　　　　　　　　　　　　　　　　　　　　　　　*Rischgitz*

THE MARRIAGE OF HENRY I

The English had naturally taken the coming of the Normans hardly. Henry I, however, who was born in England, was anxious to bind the two peoples closer together. His marriage to Matilda, sister of the Anglo-Saxon king, Edgar the Ethlin, pleased the English. As Matilda had worn the veil during her childhood, it was suggested that she was not free to marry, but the objection was set aside and the young queen duly crowned.

THE WRECK OF THE WHITE SHIP

Trouble arose in Normandy, but a treaty of peace ceded its possession to Henry who returned triumphantly to England. His only son William following him in the *Blanche-Nef* was wrecked and drowned. This tragedy was unfortunate for the English people, since Matilda, the king's daughter, was rejected by the barons, although they had promised Henry to support her after his death. Stephen, son of Adela, William the Conqueror's daughter, was chosen, and a long period of civil war followed causing much unrest.

From the picture by G. Merry

LIFE IN A NORMAN

The picture shows a Norman castle in time of peace, when life centred in the great hall, shown in one of the smaller pictures. In the centre was the great hearthstone and the smoke of the fire found its way out as best it might through a hole in the roof or high up in the wall. Windows were innocent of glass ; shutters kept out the wind, rain and light. A thick layer of rushes covered the floor. At meal times trestle tables were

THE SOLAR

THE BOWER

By permission of "Pictorial Education"

CASTLE AND MANOR

erected and long benches placed at right-angles to the table of the lord. The meal over, the lord and his guests retired to an inner chamber called the Solar. There they played chess, listened to or told stories, or settled business affairs. The ladies of the household retired to the Bower, there to occupy themselves with spinning, weaving or needlework. Village life was now more animated. The lord owned the fishing rights and the mill.

From the picture by C. W. Cope   *Rischgitz*

THE FIRST TRIAL BY JURY

Henry I was responsible for introducing trial by jury into England. The old method of " trial by ordeal " was a too rough and ready method to prove a permanent part of a system of justice. The plunging of a hand into boiling water and if it healed within a certain time presuming the innocence of the accused, may have served well in barbaric times, but the reforms of Henry I demanded a more certain form of justice than chance.

From the picture by Sir John Gilbert, R.A.   *Rischgitz*

THE BATTLE OF THE STANDARD, 1138

The reign of Stephen was one of almost continual warfare. The barons were perpetually in revolt, first supporting Stephen and then his rival Matilda. In the midst of these troubles the Scots invaded England, but at " The Battle of the Standard " the recklessness of the Scots was broken on the lances and archery of the English and they were completely defeated. The following year a treaty was concluded with the Scottish King David.

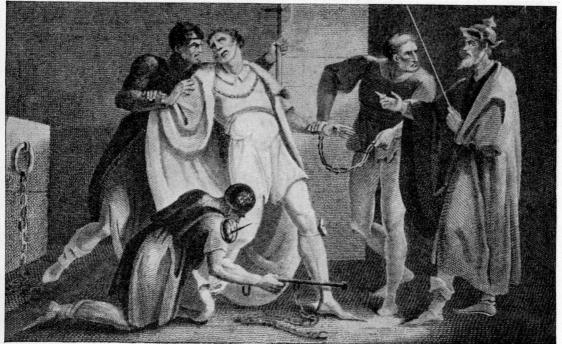

From the picture by Henry Tresham, R.A.   Kischgitz

THE IMPRISONMENT OF STEPHEN

In February, 1141, the supporters of Matilda defeated Stephen at Lincoln and took him prisoner. He was sent to Bristol Castle, and in the meantime Matilda seized what remained of the royal treasure, including the actual crown. When she arrived in London two months later her haughtiness of manner so displeased the citizens that she lost their support. Her vindictive temper turned some of her staunchest friends into formidable enemies.

to the king's court. To overcome this difficulty, Henry sent justices all over the country, with full authority to collect money, enforce military service, and in other ways carry out the rights and claims of the king. Thus the power of central government spread throughout the country and gradually broke down the attempts of the powerful barons to set up their own local courts against those of the king. Justice to-day is carried on in the same way as instituted by Henry I. There are the central criminal courts in London, and then, in addition, judges go on circuit to the Assizes to try cases locally.

ANOTHER QUARREL WITH THE PAPACY

Henry had one serious quarrel with the Papacy. The Pope claimed that he alone had the right to appoint bishops. Such a claim, if successful, left the king with no guarantee that the country would not be flooded with foreigners or otherwise unsatisfactory men, whose first allegiance would be to the Pope. With Henry's characteristic wisdom, a compromise was reached whereby the bishop received the insignia of his office from the Pope, but did homage to the king

as his immediate overlord. If we judge these quarrels by conditions to-day they may appear trivial, but, in fact, the events which occurred then have affected the whole of our history, and have led to a religious toleration which all enjoy in twentieth century Britain.

CHAOS RETURNS

Henry, having lost his son, before his death had persuaded the barons to elect his daughter Matilda as his successor. But the barons, tired of the strong rule of Henry, disregarded their oath, and chose instead Stephen, her cousin, a weak man who they knew would be incapable of keeping them in check. They were right— law and order were no more. Instead of England being ruled by one government, there were hundreds of lords of higher or lower degree each acting as if he had no government above him whatsoever. The strength of the nobility rested solely in the possession of fortified castles which became the centres of the utmost cruelty and repression. In these men and women were tortured, and from them essayed bands of unbridled blackguards to ravage the local

From the picture by J. G. Huck

Rischgitz

STEPHEN'S WIFE PLEADS FOR HIS RELEASE

Here we see the wife of Stephen appealing to Matilda for the release of her husband.   Being unsuccessful, she returned to Kent and raised such forces as to cause Matilda to leave London in flight a few days after her entry, and before her coronation.   This was the last chance she ever really had of gaining the throne, although the civil war was to continue until the country was exhausted.   She eventually retired to Normandy.

countryside. Added to this was a civil war lasting for fifteen years, while Matilda made continual attempts to assert her claim to the throne.

THE NORMAN GOVERNMENT

From all this we see that whereas the Normans had succeeded in introducing a strong system of government, it depended very largely for its success upon the personality of the king and his advisers. Under William I and Henry I it was a success, but with weak kings like Rufus and Stephen it almost collapsed. Under a strong king, the Norman castles were sources of orderly government, but the slightest weakening of the central authority and they became local seats of cruel oppression. The barons were exceedingly powerful. Their castles were strong enough to resist any attack and they controlled large retinues of armed followers. If the king was a strong man he could keep his powerful nobles in order and use their followers for his own purposes ; but if he was a weak man the barons and their followers would defy the king, quarrel among themselves and upset the peace of the land.

An example of this occurred when Henry I died and Stephen came to the throne. He proved to be so weak that Matilda asserted her claim and for many years the country was torn by civil strife. Some of the barons supported Stephen and some Matilda, but none of them really cared who was on the throne provided the ruler was not strong enough to curb their power. During this period the country was left uncultivated, and so great was the general misery that it was openly said that " Christ and His Saints slept."

The barons ruled—or misruled—their own lands independently : torturing, burning and pillaging wherever there was a chance to extort more money from the peasantry. Only the accession of Henry put an end to the nation's difficulties.

THE BREAK UP OF FEUDALISM

"AFTER the death of the first Henry, the outcome of bad government was anarchy; after the death of the second Henry the outcome of bad government was constitutional reform. And the difference is the measure of the work of the great Angevin."

This quotation expresses clearly the fact that feudalism, as we have already seen, failed to establish a state of society in which the central authority was strong enough to resist the activities of strong barons under a weak king. But Henry II, the first of the line of kings called the Angevins, set about reform in no uncertain manner. He compelled all nobles to settle their disputes in the *curia regis*, i.e. the king's court, thus breaking the power of the baronial courts. No freeholder could be sued with regard to the holding of land except in the king's court, thus placing all landowners on an equal footing and lessening the power of big landowners. The police system was reorganised, and the responsibility for bringing criminals to justice was taken out of the hands of the injured party and placed in the charge of a public jury—thus strengthening king's justice as against the local baronial courts. The jury, unlike a modern jury which tries a case on evidence submitted by witnesses, was responsible for supplying the evidence from *their own knowledge* of the crime. The Assize of Arms reorganised the military side of life and detailed to every individual his military responsibility to the king. But one reform, perhaps more than any other, served to undermine the power of the barons. The institution of scutage, a money payment in place of military service, had the effect of making the nobles less warlike. Many of them chose to pay Henry the equivalent in money for the number of armed troops which their position in life entitled the king to demand. With this money, Henry created a mercenary army independent of the barons, and since they were professional soldiers, they tended to be more efficient than any which the barons could muster. Such an army was essential to Henry, since he had many foreign possessions which needed protection. In these various ways, by bringing suits into the king's courts, by transferring feudal relations into a money payment, by organising armies independent of the barons, the king and his ministers reduced the power of the barons. But the royal government was becoming absolute by getting into its hands all political power, and this gave rise to another problem—can the power of the king be regulated so as to ensure that he shall not oppress his subjects ? The first attempts to answer this question will be dealt with in a later part of this chapter.

THE MURDER OF BECKET

Henry, as seen by the map on page 88, had many foreign possessions. It was while he was on the Continent that the furious quarrel with Becket came to a head, leading as it did to the Archbishop's murder on the steps of Canterbury Cathedral. The old quarrel between Church and State had arisen. During the reign of Stephen, the Church was the only organisation which maintained some standard of decency, but in the general disorders, certain privileges, which both William the Conqueror and Henry I had resisted, were gradually taken back. The Church courts had become so powerful that they claimed the right to try criminal cases in which the clergy were involved and which properly belonged to the secular courts. Clerics had flooded into the Church, and thus Henry was faced with the problem of a large and influential section of the community which was not responsible to the ordinary laws of the land. Becket supported the claims of the Church against Henry, but at the Council of Clarendon, held in 1164, an agreement was reached whereby no appeals were to be made to Rome, no vassals of the king were to be excommunicated and no clerics were to leave the country without Henry's consent. Clerics guilty of crime were to be tried in the secular courts, and bishops and abbots were to do homage to Henry for the vast lands which they possessed. No sooner, however, had Becket agreed, than he appealed to Rome and in fear fled the country. From abroad, Becket, with the support of the Pope and the king of France, hurled defiance at Henry, and in 1170 Henry was threatened with an interdict for having had his son crowned in the absence of the Archbishop. This was a new custom and illustrates the beginning of a principle that the king's son is the natural heir to the throne. Henry gave way, and Becket returned to England, but immediately threw down a further challenge to the king by excommunicating the bishops who had taken part in the coronation. This was too much for Henry, who in a fit of wrath said " Who will rid me of this turbulent priest ? " Certain of his followers took him at his word, hurried across to England and murdered Becket. The whole civilised world stood aghast at such an event, and so powerful was the influence of the Papacy that the spectacle was seen of an English king doing penance at the tomb of his victim, while the monks of Canterbury publicly whipped him.

AN ATTEMPT TO CONQUER IRELAND

Henry's prestige had suffered considerably by the affair of Becket, and it was necessary that he should retrieve it by some spectacular move which would make people forget. Ireland offered an ideal opportunity. He had previously promised the Pope that he would conquer Ireland and bring her back into communion with Rome. Once again, an act of intended brigandage was to be cloaked with the semblance of a religious crusade. He had allowed great earls, such as the Earl of Pembroke, Richard de Clare (known as Strongbow) and some of the Fitzgeralds to go to Ireland as the allies of Dermot McMurrough, king of Leinster, and to acquire such lands as they could. Strongbow, indeed, actually succeeded the king of Leinster. It was then that Henry felt that he ought to go personally to Ireland, as he feared the danger of a strong

THE MURDER OF THOMAS A BECKET

" Who will rid me of this turbulent priest ? " These words, spoken in anger by Henry II, led to the murder, by four faithful knights, of Archbishop Becket on the altar steps of Canterbury Cathedral. The knights set out from Normandy, where the king was staying, and, before he had time to restrain them, had committed a crime which was to shake Christendom and bring the most severe wrath of the Roman Church upon the king.

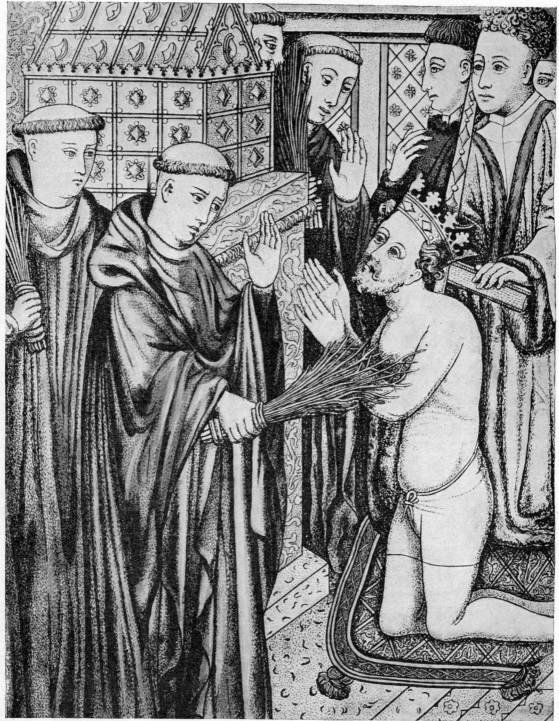

From an old manuscript   *Rischgitz*

HENRY II DOING PENANCE BEFORE THE TOMB OF BECKET

Such was the power of the Church in the Middle Ages, that the Pope could often compel kings to obey his commands. Here we see Henry being whipped by the monks as a public penance for the murder of Becket. Not only was the king so punished but Rome also imposed stern religious measures on the country. As a further conciliation Henry invaded Ireland in accordance with an old promise to bring her back to the Church.

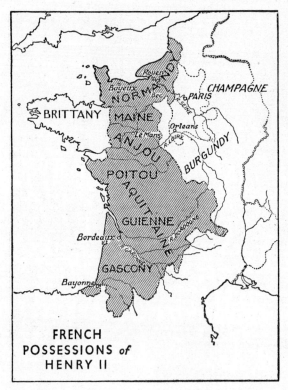

FRENCH
POSSESSIONS of
HENRY II

his Crusade. This he did by selling everything saleable, and offices of state were sold indiscriminately. He was soon away again, leaving England in charge of Chancellor Longchamp, a low-born Norman. This man was loyal to the king, but owing to the constant financial demands of his master and the jealousy of his rivals, who resented his open contempt of the English, he was unpopular. London, now increasingly interested in trade, and therefore adverse to increasing taxation, led the revolt against Longchamp in support of Walter of Contances, who became Chief Justicior. This man was succeeded by one of outstanding ability, the newly-appointed archbishop, Hubert Walter. His administration gave life to a new political class, the knights of the shire, men who were below baronial rank, a class which a little later was to compose the great bulk of the House of Commons. These knights became responsible for the maintenance of local law and order in the towns which were now assuming greater importance. In 1194 and 1198, the elective principle was first introduced by an instruction to the circuit judges to arrange for the election in each shire of four " coroners " who should decide what cases were to be reserved for the king's justice. This was a decided blow to the privileged classes, since this task had previously been done by the sheriffs. Also a committee of four knights were entrusted with the task of nominating the jury which should attend the Assizes. Certain towns were also granted the privilege of electing their own magistrates. These are small beginnings, but they mark the beginning of the end of the privileged class of over-mighty subjects—the barons. So far, however, the will of the people has found no vocal expression. We must wait for some time before the masses become articulate, although there are rumblings which we shall have to note almost immediately.

Norman state being set up which might cause trouble in the future. So to Ireland he went, and received homage as " Lord of Ireland." But before he could organise the country, he was summoned to meet the Papal legates in order to receive official absolution from the Pope for his crime of the murder of Becket. The Pope demanded harsh terms—clerics were to be tried in Church courts, and appeals were to be allowed to Rome ; such was the power of the Pope in the twelfth century. But, in spite of such a setback, Henry had built up a system of law and order which was able to stand the strain of an absentee king, as we shall see in the next section.

THE ABSENTEE KING

On the death of Henry in 1189, Richard I (called Cœur de Lion) came to the throne, but out of the whole reign of ten years he spent less than twelve months in England. Saladin had taken Jerusalem, and an appeal for help from this city set the third Crusade in motion in 1188. Kings and princes in Europe rushed to answer the call, and foremost among them was Richard. He was on the Continent when his father died, but he visited England to be crowned and to stay just long enough to raise money to finance

THE GREAT CHARTER

The danger of a too-powerful central authority is clearly illustrated by the reign of John. He used the power which Henry had created to oppress all and sundry. Magna Carta was a reply to this attempt and implies the political theory that the actions of a king may be checked by the will of the governed. The importance of the Charter can be summarised under four headings : (1) It showed that if the king did not rule as a section of the people wished (we cannot

From the picture by D. Maclise   Rischgitz

THE MARRIAGE OF STRONGBOW AND EVA

Adrian IV, the only English Pope in history, had authorised Henry II to conquer Ireland and bring her back again into community with Rome. The king was too busy on the Continent to carry out this scheme, but private adventurers from Wales, under the leadership of the Earl of Pembroke, nicknamed Strongbow, undertook the conquest of Ireland. The uncouth Irish were no match against the well-trained archers and cavalry of the invaders. Strongbow became so powerful that Henry was compelled to recall him lest he became a serious rival to his own authority. The king later accompanied him on a second expedition to Ireland.

speak of the will of the people yet) he could be made to. (2) It involved the theory that the king made a contract with the barons to rule well in exchange for their service. (This was to be considered a binding contract.) (3) The Charter included reforms and rules of government which were to regulate the relationship between the king and his nobles, and, what is important, between nobles and their sub-tenants. (4) It was a statement of rights which served as a ready reference in later times when the privileges of the people were being attacked ; it became a standard.

The possession of extensive lands on the Continent by king and nobles had the effect of a divided loyalty. Many of the nobles, for instance, were in the position of absentee landlords, and took very little part in the affairs of England. Later, Henry III (see picture on page 102) was compelled to confirm this Charter. The loss of foreign possessions during John's reign compelled the nobles to choose between England

or the Continent. Those who stayed became definitely English, and this explains the antagonism of the nobles to foreign Church influence in later history. Indeed, the serious quarrel between King John and the Pope serves to show how dangerous foreign influence might become. In fact, at one stage of the quarrel, England was actually held as a fief of Rome, and so strong was the Pope's power that he placed England under an interdict and excommunicated the king. These facts throw a clear light upon the deeply religious character of life in these days. The Church literally governed the daily lives of the people and an interdict, which forbade the holding of Church services while it lasted, cut right at the core of daily life. Excommunication, a further punishment for John, like the interdict, had little effect on him personally, since he was obviously not affected by religion, but when his barons offered to support the Pope in his threat to invite the French King to dethrone him, he faced up to the inevitable, and gave in. The signing of Magna Carta was the result of this situation.

THE ATTEMPT TO CONTROL THE KING
1216—1337

The temporary unity of the barons lasted until they had gained John's submission. They soon began to quarrel. There was no idea as yet of putting the country as a whole before personal advantage. Most of this period is occupied by the long reign of Henry III. He was an unpopular king, since the barons, having lost

Mansell

CASKET CONTAINING RELICS OF BECKET

their foreign possessions, were English in outlook and disliked the introduction of foreigners into the chief positions in Church and State. Meanwhile the Pope had consolidated the progress made in John's reign by instituting a system of Papal legates and taxation. The Great Council (old *Curia Regis*) now met regularly, and in 1258 a most important step was taken when at Oxford, Simon de Montfort tabulated a list of demands (The Provisions of Oxford) which greatly restricted the power of the king. Foreigners were to be removed; a council of bishops and nobles was set up to bring about reforms and to

control the king; and all appointments were placed in the hands of this council. Henry agreed, later resisted, and was finally defeated at the Battle of Lewes in 1272.

PARLIAMENTARY DEVELOPMENT

So far we have seen the struggle of the king to break the power of the Norman barons, and the efforts of the nobility to check the power of the king. Edward I's reign is important for a further struggle; government had developed into government for the nobility. The growth of trading, however, had invested the towns with a new importance, and there had arisen, as a consequence, a new class of people— the wealthy middle classes, who were outside the land system of feudal tenure. These now demanded a say in government, and in the Parliament of 1295 there were added two representatives of each county and two townsmen from each city to represent their respective interests. These were selected representatives and not elected by popular vote. Gradually the nobles and bishops began to sit in a separate room, and the representatives of the shires and towns elected their own "speaker" and met as a body in the House of Commons. The king had always reserved the right to institute taxation, but in 1297 Edward gave up all right of taxation except "by the common consent of the realm."

THE JEWS

During these early years the Jews were always considered fair game for financial plunder or unenlightened religious bigotry. In this period the Jews were an alien caste who were compelled to pay special taxes, and were used by the king to provide him with money, which he rarely repaid. In order to make good their losses they compelled less distinguished debtors to pay a rate of interest out of all proportion to the loan. This extortion, plus religious bigotry, was sufficient to cause their expulsion. The Church forbade the lending of money, and since trade depended upon adequate finance, no progress was possible without the Jews. The Jews were considered "infidels," without hope of salvation except through renouncing their faith and becoming Christians.

From the picture by D. Macpherson
By permission of "Pictorial Education"

PRINCE RICHARD PAYING HOMAGE TO THE KING OF FRANCE

The last years of Henry were occupied with quarrelling with his sons on the Continent. Prince Richard, with Philip of France, was in arms against his father. Here we see Richard doing homage to the French king. The two kings met later on, but Henry's spirit was broken by the rebellious attitude of his sons.

From an old manuscript   *Rischgitz*

THE CORONATION PROCESSION OF RICHARD I

Although Richard was born in England, he had spent most of his boyhood on the Continent, and for the ten years of the reign he was mainly concerned with the Crusade and wars in France. In fact, he spent only a few months in England throughout his reign. This continued absence brought about the first steps towards Parliamentary freedom from the domination of the king who was, up till then, a complete despot.

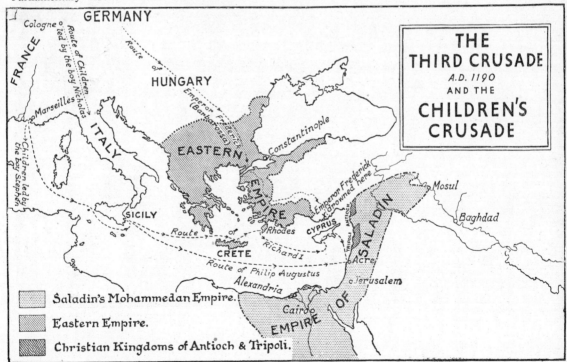

ROUTES FOLLOWED BY THE CRUSADERS IN THEIR ADVANCE UPON THE HOLY LAND

From the picture by A. Cooper   *Rischgitz*

RICHARD I AND SALADIN AT ASCALON

In 1187, Jerusalem was captured by the great Saracen leader Saladin. Richard joined the Crusade for its recapture, which was an adventure after his own heart. Although the Crusaders came within sight of the Holy City, previous jealousies and quarrels had so diminished their forces that they realised they were not strong enough to capture the city. After severe fighting Richard withdrew his men and finally sailed from the Holy Land.

From the picture by Charles Landseer   *By permission of the Tate Gallery*

PILLAGING A JEW'S HOUSE

Here we see a typical scene during a period when the Jews were pillaged and massacred for the wealth which they possessed, or for the mere fact that they were of the Jewish faith. Religious toleration was then unknown and the Jews were regarded as legitimate prey whenever their thrifty habits brought them into public notice.

From the picture by D. Macpherson

BLONDEL THE MINSTREL AND RICHARD THE LIONHEART

Richard, on returning from the Crusades, was shipwrecked and imprisoned on the Continent, the position of his prison being unknown except to his captor. Blondel, a trusty troubadour, travelled over hill and dale seeking the king, and singing the songs which he and Richard had often sung together. At last his search was rewarded by the faint sound of a voice from the window of a castle. It was Richard's. Negotiations were opened with his captor, Leopold of Austria, who was compelled to hand Richard over to Henry VI of France.

From the picture by B. West

Rischgitz

PRINCE JOHN'S SUBMISSION TO RICHARD I

Meanwhile, Prince John, taking advantage of his brother's absence had been plotting against him. He knew that Richard was a prisoner, but announced that he was dead and immediately raised a rebellion. On Richard's release, however, a large ransom having been paid, he soon forced John to submission, and pardoned his brother's treachery. They remained on fairly friendly terms until Richard's death five years later. On his death-bed Richard is said to have disregarded Arthur and declared John his successor.

From the picture by W. F. Yeames   *By permission of the Manchester Corporat*

PRINCE ARTHUR AND HIS GAOLER HUBERT

On the death of Richard, Prince Arthur claimed the crown. He fell into the hands of John, howeve who immediately imprisoned him. He was never again seen alive, and John has always been suspecte as being responsible for his murder. The disappearance of Arthur lost John the support of France

After Vernet   *Rischgitz*

THE BATTLE OF BOUVINES

John lost the great continental domains of Henry II. After his defeat at the Battle of Bouvines in 1214, he returned to England to face the angry barons. Despite his disgrace abroad he broke the promises he had made to his country and allowed his mercenaries to plunder and harass the people as they wished.

From the picture by W. Martin   *Rischgitz*

THE CHARTER OF LIBERTIES

The Barons, led by the Archbishop, drew up reforms which they were to demand from the king. Here we see them taking an oath binding them to support the reforms, and to present their claims at Christmas.

THE SCRIPTO

THE KIT

THE CHAPTER-HOUSE

A VIEW OF KIRKSTALL ABBEY, NEAR L

1 CHURCH	6 CELLARS AND DORM
2 CLOISTER	7 GUEST-HOUSE
3 INFIRMARY OR ABBOT'S HOUSE	8 CHAPTER-HOUSE
4 KITCHENS	9 CALEFACTORY OR D
5 REFECTORY	10 COMMON ROOM

From the picture by G. Merry

SCENES FROM MONASTIC

Kirkstall Abbey, founded in 1152 by Henry de Lacy, was one of the most beautiful Cistercian monasteries. These monks, a branch of the Benedictine order, practise the most rigid self-abnegation. Their monasteries

THE ABBEY CHURCH

THE CLOISTERS

THE MONASTERY: GENERAL VIEW

THE GUEST-HOUSE

THE REFECTORY

By permission of " Pictorial Education "

LIFE IN THE MIDDLE AGES

are of a simple architectural style, usually built in a valley and always on the banks of a stream. This feature is shown here, also the fish-pond in which the fish caught by the monks were kept alive until required.

After the picture by Ernest Normand   Rischgitz

KING JOHN AT RUNNYMEDE

John, realising that immediate resistance was inadvisable, is here seen signing Magna Carta, the most famous document in British history. But whilst signing he was actually planning what steps he could take to wriggle out of his solemn obligations. After a long civil war he died, according to superstition, of poisoning.

From the picture by Benouville in the Louvre
ST. FRANCIS BLESSES ASSISI
Mansell

St. Francis sent his poor friars to preach throughout the Continent, including England. Here we see him just before his death in 1226, halting before Assisi near the spot where, during his youth, he had once tended a leper.

From the picture by A. Forestier
By permission of the " Illustrated London News "
A MIRACLE PLAY IN THE THIRTEENTH CENTURY

Our first plays were versions of Biblical stories, and, as such, intended to appeal to religious sentiment and enforce the reality of sacred events, they were presented inside the cathedrals and churches. Later, they were transferred from church to churchyard or market-square. The various scenes were not all crowded on to the same stage : Heaven would be situated in the rood-loft ; Herod in a nativity play would have his special platform, and so perhaps had the Wise Men and the Shepherds, and each scene would be acted on its own stage.

From an old print   *Rischgitz*

HENRY III REVIEWING MAGNA CARTA

Although John had no intention of keeping to the clauses of Magna Carta, this document became important as a standard when liberties were attacked. Here we see Henry III reviewing the Charter and promising to abide by its clauses. He, too, forgot his pledges and extorted money until his nobles rose against him.

From the picture by Louis Ginnett   *By permission of the artist*

AFTER THE BATTLE OF LEWES

Henry's partiality to foreigners, and the general extravagance of his reign, caused the English barons under Simon de Montfort, Earl of Leicester, to take up arms against the king, who was defeated at the Battle of Lewes in 1264. The government now fell into the hands of De Montfort, who in 1265, called together a Parliament to consider the case against the king at which two knights from each of the shires were summoned.

THE FIRST PRINCE OF WALES

The reign of Edward I was mainly occupied with his attempts to conquer Scotland and Wales. In the previous reign, Llewelyn, Prince of Wales, had taken the side of the barons against the king. He now delayed paying homage to Edward on his accession and the English king invaded Wales in 1277. By 1282 Llewelyn had been killed and his brother David suffered a traitor's death. Edward now annexed the country and spent nearly a year in restoring peace and order. He also divided the land into counties similar to the English manner, and in order to encourage trade, granted charters to the merchants. When Edward's wife Eleanor bore him a son in the castle of Caernarvon, he presented the infant child to the people of Wales saying that "he who had been born among them should be their prince." The Welsh chieftains hailed their prince with delight, believing it to mean that they would have a separate independence, for at the time the young Prince Alfonso, elder brother of the child Edward, was the heir to the throne of England. Alfonso died, however, and gradually the Welshmen came to realise that their hope was only a dream. The picture shows the prince being held upon his father's shield, which is the basis of the ceremony of presenting the king's eldest son to the Welsh people, as their Prince.

From the picture by Morris

Rischgitz

EDWARD I PRESENTS HIS SON

From an old print   Rischgitz

THE PARLIAMENT OF EDWARD I

Earlier Parliaments during the reign of Edward I had been more of the nature of Assemblies, consisting of knights, citizens and other vague personalities. There was, however, a growing desire for individual representation and in 1295 Edward summoned what is known as the first complete or Model Parliament in English history. '' What touches all shall be approved by all,'' was the momentous statement contained in the writ to the Archbishop of Canterbury. The two archbishops and bishops, sixty-seven abbots, and also forty-nine earls and barons formed the Estate of the Lords. The lower clergy were instructed to send delegates who formed the Estate of the Clergy, they did not take kindly to Parliament, and after about one hundred years ceased to attend. To every county the king directed the sheriff '' without delay to cause to be elected from the county two knights and each borough two burgesses. . . .'' Thus the Estate of the Commons was established in Parliament. Later the Lords and Commons met separately to consider their proposed laws.

THE GREAT STONE CAPTURED FROM THE SCOTS

Scotland proving troublesome, Edward advanced upon Berwick. Returning triumphantly he stopped at the Abbey of Scone and seized the '' Stone of Destiny '' upon which all the Scottish kings were crowned. The stone was brought to Westminster and declared by Edward to be a sign of the conquest of the turbulent Scots. A special throne was built to contain the treasure which has formed the Coronation Chair of English kings thereafter. It symbolises the acceptance and crowning of the heir as king of Scotland and England.

From the picture by Maclise   *Rischgitz*

THE TRIAL OF WILLIAM WALLACE

Edward's success in Wales was not repeated in Scotland.   The Scots and the French were alternately helping each other in their respective quarrels with the English.   In 1296 the Scots were defeated at Dunbar, and Edward was left free to invade France.   But events were going wrong in Scotland and Edward was compelled to execute an invasion against Wallace, whom he defeated at Falkirk.   Some 1,500 Scots died on that fatal day.

From the picture by W. Bell-Scott   *Rischgitz*

THE LAST MARCH OF EDWARD I

After the trial and death of Wallace, Robert Bruce determined to secure the Scottish crown.   He possessed inadequate forces, however, and although the danger did not appear very great, Edward decided to settle the matter in person.   He advanced upon Scotland, although grievously ill, and his death at Carlisle, in 1307, changed the whole history of Scotland, since the real chance to conquer the country was irrevocably lost.

W. F. Taylor

THE ELEANOR CROSS AT NORTHAMPTON

Edward I had the deepest love for his wife, Eleanor of Castile. When the queen died her body was carried to London for burial. At every place where the coffin rested for a night the king afterwards erected a beautiful cross. There are said to have been twelve of these crosses, but only three remain—at Waltham, Geddington and Northampton. A modern replica marks the last resting place of the coffin at Westminster before its internment in the Abbey. The spot became known as Charing Cross and formed the nucleus of a village.

From the picture by Frank Craig   *By permission of C. W. Faulkner & Co. Ltd.*

THE HERETIC

Religious toleration was unknown until comparatively late in history. Heretics, who were often quite ignorant of the meaning of their acts or words, were tortured and killed by those who honestly believed that heaven could only be attained by strict conformity to one faith. Here we see a heretic being led by Church dignitaries through the streets. She may be put to the rack and if condemned, burnt at the stake.

From the picture by A. Forestier   *By permission of the " Illustrated London News "*

A GAME OF FOOTBALL IN THE MIDDLE AGES

It is believed that football first came to Britain with the Romans. A crude form of the game was well known in the twelfth century. On certain fixed days, rough football was played in the streets of London. The early Tudors enacted laws against it, but the game survived in spite of them. It became much more orderly later on.

From the picture by Marcus Stone   *Rischgitz*

EDWARD II AND PIERS GAVESTON

Unlike his illustrious father, Edward II was a weak king, and his reign was one of the most ruinous in English history. The chief causes of his misfortune were his love of pleasure and his attachment to favourites. Piers Gaveston, who was eventually murdered, was the chief of his favourites. Edward, himself, was murdered in prison on September 21st, 1327, after having been forced to abdicate in favour of his son.

From the picture by W. Allen   *Rischgitz*

ROBERT BRUCE AFTER THE BATTLE OF BANNOCKBURN (1314)

After the death of Gaveston, Edward, although brokenhearted, prepared to invade Scotland. With a powerful army, he met Robert Bruce at Bannockburn, but was hopelessly defeated by the strategy of the Scottish forces.

ROBERT BRUCE AND THE SPIDER

At one period the cause of Bruce appeared hopeless, but the story is told that as he lay in hiding from the English, he was inspired to fresh endeavours by the example of a spider which he watched patiently striving to attach the first thread of the web it wished to spin. By the year 1323 events had gone so badly for the English forces that a truce was concluded with Scotland which lasted for thirteen years.

From the picture by A. Forestier   *By permission of the " Illustrated London News "*

A MYSTERY PLAY IN A FOURTEENTH CENTURY MARKET PLACE

The miracle play performed in the church or monastery has now developed into the mystery play of the market square. As the plays moved away from the sacred precincts, control passed from the clergy to the laity. The powers of good and evil were portrayed in the form of morality plays, the characters generally explaining themselves as they came on the stage ; the powers of evil have a comic flavour as had the Devil, Herod, or Pilate in the older plays. Later, to these religious characters were added presentations of social types, and thus was the way prepared for the drama or comedy of real life. These plays were the cause of much buffoonery between actors and an audience which never failed to express its opinion, sometimes even by violence.

111

From the picture by Corbould   *Rischgitz*

THE CANTERBURY PILGRIMS AT THE TABARD INN

After the murder of Becket, his relics became an object of veneration by the faithful, and pilgrims set out from all parts to pay homage at the tomb of the Saint. Here we see a party preparing to set out on their long journey from the Tabard Inn at Southwark, to Canterbury Cathedral. The importance of Southwark (or " south works ") to medieval London was caused by the convergence of many roads crossing London Bridge and leading to the south. The inns were famous as points of arrival and departure and much of the city's life centred about these meeting places. A certain Harry Bailey is reputed to have been the landlord of the Tabard Inn at the time of these famous journeys and to have played host to the Chaucer pilgrims who numbered " wel nyne and twenty in a company." Here we see them about to set forth on the journey.

From the picture by Thomas Stothard   *Mansell*

THE PILGRIMAGE TO CANTERBURY

Chaucer has immortalised these pilgrims, in his " Canterbury Tales." The journey was a tedious affair, and to while away the time, Chaucer makes each of the travellers tell a story. Although Chaucer is remembered as the father of English poetry he played an important part in the civil life of the country. Not only was he a Justice of the Peace, but held a guardianship of two Kentish wards, and a commissionship of that part of the Thames between Greenwich and Woolwich. He also became a Member of Parliament in 1386, and yet found time to compose poetry of such style and quality as must have astonished and amazed the good citizens of London town. King Richard was a great patron of the poet and in the later years of Chaucer's life granted him a pension. Chaucer died in the year 1400, one year after his king. His remains were buried in Westminster Abbey and his tomb formed the beginning of what is now known as the Poets' Corner.

From the picture by Ford Maddox Brown

Rischgitz

CHAUCER AT THE COURT OF EDWARD III

Here is Geoffrey Chaucer, at the height of his renown, reading his famous " Canterbury Tales " to King Edward III and his court. Notice the elaborate head-dresses of the ladies and the costly jewels. With the writing of poetry and prose in English, a new era is opening in English literary history. In 1475 Caxton printed the first edition of the pilgrim's adventures, but the collected works did not appear until 1532.

From the picture by Ford Maddox Brown   *By permission of the Manchester Corporation*

THE ESTABLISHMENT OF THE FLEMISH WEAVERS IN MANCHESTER

The persecution of the Protestants on the Continent led many of them to seek a sanctuary in England. Among them came Flemish weavers, many of whom settled in the neighbourhood of Manchester and taught the English the secrets of their art. Thus out of foreign persecution was laid the foundation of England's wool trade.

From the picture by W. F. Yeames   *Rischgitz*

THE DAWN OF THE REFORMATION

The power of the Church had rested upon the absolute authority of the bishops and clergy, and since the services were in Latin and the Bible was not available for all to read, as it is to-day, the ignorant laity had no cause to question established doctrine. When Wyclif translated the Bible into English, however, the dawn of the Reformation and a revival of learning was in sight. Centuries of ignorance were nearing an end.

From an old print   *Rischgitz*

THE SEIZING OF MORTIMER

The unfortunate Edward II, betrayed by his queen, was cast into prison and there heartlessly murdered. As his son Edward III was a minor when he came to the throne, the government was in the hands of the infamous Mortimer and Isabella the young king's mother, but these two ruled the country so badly that when the king came of age Mortimer was arrested and executed. At the intervention of the Pope, Edward spared his mother, but caused her to spend the rest of her life in confinement in the country.

From the picture by Ernest Board   *By permission of " Pictorial Education "*

EDWARD III AT THE BATTLE OF CRECY

Knightly chivalry was now at its height and this spirit influenced the country as it rose to support the king and his well-loved heir in a war with France of popular memory. Here we see Edward watching his son, called the Black Prince on account of the colour of his armour, at the Battle of Crécy. "Let him win his spurs," was the king's reply to a message that the young lad was surrounded by French knights. By the end of the day the English had gained the victory and that much coveted prize, the spurs, was won.

116

From the picture by Paul Haray

by permission of " Pictorial Education "

THE EARLY USE OF GUNPOWDER

It is said that at the battle of Crécy (1346) the English brought guns into the open field for the first time. No one is quite sure who invented gunpowder. The Chinese certainly knew about it for centuries before Roger Bacon, a friar of the 13th century, is said to have chanced upon it as a result of obtaining nearly pure nitre. Even so, these early guns, called bombards, were not very deadly. " With fire, they threw little iron balls to frighten the horses " ; and the bowmanship, " so rapid that it seemed as if it snowed," won the day.

From the picture by Sir John Gilbert   Rischgitz

EDWARD III AT THE SIEGE OF CALAIS

Soon after Edward came to the throne the "Hundred Years War" broke out between England and France. Although fighting was not continuous, it lasted at intervals until the English were finally driven out of France. In 1346 Edward laid siege to Calais, and here we see the king surrounded by his standard-bearers outside the city. In the absence of explosive shells, it was no easy task to take a thickly-walled city.

From the picture by J. Doyle Penrose   "Autotype"

THE BURGHERS OF CALAIS

For many months the people of Calais held out, but at last they were compelled to give in and sent six citizens with ropes round their necks with a request that Edward should do what he liked with these, but spare the rest of the citizens. Here we see his wife, Queen Philippa, pleading successfully for the lives of these brave men.

THE BLACK DEATH AND PEASANTS' REVOLT

THE Black Death, beginning in the year 1348, increasing in volume in 1349, and dying out in 1350, but visiting the country from time to time afterwards, was one of the most dreadful pestilences that has ever befallen this country. The disease was the bubonic plague, and it spread rapidly from one town, monastery or country district to another throughout England. Although no exact figures are available, it has been estimated that one of every two persons died. Thus, half the population, including the highest in the land, was swept away. Churches were denuded of clergy, the monastic lands could not be looked after because of a lack of labourers, and, in fact, the whole structure of life, as it had existed before the plague, was changed.

Immediately labourers, who were quick to realise the increased value of their services, began to demand higher wages, and at first the employers had no option but to grant them. But the government was entirely in the hands of the upper classes, and as soon as the worst stages of the crisis had passed the king issued a proclamation that labourers were not to demand wages higher than those in operation during the year immediately preceding the Black Death. In 1351 Parliament went a stage further by the issue of the Statutes of Labourers, which was an attempt to force labourers back into a state of semi-slavery. The labourers were naturally angry that they were not permitted to ask for the wages which the increased value of their services appeared to justify, and thus, for the first time in English history, there was a definite clash between capital and labour, although many centuries were to pass before the workers were organised for effective action.

THE BREAK UP OF FEUDALISM

Not only were the labourers affected by the Black Death, but the landowners, too, had their troubles. There was now a dearth of tenants to work the large estates, and the big landlords were compelled to reduce rents in order to tempt their tenants to remain on their estates. Under the old feudal system, tenants (or villeins as they were called) were bound to one landlord and were compelled to perform two or three days' work each week free for their master. Now, however, the landlords were only too pleased to accept money payments in exchange for this forced labour, and, further, the tenants freed themselves from the burden of being tied for life to one landlord ; thus the villeins became labourers or tenants, who might or might not be prosperous but who were at least free. The Black Death, with all its horrors, had served one good purpose : it had freed the English people from much of the slavery of the feudal system.

A CORRUPTED LEGAL SYSTEM

But the ruling classes had not learnt their lesson, and instead of introducing legislation which would have led to a general improvement in the conditions of the people, taxes were increased, the judges were open to bribery, and the king's officers throughout the country violated the rights of the people. Discontent grew, and this was encouraged by popular preachers who travelled through the country discussing the conditions of the time in their sermons. Rhymes portraying the misery of the time were spread from mouth to mouth, one of the most famous of which was :—

" When Adam delved and Eve span,
Who was then the Gentleman ? "

In 1379, Parliament, ignoring this growing voice of discontent, introduced a new type of tax called a poll tax. Previously taxes had been laid upon land, personal possessions and exports and imports, but now a tax was levied upon every person over the age of twelve years. No one could now escape, but to make matters worse, when the first tax did not produce the expected amount, commissioners were sent round the country to levy a further tax. This second tax was in 1381, and was the spark which set fire to a general conflagration. In one village after another the tax collectors were attacked and there was an outbreak of rioting. Manor houses, castles and monasteries were attacked, and the rioting spread throughout most of the south-eastern part of England. At the same time, bodies of rioters set out for London to petition the young king, Richard II, to redress their wrongs. They had no difficulty in entering London, since many of the citizens, and, indeed, several members of the Council, were in sympathy with them.

The movement threw up a born leader in the person of a man called Wat Tyler, and under his guidance London was at the mercy of the rioters for three days. They burned the city palace of the Duke of Lancaster and a number of other buildings owned by unpopular nobles. They invaded the Tower, seized and beheaded Archbishop Sudbury, the Lord Treasurer, and some lower officials. They attacked foreigners and unpopular citizens and put many to death.

WAT TYLER'S MURDER

In the meantime, the fifteen-year-old king agreed to meet the rebels at Mile End, a village just east of London. Here 60,000, with Wat Tyler at their head, assembled to present their grievances and to ask that their wrongs should be righted. They demanded freedom from serfdom, the abolition of compulsory labour services, low rents, the repeal of the Statutes of Labourers, and other reforms, and a general pardon for the rebellion. The king agreed to all their demands without, however, having any intention of keeping his promise. Many of the rioters then returned home, but some remained with their leader to make further demands of the king on the following day. The king, attended by the Lord Mayor, met them at Smithfield in the evening. Wat Tyler rode forward to present his demands to the king, but a serious dispute arose, and the discussion became so violent that several nobles, fearing for the safety of the king, rushed forward and stabbed Tyler to death. The bravery of the king saved what might have been an ugly situation. Rushing towards the rebels he cried out—" Are you seeking a leader ? I will be your leader." Bewildered by the events, the ignorant peasants followed the king outside the city gates, where they were surrounded, disarmed and sent home.

Immediately after the rebellion, repressive measures were introduced by Parliament, and all the liberties which the king had promised were withdrawn by proclamation. This first attempt by the people to rebel against oppression had undoubtedly proved a failure if it is assessed by immediate results, yet there is little doubt that serfdom passed away quicker than it would normally have done if it had not been for the efforts of Wat Tyler and his rioters.

WYCLIF AND THE LOLLARDS

But other forces were at work which in due time brought about radical changes. John Wyclif, a clergyman, launched his attack upon the wealth and religious indifference of the Church at this time. He accused the priests of the parishes of being neglectful of their charges, and the monks of being lazy, ignorant and avaricious. Since the Church and the State were so closely knit together, this was a direct attack upon the established order. He taught that no man had any right to property unless he obeyed the will of God. Poor priests were sent out to preach the Gospel and to do just the work which the Church and the monks had neglected. The preaching of the Gospel, however, was dangerous to the well-being of the established order. The followers of Wyclif, or " Lollards " as they were called, became so dangerous that the established Church persecuted them for heresy, and these persecutions were backed up by Parliament which brought in strict laws against heretics. The government was not very concerned with the religious views of the Lollards as such, but they realised that the spread of these new doctrines would lead inevitably to an attack upon the State.

Wyclif and his followers preached and wrote largely in English, and in doing so they were appealing to all classes of the community. The language of the common people, instead of the Latin of the scholars, was in the fourteenth century fast becoming the language of all Englishmen. In 1362 a law was passed requiring that the pleadings in the Courts should for the future be carried on in English. This was a tremendous advance in justice since prisoners could understand the proceedings of the courts.

If it had not been for the useless wars on the Continent, it is conceivable that much might have been done to improve conditions, but war, especially when it is unsuccessful, is expensive, and the government was compelled to resort to every means to raise money, and to suppress all movements which might be dangerous.

There was gradually arising a realisation that the old order, which rested upon the slavery of the masses for the benefit of the few, was unjust and not in accordance with the Gospel which people were now beginning to read. Progress was slow but the movement which started with the Peasants' Revolt progressed until the government was unable to resist the will of the people.

From the picture by Paul Hardy

By permission of "Pictorial Education"

RICHARD II AND PRINCESS ISABELLA OF VALOIS

Richard II was only a boy of ten years when he came to the throne. He was soon to face trouble, for the long wars had led to increased taxation and the conditions of the labouring classes were growing steadily worse. The Hundred Years War dragged on, but in 1396 he made peace and in his sixtieth year was affianced to the young Princess Isabella of Valois. The crown which the king is holding he is destined to resign to his cousin Henry of Lancaster, there being no heirs by his former wife, Anne of Bohemia.

From an old print   *By permission of the Waverley Book Co.*

RICHARD II MEETS THE INSURGENTS

Murmurings against injustices led to definite revolts, and here we see the young king meeting the insurgents.

From an old print   *Rischgitz*

THE DEATH OF WAT TYLER

Wat Tyler, one of the leaders, proved truculent, and the Lord Mayor, fearing for the safety of the king, struck him down.   The king showed bravery, but unfortunately he made promises to the insurgents which he never kept.

From an old manuscript   *Kischgitz*

JOHN BALL AND THE KENTISHMEN

This page from an old book shows John Ball, a priest, addressing the Kentishmen who had marched to London to state their grievances. "When Adam delved and Eve span, who was then the Gentleman?" was the basis of his appeal. "Things" he said, "will never go well in England so long as goods be not in common." Richard promised to right their wrongs, but after they had safely dispersed, these promises were either forgotten, or his evil counsellors were too strong to enable him to carry out his intentions. But the voice of the people could not be silenced for ever, and in due course oppression gave way to justice.

From the Froissart Chronicles   Rischgitz

RICHARD II PRONOUNCING SENTENCE OF BANISHMENT

Medieval punishments were often extremely brutal, the death penalty being applied to innumerable petty offences. Sentence of banishment, by which a person was cut off from all that was dear to him, was used against high or low. Those who differed from the king and his advisers were often banished for a period of years, or even for life. Unlike to-day, there were no Courts of Appeal to which the condemned could apply.

From an old manuscript   Rischgitz

RICHARD II's ARMY LANDS IN IRELAND

By the " Statute of Kilkenny" in 1366, all intercourse between the English and Irish had been cut off. The Irish thus left to themselves had been getting badly out of hand, and such interests as the English had retained were seriously endangered. In 1394, therefore, the king visited Ireland, and by his presence and energetic measures did much to make the English power safe and more or less agreeable to the unfortunate Irish.

From the picture by Sir J. Gilbert

Riscngitz

RICHARD II RESIGNING THE CROWN

Towards the end of his life, Richard sought to govern as a despot and by 1398 he had dispensed with Parliament. While Richard was away on his second trip to Ireland, Henry of Lancaster landed to claim the estates of his father, John of Gaunt, the third son of Edward III. The discontented nobles rallied to him and on Richard's return he was compelled to resign his crown. The king realised that he was not strong enough to resist.

From an old manuscript   *Rischgitz*

TWO TRAVELLERS FOLLOWED BY ESCORT OF ARCHERS

The two travellers are the Duke of Exeter and the Duke of Surrey who are on their way to meet Henry of Lancaster at Chester, having been sent by Richard II to announce that he was prepared to renounce the crown.

From the Froissart Chronicles   *Rischgitz*

THE CORONATION OF HENRY IV

Richard died of starvation (probably murdered) in prison in 1400, and Henry IV was recognised in place of the despised king. He had no clear title to the throne, and he had no means to buy military support. Though successful in crushing rebellion, Henry was obliged to submit to the guidance of a council, and he became more dependent on Parliament than any other previous king. Temporarily the barons had regained power.

HENRY'S MOST POWERFUL ENEMY—"HOTSPUR"

By refusing to ransom his brother-in-law, the king made an enemy of the powerful Sir Henry Percy, called the "Hotspur of the North." He was fond of fighting, and Shakespeare in his play causes him to say : " He that kills me some six or seven dozen Scots at a breakfast, washes his hands, and says to his wife, Fie upon this quiet life ! I want work." He rebelled against the king, but was defeated at the Battle of Shrewsbury, 1403, and killed. The actions of men in these days were largely governed by a lust for personal power.

PRINCE HAL AND THE JUDGES

Prince Henry, who was soon to be king, had the reputation of having been, before his accession, wild and dissipated, wandering the streets of London at night, and robbing his own tax-gatherers as a practical joke. Even the judges could not tame him, and the picture shows the young prince threatening the court before which he has been brought for punishment. But as Henry V he became one of the most serious, courageous and popular of English kings. His life is well told by Shakespeare in his two plays *Henry IV* and *Henry V*.

From the picture by A. Forestier *By permission of the Waverley Book Company*

LONDON IN THE MIDDLE AGES

This picture should be compared with that on page 36. It will be noticed that the Tower of London has taken the place of the Roman buildings and that only the outside wall of the city remains. Instead of the Roman temple there is now a Christian Church, and London Bridge has taken yet another of its many transitions to the present structure. As yet, however, barges and steamers had not appeared on the river.

From the picture by George Clausen, R.A. *By permission of John Swain & Son Ltd.*

READING WYCLIF'S BIBLE

In 1378, John Wyclif, rector of Lutterworth in Leicestershire, began to translate the entire Bible into English. When the great work was finished it was copied and circulated by the " Poor Priests " whom he had organised to take the place of the Friars who had become wealthy and lazy. The fear of persecution necessitated the reading of the Bible in secret places. Here we see a group of people gathered to hear the gospel in English.

From an old manuscript   *Rischgitz*

A MEDIEVAL TOURNAMENT

Magnificent indeed was the armour of the knight as he tilted at the tournament. The seats were crowded with bejewelled spectators in gorgeous costumes and dresses. Often these knights fought for the hand of a fair lady. The tournament over, the night was spent in feast and dance, and the retelling of former deeds of valour.

From the picture by Sir J. Gilbert   *Rischgitz*

THE MORNING OF AGINCOURT

Being descended from Queen Isabella, the wife of Edward II, Henry believed that he was the true heir to the throne of France, and his subsequent claim led to the renewal of the Hundred Years War in 1415. He crossed to France with 15,000 men and defeated the French at the Battle of Agincourt against tremendous odds. The morale of the French was completely broken, and Henry followed up his success until the throne of France was within his grasp, but as will be seen later, no English king was destined to wear the French crown.

From the picture by William Kent

Rischg tz

THE MARRIAGE OF HENRY V TO KATHERINE OF FRANCE

By 1420 the French were glad to sign the Treaty of Troyes by which the Dauphin, son of the mad king of France was disinherited, and Henry was declared ' heir of France,' and was married to the Princess Katherine, the French king's daughter.   While the king lived, Henry was to adminster the country in his name and on his death was himself to become king.   But his death in 1422 robbed him of the Crown, and six weeks later the French king also died.   But for Henry's death, the marriage shown above might have changed European history.

From the picture by D. W. Wynfield   *Rischgitz*

DICK WHITTINGTON—LORD MAYOR OF LONDON TOWN

Wars, even in the Middle Ages, were costly affairs, and Henry V had to borrow much money to carry on his campaigns in France. Whittington was a wealthy Lancashire merchant and had lent the king considerable sums. Here we see him at a banquet burning the bonds of the king's indebtedness, but he will be remembered more for his famous cat. "Turn again Whittington, Lord Mayor of London Town," is well known in England.

From an old manuscript   *Rischgitz*

BESIEGING A WALLED CITY

The taking of a city was a very lengthy business in the Middle Ages. This picture shows all the means at the disposal of an attacking force, but even with the invention of gunpowder, the thickness of the walls was proof against a quick decision. Starvation was the really effective weapon, but this often took months before a city surrendered. Meanwhile, the attackers camped outside the city walls until the citizens submitted.

From the picture by Opie

Rischgitz

THE CORONATION OF A BOY KING

Henry VI was less than a year old when he succeeded to the throne, and also to his father's rights under the Treaty of Troyes. While still a child he was crowned, first in Westminster Abbey and then at Paris. But the Dauphin refused to acknowledge Henry or the Treaty of Troyes, and war with France broke out again. England was losing her ownership of France. Henry's court was established for a year at Rouen, and Normandy was gradually becoming the only English possession. Soon only Calais would remain.

From the picture by Stephen Reid

THE PARLIAMENT OF HENRY VI AT READING

In this picture, Henry VI can be seen sitting on his throne in the Parliament which was held at Reading. At this period there was much unrest among the agricultural population. It was in Henry VI's reign that the first " enclosures " of common land took place—a movement that was to deprive all the poorer people of grazing land. Personal liberty was almost extinguished by the constant practice of arbitrary imprisonment.

From the picture by Paul Hardy

By permission of "Pictorial Education"

FALCONRY IN THE MIDDLE AGES

Falconry was a sport reserved for the king and nobles, and no poor man might even keep a hawk. The birds were chosen carefully, and had perches in the bedroom and hall of their owners. They were attached to the wrist by a leather or silk strap. When the falcon had made a kill, it returned again to its owner. In the picture can be seen the decorative hoods covering the eyes of the birds to prevent them unexpectedly flying after prey.

From the Statue at Dowrany by H. Chapu   Mansell

JOAN OF ARC—THE SAVIOUR OF FRANCE

During Henry's minority the Duke of Bedford looked after his interests as Protector of the Realm.   He fought in France, and with such success that in five years the English had got possession of most of the country north of the Loire.   They then pushed on in an attempt to capture Orleans, and if this fell, nothing could save France.   The Dauphin was weak and the French cause appeared hopeless, when there arose the " Maid of Orleans," who claimed that she had received a mission from God to come to the aid of her country.

From the picture by Lenepveu   *Rischgitz*

FROM TRIUMPH TO MARTYRDOM

Clad in white armour, the Maid put fresh vigour into the French and struck terror into the hearts of the English. Orleans was saved, and then she led the troops from victory to victory until she saw the Dauphin triumphantly crowned in the Cathedral of Rheims. But her own people betrayed her and delivered her to the English to be burnt as a witch. Her cause triumphed, however, and by 1453 the Hundred Years War was ended and England had lost her possessions on the Continent. Freed from the Continent, England was able, later, to build an Empire. Nearly five hundred years after the maid was canonised and is now regarded as a revered saint.

From the picture by A. Forestier   *By permission of " The Illus. London News "*

A TRAVELLING THEATRE OF THE MIDDLE AGES

Actors of medieval days were members of the various craftsmen's guilds. With a large waggon on which scenery was erected to make a stage, the players went from town to town, village to village, performing mystery, miracle and morality plays. The appearance of the players was an important event, and everyone, including the officials of the place, crowded the streets to witness the play. The picture shows a scene in the performance of a mystery play about the sacrifice of Abraham, the players' cart stopping in front of the mayor. The street is crowded with interested onlookers, and it is clear that the occasion is one of great importance. Having so little room for "action" these early dramas concentrated upon vivid and forceful speech.

From the picture by A. Forestier

By permission of "The Illus. London News'

BEHIND THE SCENES OF A MEDIEVAL PLAY

The mystery play is preserved to-day in the famous Passion Play produced once every ten years at Oberammergau by the villagers, and in various Christmas mystery plays. The morality play, too, is preserved in the old play entitled *Everyman* which is revived at intervals. The morality plays, as their title suggests, were designed to teach the ultimate triumph of good over evil, the characters being personifications of human virtues and vices. The picture shows the "effects" being produced in a scene depicting hell. Note the ingenious contrivances for "noises off." Hell was often deliberately comic. With the development of facilities for scenic effects, the plays became more ambitious and from such small beginnings has the theatre of the modern world grown.

From the picture by Paul Hardy

By permission of " Pictorial Education "

HENRY VI BUILDING ETON COLLEGE

Henry was a weak king and was constantly faced with the ever-increasing power of the nobles, especially the Earl of Warwick, who, it is said, had at his different castles upwards of thirty thousand men in his service. In the acts of peace, however, he showed more promise, and here we see him taking an active interest in the building of Eton College. As yet, individual craftsmanship had not been supplanted by mass production, and men worked with an affection and pride in the masterpieces they created. Their work defied Time.

From the picture by Sir John Gilbert   *Rischgitz*

THE MURDER OF A DUKE

The stage was being prepared for the outbreak of civil war. One of the king's most powerful opponents was the Duke of Gloucester, and in 1447 the court party decided to strike a blow at their enemies by his arrest. Soon after he died in prison, but many believe that he was murdered with the full knowledge of the king.

From the picture by Charles Lucy   *Spencer Arnold*

JACK CADE'S REBELLION

In 1450, a rebellion broke out in Kent led by a man called Jack Cade. Whereas Wat Tyler's revolt, seventy years before, was almost purely social in character, this was almost wholly political. He entered London with 20,000 men, but after three days of riot and murder the rebellion collapsed. During another rebellion soon after, Cade was captured and died of the wounds which he had received. Here he is seen holding court.

From the picture by Henry A. Payne By permission of The Fine Arts Publishing Co. Ltd.

THE WAR THAT STARTED IN A GARDEN

So long as the English nobles had France for a fighting ground, and French captives to hold for heavy ransom, they were content to let matters go on quietly at home. But with the loss of all possessions on the Continent, the warlike nobles had no outlet for their energies except in England. The rebellion of Jack Cade had served to show the extent of the rising anger against misgovernment which the reign of Henry VI had engendered. Richard, Duke of York, had designs on the throne, and while the king remained without a son he was prepared to wait. But the birth of a son to Henry changed the whole situation. The Duke of Somerset, a descendant of the House of Lancaster, had maintained the traditional feud against the House of York by accusing Richard of being a traitor. Matters came to a head when in a garden Richard plucked a white rose, whereupon his rival plucked a red rose. It was thus that the Wars of the Roses commenced. The nobles now pillaged each other, and in the process the needs of the people were forgotten. The first blood was shed at St. Albans in 1455, where the Yorkists proved victorious, and again at Northampton in 1460, when Henry was taken prisoner and his wife, Queen Margaret, fled with the young Prince Edward to Scotland. Richard now demanded the Crown, but a compromise was reached whereby Henry agreed that Richard and his heirs should succeed him. But Queen Margaret refused to see her son set aside and raised an army to attack the Yorkists, and at the battle of Wakefield in 1460 she proved successful and Richard was slain. But next year, at Towton, the Lancastrians were defeated, and the Earl of Warwick placed Edward on the throne.

From the picture by J. H. Amschewitz
By permission of the Gresham Committee

THE ROYAL PRISONER

The Yorkist leader, Edward IV, escorts his prisoner, Henry VI, to Barnet, where the Lancastrians have mustered for battle. His object is to safeguard himself should Warwick be victorious. During the whole of Edward IV's reign the war went on with varying success to either side, but undeniable loss to the common people who had no real part in these family quarrels. The people's power to vote had been restricted, and the House of Commons had ceased to be democratic even in a moderate degree. Its members were all property owners elected by property owners. Added to this, the rival armies lived by plundering the villages as they passed.

From the picture by J. A. Houston

Spencer Arnold

THE DEATH OF "THE KING-MAKER"

After Edward had been on the throne for a few years, he quarrelled with the Earl of Warwick, who thrust him from the throne and restored Henry VI. But at the battle of Barnet in 1471, Warwick was killed, and Henry suffered one of those mysteriously sudden deaths which most people suspected as murder. In the same year, at Tewkesbury, Edward was slain, and Queen Margaret herself taken prisoner, but after paying a ransom was allowed to return brokenhearted to France. Prince Edward, a lad of twelve, came to the throne as Edward V. The power of the Earl of Warwick was so great, that he has been called "the King-maker."

144

From Strutt's "Dress and Habits"   *Rischgitz*

LABOURERS IN THE FIFTEENTH CENTURY

Laws were passed in the fifteenth century enforcing the social barrier, as far as dress was concerned. The poor labouring class, for instance, might not buy cloth above two shillings a yard, and were for the most part restricted to coarse flannel and linen girdles. The nobles, however, became most elaborate in their attire. No gentleman would think of appearing in a costume of one hue only. Parti-coloured effects grew in favour, even to the point where tights were of a different shade for each leg, and the shoes were of contrasting materials. About this time men began to cut the hair short, even cropping it close to the head. The hat with the rolled brim was worn.

A FIFTEENTH CENTURY BEDROOM

Linen sheets and blankets were now used for beds, and the feather bed had been introduced from France. These beds were handed down from generation to generation. Dress showed the influence of the French court, being short-waisted and long skirted, but attention was mostly centred upon the head - dress. Wire frames were bent in most fantastic shapes, covered in heavy brocades and draped in flowing veils. Turbans and box-like creations were supported on the heads of their wearers, the style of which was no doubt influenced by the oriental interests of the period and copied from spoils brought back from the distant East.

From an old manuscript   *Rischgitz*

From an old manuscript   *Rischgitz*

TAKING TOLL IN THE FIFTEENTH CENTURY

Travelling was dangerous and uncomfortable in the Middle Ages. Here is some advice given to a traveller arriving at an inn . . . . " Undress and wash your legs and then dry them with a cloth, and rub them well for *love* of fleas, that they may not leap on your legs, for there is a pack of them lying in the dust under the rushes." Almost every bridge, road or gateway had its toll which was exacted from travellers. Occasionally this money was applied to improvement, but more often to embellish the already large profits of the owner.

From the picture by Paul Hardy   *By permission of " Pictorial Education "*

THE INVENTION OF PRINTING

The most important event in this period was the introduction of the printing press into England by William Caxton. This invention more than any other served to break down the privilege of learning which had been guarded jealously by the few, and to produce a revolution of thought which was eventually to lead to the rise of democracy. Books made by hand by the monks and scholars could be produced only in small numbers—now machinery could make learning available to the masses. Education was to free the masses from serfdom.

From the picture by Millais

Rischgitz

THE PRINCES IN THE TOWER

The ambitious, unscrupulous and cruel Richard, Duke of Gloucester, was appointed Lord Protector during the minority of his nephew the boy king, Edward V. Richard, on the pretext of protecting the lad, had him lodged in the Tower, and later he was joined by his younger brother. Meanwhile, those who might have assisted the young princes were arrested, and at least one of them, Lord Hastings, executed. Richard's plot to seize the crown was taking its deadly course, and he was already scheming one of the wickedest acts in history.

From the picture by James Northcote, R.A.

Spencer Arnold

THE MURDER OF THE PRINCES

At last, and only three months after Edward's succession to the throne, Richard was ready to play his final card —the murder of the young princes. The exact manner of the crime is not definitely known, but two bodies corresponding to those of the youths have since been discovered in the Tower. Having cleared his rivals out of the way, Richard seized the crown and reigned as Richard III. Two years later, he met his match at the Battle of Bosworth, where he was defeated and killed at the hands of Henry Tudor who became Henry VII.

THE EARLY TUDOR PERIOD
1485-1547

After a period of chaos, nations are often ready, through sheer exhaustion, to accept the rule of an autocracy. The long and useless civil wars between the Houses of Lancaster and York (the Wars of the Roses) had dissipated the wealth of England and had undermined very seriously the gradually increasing power of a semi-democratic central authority. Henry VII, the first of the Tudors, started a form of government which was in every way a despotism. His doubtful claim to the throne through conquest in battle led to two attempts to usurp the Crown, but the leaders, Lambert Simnel and Perkin Warbeck, were easily defeated, and the way was cleared for a strong government centred in the personality of the king.

FOREIGN POLICY

England's relations with the Continent in the history which we have previously reviewed largely rested in the interest which individuals took in their private possessions abroad. In other words, they were personal rather than national possessions. Unsuccessful attempts at European conquests were made from time to time, but now we see an entirely new departure which may be called for the first time—diplomacy. Diplomatic marriages of Henry and members of the Royal Family strengthened the position of Henry at home and abroad ; the king, for instance, married Elizabeth of York and thus united the rival houses of Lancaster and York. Arthur, his son, married Katherine, daughter of the king and queen of Aragon and Castile ; and on his death, a few months after, Katherine was married to the king's second son, Henry ; Margaret went to Scotland as the wife of James IV ; Mary, however, was too young to marry at this stage, but she was married later to the King of France. The use of royal marriages in diplomacy lasted until comparatively recent times.

THE PRESERVATION OF ORDER

The ruthlessness with which Henry VII put down rebellions and attempts to usurp the throne, is best viewed in the light of the terrible disorder during the Wars of the Roses. The nobility had suffered severe losses, many estates had been forfeited to the Crown, and the king became so powerful that the landed nobility were no longer able by their numbers and possessions to overawe the Crown. The new established Court of Star Chamber provided means by which the powerful nobles could be brought to justice without being in the position to bully the judges, as had been the case in the local courts. The growing practice of the nobles to keep large bands of liveried retainers was checked, and thus any noble who was compelled to appear before a court of justice had no longer the support of followers who could, and often did, interfere with witnesses and subvert the course of justice.

But a strong government must have ample funds at its disposal, and Henry soon set about replenishing the depleted coffers of the State, and in this he was helped by his able ministers, especially his chancellor Morton. War is costly, therefore war was to be avoided ; exact accounts were demanded from all officials ; and " Morton's Fork " extorted money from the profligate on the supposition that they could afford to retrench, and from the frugal, since it was assumed that they must have saved enough to spare some for the king.

DECREASE OF THE POWER OF PARLIAMENT

With the increase in the king's purse, there was a corresponding decrease in the power of Parliament. The House of Commons was largely representative of the new and wealthy middle classes, and their interests and the king's were the same, and since the Speaker of the House was chosen from the king's household, no legislation was initiated that went against the interests of Henry or the middle classes. The middle classes, too, would support the king's peace policy, since, apart from those definitely engaged in the manufacture of materials for war, the trading classes thrive in times of peace and lose during war time.

THE NEW WORLD

(a) *The Merchant Adventurers.*

Heretofore, trade had been carried on very largely by foreigners, but now Henry made treaties with foreign countries by which Englishmen

From the picture by Denis Eaen   By permission of The Fine Arts Publishing Co. Ltd.

HENRY VII—THE FIRST OF THE TUDORS

The advent of Henry VII to the throne not only started a new line of kings and queens—the Tudors—but marks the beginning of a new and glorious era in British history. During this period a great new world was discovered—a world which opened up vistas of wealth beyond the imagination of men in the Middle Ages. There was a revival of learning when scholars rediscovered the glories of Ancient Greece and Rome, and by means of the printing press made this learning available to the common people. The above picture of Henry VII is meant to typify this Age of Discovery. It is, as it suggests, an age of youth and great adventures.

From the picture by J. H. Amschewitz   By permission of the artist

THE FIRST WHITE MAN TO LAND IN SOUTH AFRICA

The Portuguese had spent many years trying to find their way round the west coast of Africa. The Turks had taken Constantinople and were therefore in a position to control the supplies of goods coming from the East. They taxed merchants heavily before they would allow them to pass through on their way to the West. In 1486, Bartholomew Dias rounded the Cape of Good Hope and thus showed the way to India. Here we see him taking leave of the King and Queen of Portugal. On the left, members of the crew are taking on board the stone cross which was later erected on the shores of the Cape to record his adventure.

were admitted to buy and sell, on equal terms. The " Merchant Adventurers " as they were called, were a loosely organised band of English merchants trading in the Netherlands— Henry granted them a charter and gave them complete control over the affairs of their trade at home and abroad. The conquests of the Turks in the Eastern Mediterranean had cut off the old routes to India, but Portugal had discovered a new way round the Cape of Good Hope. Thus while foreigners came less to England, English

traders began to visit ports on the Mediterranean and Baltic seas and to the shores of the continent directly opposite England. Bristol became the centre of English activity, and Cabot, with the backing of Henry, set out on his famous voyage of discovery. England had now new interests and ambitions in the unknown western world.

(b) *The Renaissance or Revival of Learning.*

Beliefs are often largely based upon tradition, and traditional beliefs are usually the result of the ability of the few to make the majority accept what has been thought out for them. Any thinking that was done in the Middle Ages was almost entirely in the hands of the Church. Education, such as it was, was dispensed by the monks or other members of the Church. This was natural, since the Bible and other books were written in a tongue (Latin) which only the clergy and lawyers understood. Therefore, the laity believed what they were told to believe, and no question was ever raised as to the logic of accepted beliefs. Suddenly, however, the whole outlook of thinkers was changed by the dissemination of knowledge which followed upon the capture by the Turks of Constantinople, the surviving centre of culture. Learned men were forced to find fresh homes, and many of them crossed into Italy, France, and Germany, and from these places their influence extended to England. Contact with early Greek thought, and the subsequent translation of the Bible into German and English,

led certain eminent men to test the beliefs which had been handed down to them for so long. Luther in Germany ; Wyclif in England ; and many others began to doubt not only the political authority of the Pope, but the very fundamental principles upon which the Catholic faith was based. This was to lead to a demand for a reform of obvious abuses, and eventually to break away from Rome, which was as complete as any event in English history. The spirit of the age is well exemplified in the virile writings of Chaucer (the father of English literature), and the introduction of printing enabled the new knowledge to be spread more widely than before the time of Caxton, the first English printer.

ACCESSION OF HENRY VIII

This reign may be conveniently divided into two parts—that which corresponds to the influence of Wolsey, and the period covered by

From the picture by F. Pradilla

By permission of The Ladies' Carlton Club

THE SURRENDER OF GRANADA, 1492

For nearly eight centuries the Mohammedans and Christians had been at war. The long struggle ended with the capture of Granada from the Moors by Ferdinand and Isabella of Castile, and thus Spain was free to develop her great exploration feats, which were to end, however, with the final defeat of the Spanish Armada in the reign of Elizabeth. Here we see the Moorish king riding down from his palace, the famous Alhambra, to deliver the keys of the city of Granada to King Ferdinand. Queen Isabella sits proudly on her white horse watching the conquered infidels acknowledging the might of Spain's great army.

Henry's quarrel with the Pope following the failure of Wolsey to settle the divorce question according to Henry's demands.

(a) Immediately on his accession, Henry married his widowed sister-in-law, Katherine— an event which was to have far-reaching results. The position may be summarised as follows :—

(1) The Pope was struggling to maintain his position in European countries many of which were showing signs of straining at the leash— therefore, friendship with the powerful Catholic father of Henry's wife Katherine was essential ; (2) Henry, married to the daughter of a powerful king, was without a male heir to the throne, and (3) Wolsey, as Papal legate, found him-

self on the horns of a dilemma—could he serve two masters, the King and the Pope ?

The Pope and Wolsey attempted procrastination, but Henry, becoming suspicious of Wolsey's intentions, removed him from office in 1529, on the charge that his acceptance of the office of Papal legate was illegal. A year later he was summoned to London on a charge of treason, but died when on his way to London to answer this new attack.

(b) *The Political Reformation.*

With the fall of Wolsey, Henry took matters into his own hands, and in this he was helped by the increasing growth of the national life of the community. People were no longer willing to

From the picture by R. Balaca   *Mansell*

THE RETURN OF COLUMBUS

Christopher Columbus, a Genoese sailor, had settled in Portugal. After much study he became convinced that the world was round like a ball and not flat like a penny, and that there was land across the western ocean and the land must be India. In 1492 he set out to find India, but sailed too far west and accidentally discovered land (the Indies) which he mistook for India. Here he is seen at the court of Isabella and Ferdinand on his return from his wonderful voyage which lasted two hundred and twenty-five days. Note the captives on the right, and the heap of treasures on the left which are being offered to their Spanish majesties by the explorer.

From the picture by J. H. Amschewitz   *By permission of the artist*

VASCO DA GAMA REACHES INDIA

Another Portuguese, Vasco da Gama, twelve years after Bartholomew Dias had rounded the Cape of Good Hope made the longer journey and actually reached India. When news of his great voyage reached King Manuel of Portugal, he wrote with pride to the king and queen of Spain, saying : "They did reach and discover India, and other kingdoms . . . they entered and navigated its sea, finding large cities, large buildings and rivers and great populations, among whom is carried on all the trade in spices and precious stones which are forwarded in ships to Mecca, and thence to Cairo, whence they are dispersed throughout the world." These early pioneers suffered from the ridicule of the people, but their work has glorified their names for ever.

place so much political power in the hands of a Church the head of which lived in a foreign country. Their interests were centred in trade, agriculture and manufacture, and in learning, art and travel. Therefore, Henry ignored the Pope and turned to Parliament, where he found this growing sense of national independence amply reflected.

THOMAS CROMWELL

A new figure came on the scene to sway the destinies of England. This was Thomas Cromwell, Wolsey's secretary, who served his master faithfully until the latter's end. His was a life devoted to one purpose only : to raise the king to a peak of eminence far above the powers of the Church or of the Parliament.

By his machinations he was instrumental in assisting Henry to take the title of " Supreme Head of the Church of England on earth " and to elect himself as Vicar-General or Vice-regent of the king in all ecclesiastical matters. From this vantage point he struck at the Catholic Church. He was responsible for the execution of

Sir Thomas More for refusing to acknowledge the legality of the king's divorce ; and in his furious campaign against Catholicism he spread death and disaster throughout the country. For ten years he stood behind the throne of England directing the king's power. The Reformation was beginning, but it was shadowed by terror of an utterly ruthless man, who was prepared to wade through blood to achieve his ambitions.

But his arrangement of Henry's unwilling marriage with Anne of Cleves proved his undoing. The king turned against him and he was executed in 1540, on the very day that the king married Katherine Howard, only four days after his marriage with Anne had been annulled.

THE SUPPRESSION OF THE MONASTERIES

There were six stages in the development of the Reformation. In the first place, Henry assumed the title of " Defender of the Faith " by Act of Parliament, thus the Church became subordinated to the State. This led inevitably to a separation from the Papacy. The third stage has

From the picture by J. H. Amschewitz   *By permission of the artist*

VASCO DA GAMA SIGHTS THE CAPE

Imagine the thrill which Vasco da Gama must have experienced when he first sighted the Cape of Good Hope. Months of anxious toil against the fury of the sea was now crowned by success, and da Gama was within striking distance of his goal. No longer could the infidels cut off the abundant riches of the East from the Western world, or continue to levy tribute on such goods as they thought fit to allow through their territory. Here he is seen clinging to the rigging as the angry seas sweep over his tiny ship.

brought the greatest criticism of Henry's reign—the suppression of the monasteries. Throughout the Middle Ages the monasteries had been the centres of learning and of charity. But as time went on, they accumulated considerable wealth, and many of them ceased to perform the duties for which they were originally founded. Henry, faced with the need of money, cast covetous eyes upon this wealth, and although certain monasteries certainly needed suppressing or radical reform, the king's motive was plunder. Had the money which he obtained been used for the furtherance of education, the English would have been educated during a period of two centuries before the Industrial Revolution of the eighteenth century. As it was, the machine age arrived too soon for the influence of education to have any controlling

effect. It is only now that we are, through education, beginning to repair some of the damage done in those early days. At stage four, the common use of the Bible and of Church services in English, Henry wished to stop. He made it quite clear that his quarrel was with the Pope and not with the Catholic religion, and to emphasise this view he issued the "Act of Six Articles," in which was reaffirmed the principal doctrines of the Catholic Church. Acts of Parliament, however, were not sufficient to stem the flow of new ideas, and the purely political reformation of Henry VIII was to lead after his death to an acceptance of the two final stages. These were, a simplification of ceremonies and a change in long-accepted doctrines.

The remaining years of Henry's reign were

From the picture by Veloso Salgado

By permission of the Sociedade de Geografia de Lisbon

VASCO DA GAMA AT CALICUT

It took da Gama a month to sail from Mozambique to Calicut in India. There he met the ruler and tried to exchange his goods for spices, but the Indians laughed, as they wanted only gold, silver and scarlet cloth. Indeed, some of his men were taken prisoners, but were eventually released, and da Gama set sail again for home. After many privations he reached Portugal to tell his king how he had found the sea road to India.

From the picture by Ernest Board · Copyright of the Corporation of Bristol

JOHN CABOT, A FAMOUS ENGLISH EXPLORER

The English were not long in following the example of Portugal and Spain. Early in May of 1497 John Cabot set out on a voyage of discovery in the " Matthew " of Bristol. The merchants of Bristol had for long believed that there were islands to the west of Ireland. After seven weeks land was sighted and Cabot thought that he had reached China, but had in fact reached " New-found-land," as he called it. Thus Newfoundland became England's first colony overseas, since he took possession of the country in the name of Henry VII. Although late in the field, the English eventually outstripped the Spanish and Portuguese.

mainly concerned with his successive marriages, and his early popularity with the people was so strained that few mourned his death in 1547.

THE CONDITIONS OF THE PEOPLE

The relations between employers and employed, as we saw in the chapter dealing with the Peasants' Revolt, were just changing. By Tudor times, the rates of wages provided for in the Statute of Labourers could no longer be enforced. The Government, however, was determined not to leave the masters and men to settle their differences by themselves. In 1563, Parliament passed an act known as the Statute of Artificers. This act required that trades engagements should be by the year, and that no employer was to be allowed to discharge his workman, nor any workman to leave his employer except at the end of a year of service, and after three months' warning. Every workman was compelled to serve seven years' apprenticeship and was not allowed to leave his home district without official permission from the authorities. Hours of labour were also strictly regulated, and wages were to be settled each year by the justices of the peace. In the summer the workman commenced work at five in the morning and finished at seven or eight in the evening, and in the winter from dawn to dark.

In spite of all these regulations, however, pauperism was considerable. The monastic system at its best, and the old feudal system with

From the picture by Tom Mostyn

By permission of F. G. Robinson

BRISTOL WIVES ARE TOO WELL DRESSED

After the Wars of the Roses, the king's exchequer was in a very low state, since money had been squandered on this futile succession of battles. Henry VII, with the assistance of his Chancellor Morton, determined to repair these losses by taxing the people. " Morton's Fork," as it was called, served to tax both the extravagant and the thrifty, since it was maintained that if a person spent too much he could afford to cut down his expenditure, and if he spent too little he had a surplus to give the king. On a visit to Bristol, the merchants decked their wives in their finest array in honour of the king. Henry fined them for their extravagance.

From the picture by F. Cadogan Cowper, A.R.A.

THE NEW LEARNING

This is a symbolic picture representing the spirit of the New Learning which reached its height during the Tudor period. The Middle Ages were now fast passing away, and with them the restricted possession of such learning as existed in the hands of the few scholars who possessed the key to knowledge. Men and women were beginning to question the old order as to whether it represented the best of all possible worlds.

Rischgitz

A TRIAL OF WEIGHTS AND MEASURES

As trade increased, the rough-and-ready methods of barter must give way to a system which is more exact.
It becomes important that money values should be stabilised, and that weights and measures should be accurate.
Here we see a trial of weights and measures, which served to standardise these for the whole country, and to
check any which may have become defective through deterioration or rendered inaccurate by dishonest traders.

From an old manuscript

Mansell

HENRY VII FOUNDS KING'S CHAPEL

Henry VII encouraged all forms of learning. This picture, a page from an old manuscript, shows the king giving indentures to monks for the founding of King's Chapel. Tudor architecture represents one of the great periods in the history of building. This period also marked the eve of literary appreciation.

all its faults, were based upon the responsibility of the community for all within that community. When the monasteries ceased to do the work for which they were founded, and the feudal system began to break up, no organisation was available for the care of those who needed assistance. Private charity had broken down, and paupers, left to their own devices, travelled up and down the country, gathering in large numbers on the outskirts of the larger towns and indulging in all forms of lawlessness. The government had attempted to deal with the problem, but with little success. Soon after the passing of the Statute of Artificers, however, a law was passed " to the intent that idle and loitering persons and valiant beggars may be avoided, and the impotent, feeble and lame, which are the poor in very deed, should be hereafter relieved and well provided for." Collectors were to be appointed in each parish whose duty it was to discover the numbers of the real paupers and of those who were in a position to help. From the latter the collectors were given power to exact a weekly sum for the proper upkeep of the paupers. Those who were not paupers were forbidden by law to beg publicly in the future.

THE FIRST ENGLISH POOR LAW

It was easier to legislate for than to solve the problem of pauperism. In spite of penal laws, vagabonds still persisted, and law followed law to suppress them. According to one law, any person declared to be a vagabond shall be " stripped naked from the middle upward and shall be openly whipped until his or her body be bloody." According to another law the sturdy beggar was to be " greviously whipped and burnt through the gristle of the right ear with a hot iron of the compass of an inch about."

Then towards the end of Elizabeth's reign, all this petty legislation was collected into the Poor Law of 1601, which remained the established law of England down to 1834. Houses of correction were to be built to which those who were unable or unwilling to find work were to be confined and compelled to work. For the poor who could not work almshouses were built. Overseers of the poor were established in each parish, and all people of any means were taxed to supply the money to support this system. Thus was established for the first time the principle that the State was responsible for the poor and was the beginning of State social legislation.

After Holbein   *Rischgitz*

"BLUFF KING HAL"

"The world owes some of its greatest debts to men from whose memory it recoils." Henry VIII, no matter what the motive, lifted England up out of the old medieval ruts and placed her squarely and securely on the new highway of material progress. Though political freedom diminished, order and peace came from the iron hand of absolute power. His reign brought forth religious reforms which altered the whole aspect of English life for ever. He dominated his country yet was at all times an object of affection to his people.

Mansell

A PRISONER IN THE TOWER

Sir Walter Raleigh said of Henry VIII—" If all the pictures and patterns of a merciless prince were lost in the world, they might all again be painted to the life out of the story of this king." This interesting picture shows a prisoner in the Tower, that building which for centuries had been the scene of countless tragedies. Imprisonment, torture, and death befell the sad victims whose offences brought them to the grim fortress. Great men and women came in shame to the narrow gateway in the foreground known as the Traitors' Gate. Henry's own queen, Anne Boleyn, entered the Tower for the last time through this fatal archway.

From the picture by John Faed   *By permission of the Wolverhampton Art Gallery*

THE MORNING BEFORE FLODDEN

In 1513 Henry invaded France, and the Scots, who were still the implacable enemies of the English, took the opportunity of invading England in order to assist their allies the French. At the Battle of Flodden, the English general, Lord Surrey, surrounded the Scots and inflicted such a crushing defeat that few survivors were able to make their way back to Scotland. During the encounter, James IV of Scotland was slain.

Rischgitz

LUTHER BURNING THE PAPAL BULL

Martin Luther, the German religious reformer stirred the world with his doctrines against the Roman Church. Eventually the Pope issued a Bull of Excommunication against him and his followers, but refusing to be intimidated the monk publicly burned the Bull together with other documents to show his defiance.

From the picture by Sir John Gilbert   *Rischgitz*

HENRY VIII AND WOLSEY

Henry VIII had the faculty of choosing able men for his ministers. The most famous was Thomas Wolsey who rose from humble beginnings until from 1514 to 1529 he almost ruled England. He fell from power through his inability to secure a divorce for Henry from Katherine of Aragon and after a short period was sent into retirement at his palace at Esher. With the exception of Bishop Gardiner in the reign of Mary, he was the last great clerical statesman. Since then all high ministers of the Crown have been laymen.

After the picture by A. Johnstone   *Rischgitz*

WILLIAM TYNDALE TRANSLATING THE BIBLE

The Tudor period produced great men—Tyndale and Coverdale gave England the Bible in Tudor English, Cranmer the Prayer Book, and Latimer the soul of the popular movement which was to demand so much sacrifice and claim so many martyrs. The Bible, as Tyndale wished, became familiar even to " the boy that driveth the plough,'' and brought religion into the humble homes of English peasantry throughout the land.

After Holbein (?)   *Kischgitz*

HENRY EMBARKS FOR FRANCE

The greatness of Cardinal Wolsey was seen to best advantage in his realisation of the futility of continuing a succession of continental wars which, in the past, had only succeeded in draining the wealth of England. France and Germany were becoming rivals and Wolsey's plan was to maintain a balance of power. In 1520 Henry set out for France on a mission of peace amidst scenes of great enthusiasm and acclamation.

After Holbein (?)   *Kischgitz*

THE FIELD OF THE CLOTH OF GOLD

The King of France and the Emperor Charles V of Germany vied with each other in seeking Henry's alliance. The Emperor visited England to meet the English sovereign, while the King of France arranged an interview in his own dominion, known from the magnificence of the occasion as the " Field of the Cloth of Gold." England was soon to become one of the foremost nations of Europe, and to dominate foreign affairs.

After Holbein   *Rischgitz*

HENRY VIII AND THE BARBER SURGEONS

This interesting picture shows the king presenting a charter to the barber surgeons. Royal patronage was sought by all sorts and conditions of trades, and unless a person belonged to such a recognised body he would be unable to practise his trade. The foundations of commerce were greatly strengthened by Henry's patronage.

From the picture by Sir J. Gilbert   *Rischgitz*

WOLSEY'S QUARREL WITH BUCKINGHAM

The more powerful Wolsey became the more enemies he made. One of the most important of these was Edward, Duke of Buckingham. Although Henry had been married to Katherine for a long time, apart from a delicate girl there were no children. Buckingham, therefore, as a descendant of Edward III, might cause trouble if the king died without issue. He was executed in 1521, on a charge of supposed treason.

From the original painting by Vivian Forbes　　　　　　*By permission of John Swain & Son Ltd.*

WOLSEY AND HIS RIVAL SIR THOMAS MORE

A serious crisis was now arising as Henry was determined to rid himself of Katherine, and offered as an excuse, that since she was the widow of his elder brother, Arthur, the marriage was invalid. Wolsey was in favour of the divorce as he wished the king to marry a French princess, but Sir Thomas More, who was eventually to succeed him, did not agree with his policy, and opposed the Cardinal by every possible means.

After William Bromley　　　　　　*By permission of the Manchester Corporation*

KATHERINE AND THE CARDINALS

Henry appealed to the Pope to annul the marriage. This the Pope did not wish to do, but he agreed to send delegates to England to try the case with Wolsey. Here we see the Pope's representatives interviewing Katherine, who throughout maintained her rights as a wife and rejected any suggestions for a compromise.

From the picture by Frank O. Salisbury.   *By permission of the Fine Arts Publishing Co. Ltd.*

KATHERINE APPEALS TO HENRY

Meanwhile Henry had fallen in love with Anne Boleyn, a lady-in-waiting at the court, and turned a deaf ear
to the pathetic appeals of his wife. The Pope then ordered that the trial of the case should be transferred
to Rome, and actually commanded Henry to appear in person. This infuriated the king who blamed Wolsey
for the delay. At last, to secure his will, Henry declared himself supreme head of the Church of England.

After Westall   *Rischgitz*

THE FALL OF WOLSEY

The failure to obtain the divorce cost Wolsey Henry's favour, and he was banished from the court. In 1530, he was summoned to London to face what he believed to be a charge of high treason, but he died in Leicester Abbey on his way from York, although Henry sent three of his own physicians to attend the Cardinal. Shakespeare has these words in his play: " O, how wretched is that poor man that hangs on princes' favour.''

After J. Nash   *Rischgitz*

HENRY AND ANNE BOLEYN

Henry decided to ignore the Pope, and to ask Archbishop Cranmer to try his case. This was done and, of course, resulted in the king's favour. Immediately he married Anne, and within a few weeks she presented him with a daughter, Elizabeth, the future queen of England. Mary, his daughter by Katherine, was declared illegitimate, and treated with the utmost humility and disgrace by the new queen and her supporters.

From the picture by William Peters, R.A.   Spencer Arnold

CRANMER BAPTISING PRINCESS ELIZABETH

Princess Elizabeth was baptised by Archbishop Cranmer, who is here seen performing the ceremony. Unfortunately Anne had behaved indiscreetly and thereby aroused Henry's jealousy, and before she could present him with a son, she was executed. Two days afterwards Henry married Jane Seymour, and by her he had a son, born in 1537, but the queen died soon after his birth. He remained for two years a widower.

From the picture by J. R. Herbert   Kischgitz

SIR THOMAS MORE IN THE TOWER

Sir Thomas More had refused to accept the Act of Parliament which had settled the succession on the children of Henry and Anne and was sent to the Tower, together with Fisher, Bishop of Rochester. Both were executed, and Thomas Cromwell became the king's chief adviser and by his aid attacked the monasteries.

From the picture by Stephen Reid   *By permission of the artist*

THE VISITATION OF A MONASTERY

At this time there were in England more than six hundred monastic houses, many of which had become extremely wealthy. They had done good service as retreats for men of peace and learning, but with the rise of new universities much of their educational value had departed. Cromwell sent round a commission to discover the amount of wealth possessed by the monasteries, so that he might seize it for his royal master.

From the picture by Sir George Harvey   *Spencer Arnold*

READING FROM A CHAINED BIBLE

Henry cast greedy eyes upon monastic wealth, and although many houses had fallen into a dissolute state and deserved dissolution, the motive was personal plunder, since little of the wealth thus acquired was devoted to education, but was divided between the king and his courtiers. Meanwhile, the Bible was read with avidity, but Henry later prohibited its reading by the '' lower sort of people,'' who were to him but slaves of his will.

THE ELIZABETHAN PERIOD

WE have seen that Henry VIII had no intention of introducing a doctrinal reformation, but after his death, Edward VI, who was a minor, came to the throne, and the Duke of Somerset who had been declared Protector during the young King's minority, thereupon determined to force the last two stages of the Reformation upon the people. Changes in religious customs were introduced rapidly—crucifixes and images of saints were destroyed ; stained glass windows picturing figures of Christ, the Apostles and Saints, were removed ; the use of holy water was forbidden ; clergy gave up the use of coloured robes ; fasting became less general; clergy were allowed to marry ; penances were no longer imposed ; and pilgrimages were forbidden. The final stage was reached in 1548, when the Act of the Six Articles was repealed, and the new faith of the Protestant Church was codified into forty-two articles, and these took permanent shape in the " Thirty-nine Articles " of the present Prayer Book. The Act of Uniformity (1552) ordered the English Prayer Book to be used in all churches and all people were compelled to visit their parish church on Sunday.

ENCLOSURES OF LAND

This was, indeed, a period of upheaval. While religious beliefs were undergoing such transitions, changes of no less importance were taking place with regard to the land system. During the Middle Ages, England had been in the main a country of small peasant farmers, each raising sufficient to feed himself and his family, and maybe a little over to sell. At the other end of the social scale were the big feudal landowners, who relied upon forced labour to work their demesnes. This system, with its admitted evils, nevertheless, represented productions for *use* and not for *profit*. Now, however, a new type of farmer came into existence. He rented large tracts of land which he enclosed with fences and used for sheep farming, which was much more profitable. Small farmers were evicted from their holdings wholesale, and since one man could look after many hundreds of sheep, much unemployment resulted. The old village life was broken up ; farmers and their families became paupers ; houses disappeared ; the church became a ruin

and there was nothing left but a sheep-cot and a few herdsmen's hovels. Attempts were made to restrict sheep-farming, but they proved of little avail. The Duke of Somerset realised the danger of the situation and had a keen desire to help the peasantry, but they became so restless, that he was compelled to use force, and in one insurrection over 3,000 men were killed. The new sheep farmers had powerful friends, and Somerset was deposed for his friendliness to the poor, and the Duke of Northumberland, a man after their own heart, took his place. There was no more talk of resistance to enclosures. Fortunately, the acuteness of the problem was lessened by the increase in manufacturing, for many of the farm-labourers were able to find work in the new industries.

QUEEN MARY

It is not the duty of any historian to make out a brief for any person who has played a part upon the stage of history. Therefore, personal, religious or other views must not be allowed to warp an impartial judgment of historical facts. Queen Mary came to the throne immediately following an upheaval in religious affairs which had been brought about by political action. The people were still Catholic at heart, and as yet had been little affected by these changes. Immediately the throne became vacant, however, there was a plot by the Duke of Northumberland to place Lady Jane Grey on the throne and so preserve a Protestant succession to the exclusion of Mary. No sooner had this been suppressed, than Mary was faced with the rebellion of Sir Thomas Wyatt, which had as its object the placing of her sister, Elizabeth, on the throne. It should be remembered that at this time, there was only one accepted method for dealing with enemies—execution—and this was employed by Catholics and Protestants in turn. Toleration was unknown, since undemocratic government cannot allow an energetic opposition (cf., modern Italy, Germany and Russia). This is not an excuse for intolerance, but an explanation of its causes.

THE QUEEN'S POLICY

With the object of strengthening her position, as a Catholic queen, Mary married the Catholic

From the picture by Ernest Board

By permission of the Fine Arts Publishing Co. Ltd.

LATIMER PREACHING TO EDWARD VI

After Jane Seymour, on the advice of Cromwell, Henry married Anne of Cleves, but he did not like the look of her when she came to England, and so she was divorced and Cromwell was executed for his mistake. On the day of his execution, the king married Katherine Howard, who was duly executed on a charge of immorality and succeeded by the sixth wife, Katherine Parr, who, fortunately for herself, outlived the king. In 1547 the king died, and since no other child had been born, Edward, at the age of ten years, the son of the third wife, Jane Seymour, came to the throne with a legacy of a " Reformed Church which by Act of Parliament had been separated from Rome.'' But Henry, while desiring to repudiate the influence of the Papacy, had no desire to change the religious character of the Church, and, in fact, resisted all attacks upon the Catholic faith. On his death, however, the young king's advisers, among the foremost of whom were Archbishop Cranmer and Bishop Latimer, determined to take the Reformation a stage further by the issue of the first Prayer Book in the English tongue (1549). The new nobles who had become rich at the expense of the Church had enclosed large tracts of land, thus depriving the small farmers of their livelihood. Ket, a Norfolk farmer, led a rebellion against " enclosing,'' and here we see Latimer preaching to Edward against this practice. In the reign of Queen Mary, Cranmer and Latimer were put to death for heresy at Oxford, where there is a memorial to them.

Philip of Spain, in whom she thought she would find a strong ally for her furtherance of the Catholic faith. Her undoubted love for him was not reciprocated, and after a short stay in England he returned to Spain. Left alone, and with her love spurned, a curious psychological change took place—she sublimated her natural passions by a religious fervour only exceeded by the brutality with which she carried out her schemes. Through her influence, Parliament repealed the legislation of Henry VIII and Edward VI in so far as it gave support to Protestantism. She revived the persecuting statutes against heretics. The old relations with the Pope were resumed but the monastic lands were left in the hands of their new owners. This latter fact shows the enormous economic change which had taken place. The queen dared not attempt to dispossess the new type of landowner— even in the name of religion. Not only were people expected to *act* alike in religious matters, but by the use of burning and torture they were compelled to *think* alike. But the queen's cruelty

was the cruelty of sincerity, and never, like her father's hangings, beheadings and burnings, the result of tyranny, indifference or caprice. In other words, Mary was a sincere, religious woman, who believed that there was only one way to salvation, and that any steps, no matter how cruel, were justified in the attempt to save a soul.

FOREIGN POLICY

Philip's idea in marrying Mary was to drag England into the continental war between Spain and France. Although England was still averse from entering continental politics, at last Mary was persuaded to send troops to the aid of Spain. This was a ghastly blunder, and as a consequence of defeat, England lost Calais. The loss of pride was greater than the actual loss of Calais, since with the rise of trading interests in the Netherlands, Calais had become of very little importance to England. But it was a blow from which Mary never recovered, and she died, to use her own words, "with the name of Calais written on her heart." So ended an unfortunate reign.

From the picture by John Pettie   Rischgitz

EDWARD VI IN COUNCIL

The Duke of Gloucester had shown sympathy with the rebellions against enclosures which were arising all over the country, but the Duke of Northumberland was determined to put them down, and as a first step had Somerset charged with high treason and executed. He then allied himself with the extreme Protestant party, and in the second year of the reign the whole character of the Mass was changed. The Communion Service was to be considered as a memorial of Christ's death, and not, as in the Mass, the transforming of Bread and Wine into the actual Body and Blood of Christ. When the young king was dying the Duke of Northumberland persuaded him to make a will leaving the crown—which he had no right to do—to Lady Jane Grey.

A BUSY PORT IN

Year by year during the Tudor period, the spirit of adventure had been growing stronger, and especially during the reign of Queen Elizabeth when the great deeds of Hawkins, Frobisher, Drake and Raleigh were on every lip. The discovery of the New World had opened up visions of untold wealth, and few were the men, and even boys, who did not long to sail the Spanish Main in search of adventure and fortune. The English "sea-dogs" had struck terror into the hearts of their foes, since English ships were sailing North, South, East and West in search of new lands and fresh openings for trade. What wonderful tales the parrot

TUDOR TIMES

in the picture could tell of lands across the sea ! It is impossible fully to appreciate the boldness of these Elizabethan sailors unless we realise that many of the ships in which they sailed on their voyages of discovery were no larger than a fishing vessel of to-day ; that their nautical instruments were crude and inefficient ; that it was difficult for them to keep their food and water for long in decent condition ; and that disease was almost a greater enemy than the sea itself. It is only when we realise these things that the magnificent daring of the Elizabethan sailors may be properly understood and fully appreciated at the present day.

From the picture by Holbein   *Rischgitz*

EDWARD VI GRANTING A CHARTER

Here we see the young king granting a charter.   He had never been strong, and in 1552 he had measles, followed by small-pox, and subsequently died of consumption in 1553, at the age of 16.   In his short life he seems to have been a good, serious youth, but the schemers who surrounded the throne gave him little peace of mind or opportunity to develop a definite personality of his own.   Mary, his step-sister, followed him on the throne.

ELIZABETH—HER DIFFICULTIES

Mary the Catholic was succeeded by her Protestant sister Elizabeth.   An Act of Parliament declared Elizabeth to be the true and lawful heir to the throne, but her position was full of difficulty, if not peril.   Mary Stuart of Scotland, now queen of France, claimed the throne through descent from Henry VII.   She based her claim on the plea that the Pope had not recognised the marriage of Henry VIII and Anne Boleyn, of which marriage Elizabeth was the issue.   In this she was supported by France and Rome.   Scotland maintained a position of isolated independence and was certainly not friendly, while Ireland,

being still Catholic, was willing to join in any attack upon a Protestant sovereign.   Philip of Spain had hopes of marrying Elizabeth, and in doing so saw a possibility of annexing England to his own domains.

The religious problem was bristling with danger ; the country was hopelessly divided— in the north there were many powerful families who remained Catholic, while in the southeast counties the Protestants supported the reformed church.   Further than this, the new order of Jesuits was attempting to bring England under the complete rule of Rome, while the Puritans were aiming at the destruction of every vestige of Romanism that still remained in the Church.

No sooner was Elizabeth's accession announced than the Pope declared her illegitimate, and ordered her to lay aside her crown and submit to him. Elizabeth and Parliament replied to this attack by enforcing the Act of Supremacy and a new Act of Uniformity. The power to deal with rebels was placed in the hands of the High Commission Court, and it was by this means that many Catholics and Puritans were put to death on charges of treason. The whole object of this policy was to maintain a balance between the old and the new, and this undoubtedly saved a religious civil war such as had rent France in pieces, split Germany and Italy into petty states, and resulted in Spain in the setting up of the Inquisition, and of subsequent intellectual death. It is interesting to note that no nation has survived the suppression of individual liberty of thought. It should be remembered that, unlike Mary's reign, there was no attempt to make people believe the same, but for the sake of national unity people were to show an outward conformity, i.e., Catholics and Puritans were condemned for *treason* and not heresy. Elizabeth and her advisers were not religious fanatics, but they realised that a religious war would prevent the building up of national unity which alone could resist successfully a foreign power—especially Spain.

THE MARRIAGE QUESTION

The diplomatic consequences of marriage have been mentioned before, but at no stage of English history has it been fraught with so much importance as during the reign of Elizabeth.

Her dilemma may be summarised as follows :—

(1) Her marriage to an English subject, whether Protestant or Catholic, would alienate the sympathies of those who did not hold the religious convictions of her husband. This ruled out the Earl of Leicester who, it has long been suspected, had claims to her real love.

(2) If she married Philip II of Spain, she would antagonise (*a*) the Protestants of England, (*b*) France, the bitter enemy of Spain, and (*c*) she would reawaken the fear that Spain would dominate England and make her a vassal state.

(3) The Duke of Anjou, son of Henry II of France, proposed, but being a Catholic he was repugnant to English Protestants, and such a marriage would arouse the enmity of Spain.

Thus she developed a policy of apparent fickleness, playing off one suitor against another.

The key to all her policy was procrastination, when she was forced to make a definite move— compromise. England owes a debt of gratitude to a queen who placed the interest of her country before her natural desires as a woman.

MARY QUEEN OF SCOTS

No impartial historian can fail to come to the conclusion that Elizabeth was in danger of her life throughout her reign. No sooner was one plot discovered than another took birth, and the most dangerous of them all was the attempt to place Mary Queen of Scots on the throne. In 1561 Mary Stuart returned to Scotland and assumed the Scottish crown, and immediately asserted her right to the English throne. She was never popular in Scotland, since the people were very suspicious of the activities of a Catholic queen, and after the murder of her husband, Darnley, she was compelled to seek refuge in England, to the infinite embarrassment of Elizabeth. On the Continent a Catholic reaction had set in ; the king of France had ordered a massacre of Protestants on St. Bartholomew's Day and the Pope had ordered a solemn thanksgiving for the slaughter ; William the Silent, who had driven out the Catholics from the Netherlands had been assassinated by a Jesuit fanatic ; and the Pope had excommunicated Elizabeth and released her subjects from allegiance to her (1570). In the midst of all this, Mary Stuart was involved in a plot to assassinate Elizabeth, and to place herself on the throne as a Catholic queen. Whether she was merely a tool or an active co-operator in the scheme is uncertain, but Elizabeth's ministers decided that the queen's safety depended on the removal of such a powerful claimant to the throne. In 1587 Mary Stuart was beheaded.

THE ARMADA

At the Scottish queen's death, she bequeathed her dominions, including her claim to England, to Philip II of Spain, instead of to her son, James, who was a Protestant. Philip with the encouragement of the Pope, decided to invade England, conquer it, annex it to his dominions, and restore the religion of Rome. The eventual results of this scheme are too well known to bear reiteration here, but it is interesting to note that the names of some of the most famous Catholic families are to be found amongst those who stoutly resisted the Spanish attempt at invasion. England had become a nation, and when she was in danger, the Catholics chose to defend their

From the picture by Antonio More   *Rischgitz*

MARY TUDOR—A CATHOLIC QUEEN

Mary, the daughter of Henry VIII and Katherine of Aragon, was a woman of plain features, but like all the Tudors, possessed a resolute spirit and staunch courage. Declared illegitimate by Act of Parliament her early life had been one of embitterment, and the views which she so stoutly supported were by no means popular. Owing to the conflict between her and a large section of the country her reign was a very unhappy one.

country, even against the foremost Catholic power.

INSURRECTION IN IRELAND (1595)

Since the partial conquest of Ireland in the reign of Henry II, the condition of that country was deplorable. The native chiefs quarrelled amongst themselves almost incessantly; the English attempted to force a religion upon the country which the people detested; and the greed and misgovernment of the rulers added considerably to the general misery. In the words of Raleigh, "The country was a commonwealth of common woe." The object of the government following on the rebellion was "not to subdue but to destroy," and the thoroughness of the policy ended in the final submission of the starving remant of the Irish people. It is a black page in English history.

AN EXPANDING WORLD

The later Tudor period is one of continual expansion both in the world of fact and in the world of ideas. Increasing interest in trade led men to make magnificently bold journeys of discovery; the rediscovering of the literature of the ancients breathed new life into the realm of letters.

In 1492, Christopher Columbus braved the unknown waters of the Atlantic and after fighting mutiny, disease, and, greater than anything else, the sea itself, he eventually landed at the West Indies. Later, Amerigo Vespucci landed on the mainland and the new world, named America after him, first became known. Other famous voyages were made to Newfoundland, India, Africa and the Spice Islands. Newfoundland became the first English overseas colony; the Cape of Good Hope was rounded by the Portuguese who reached India. Men's minds were

LADY JANE GREY OFFERED THE CROWN

The ambitious Duke of Northumberland had married his fourth son, Guildford Dudley, to Lady Jane Grey, the grand-daughter of Henry VIII's sister Mary. On the death of Edward, the Duke attempted to rally the Protestants against the Catholic Mary, and had Jane Grey proclaimed queen, but she was never recognised.

From the picture by W. F. Yeames   *Rischgitz*

LADY JANE GREY IN THE TOWER

Mary was opposed to Lady Jane's accession and at once raised an army in Norfolk where the Catholic party was strong.   Northumberland was unpopular in the country and the people were, on the whole, antagonistic to the changes in religion, since they were still Catholic at heart.   Northumberland, therefore, found little support and Mary succeeded in having him arrested and executed—Lady Jane was sent to the Tower.

being opened to the possibilities of these great new worlds which the resolute explorers were opening up.

Just as men's minds were being stimulated by the new discoveries of the external world so were they stimulated also from within by the range of new thoughts which came from Italy. This Renaissance, or rebirth of learning, meant that the outworn philosophies and writings of the Middle Ages were giving way before the new " humanism "—that is to say the more vigorous and beautiful learning of the ancient Greeks. This cultural advancement was again increased by the existence of the printing press, the invention of which meant that more people could obtain books owing to the reduction of prices, and learning, previously confined to the few, now for the first time began to be widespread.

Apart from these developments there is another factor which is of extreme importance—the Reformation. As has been pointed out, this came about not so much because of religious, but political reasons.   Henry VIII had quarrelled

with the Pope and the throwing-off of foreign influence gave a great impetus to national feeling. England was becoming a great power and men were beginning to be proud of being Englishmen.

These three factors, the discovery of new worlds, the revival of learning, and the growth of the political or religious quarrels of the early Tudor period, because, coming to a peak as they did in the reign of Elizabeth, produced such a feeling in the country as had never been known before and perhaps never since. The narrow ideas of medieval times were disappearing : there was a feeling of progress in the air : a feeling of growing vitality and conscious greatness which overcame the might of Spain and laid the foundations of England's present greatness—her tolerance and her mighty Empire.

A MIRROR OF THE TIME

The vitality of the Elizabethan period is expressed in its literature, a literature in which form is sacrificed to vigour, and realism to romance. This is not to say that writers relapsed into wild extravagance. Far from it, for though Shakespeare talks of the sea coast of Bohemia, and transplants Warwickshire yokels to a French court, his plays are full of sayings which are not only true of his own time, but true of all time. The point is, that though the setting of Elizabethan literature is often founded on fantasy, its substance is based on hard facts, wide experience and acute observation.

The drama, which had its origin in the mystery, miracle, and morality plays, was first freed from its religious and didactic restraints, then developed by Lyly, Marlow, and others until it reached a peak which has never since been attained. In the writings of the immortal Shakespeare, poetry, which had been moribund since the time of

Chaucer, was revived by the Renaissance, and Wyatt and Surrey paved the way for the unrivalled lyric writers of the period. Though there was little prose fiction as we know it to-day, prose writing, as Sir Walter Raleigh has shown, was by no means an unknown or imperfect art.

Through this literature, which acts as a perfect mirror of the time, there shines one figure, and that figure is Spenser's Faerie Queene, Elizabeth herself. For her, men fought and died; inspired by her, men wrote some of the most beautiful poetry the world has ever known. This literature, which is centred round Elizabeth, is magnificent because it expresses the spirit of the time: a mixture of humour, courtliness, adventure, and romance. Such was the period and such was its literature.

From the picture by P. Delaroche   Mansell

THE EXECUTION OF LADY JANE

Mary wished to marry Philip, son of the Emperor Charles V, but although he was a Catholic, even the English Catholics were opposed to the marriage of an English queen to a powerful foreign prince. Sir Thomas Wyatt, the Duke of Suffolk, the father of Lady Jane Grey and others, rose in rebellion, but this was crushed and Mary felt that such a dangerous rival as the Lady Jane were better executed, and such was her very tragic end.

From the picture by Byam Shaw, R.I.   *By permission of the Fine Arts Publishing Co. Ltd.*

QUEEN MARY AND PRINCESS ELIZABETH ENTER LONDON

Mary, although she hated her sister Elizabeth, was anxious at first to maintain a semblance of sisterly affection, and here we see them entering London after the suppression of the rebellion. London, although more inclined to the Protestant cause, welcomed the new queen when it was realised that Northumberland had failed and that the country as a whole was rallying to the cry of " God save Queen Mary ! " But Mary suffered from ill advice, and instead of consolidating the enthusiasm with which she was at first received, she only succeeded in turning this into hatred. Her chief adviser was a man called Renard, who was merely the tool of the Emperor Charles, and was scheming for the marriage of Mary to his master's son. It was this man who had advised the execution of Lady Jane Grey, an act which Mary, at least at the beginning of her reign, would not have committed on her own accord, and which is one of the most terribly tragic events of English history.

From the picture by E. Leutze   *Spencer Arnold*

PRINCESS ELIZABETH IN THE TOWER

Renard went a stage further, and poisoned the mind of Mary against her sister Elizabeth by associating the princess with the Protestant plots, thus persuading the queen that here was a serious rival to the throne. He would have had Elizabeth executed, but Mary steadfastly refused to take this course, and instead sent her to the Tower.   Nothing could now prevent the marriage of Philip of Spain to Mary which was very unpopular.

From the picture by Hayter   *Rischgitz*

LATIMER PREACHING AT ST. PAUL'S CROSS

Here we see Latimer, that sturdy defender of the rights of the people, preaching one of his famous sermons at St. Paul's Cross, for which conduct he was soon to pay the penalty at the stake.   Mary, childless, and deserted by her husband who had returned to Spain, adopted religious intolerance as a consolation for her sorrow.   She felt that her life's work was now to uproot Protestantism, and to substitute full Catholicism.

From the picture by Stephanoff   *Rischgitz*

CRANMER'S FAMOUS RECANTATION

Among the more famous of the Protestant martyrs were Cranmer, Latimer and Ridley. Cranmer, Archbishop of Canterbury, was a man of gentle character whose physical endurance was not equal to the strain of facing the inquisitors who had been charged with the task of uprooting Protestantism. In a moment of weakness he renounced his faith but later recovered his courage and made a public recantation of his betrayal of faith.

From a contemporary engraving   *Rischgitz*

MARTYRS AT THE STAKE

"Be of Good Comfort, Master Ridley. Play the man : we shall this day light such a candle, by God's Grace, in England, as I trust shall never be put out." With these words, the sturdy reformer Latimer offered a word of cheer to his companion, Ridley, Bishop of London, who at Oxford was burnt with him at the stake. Thus did these great and brave men die a terrible death rather than renounce the faith in which they believed.

From tne picture by F. Goodall   *Rischgitz*

CRANMER AT THE TRAITOR'S GATE

Cranmer lasted a year longer, but in 1556, he, too, was burnt at the stake in Oxford. Here we see him passing through the dreaded Traitor's Gate of the Tower, and in the picture on the previous page he is seen thrusting '' the unworthy hand '' which had signed the recantation into the fire to be burned first. The Martyrs' memorial standing outside St. John's College, Oxford, commemorates the martyrdom of Cranmer, Latimer and Ridley.

From the picture oy R. Caton Woodville   *By permission of " The Illustrated London News "*

" YOUR HUSBAND—OR YOUR CHILD "

This picture tells its own dramatic story—shall the mother sacrifice her husband to the Spanish Inquisitors to save her child ? Mary's unpopular Spanish marriage involved England in a war with France, as a result of which we lost our only remaining French possession, Calais. Mary died in 1558, with, as she said, the name of Calais engraven upon her heart. Much happier days were to follow under Elizabeth.

ELIZABETH—" THE VIRGIN QUEEN "

The reign of Elizabeth marks one of the greatest periods in England's history, for it was during this period that the might of Spain was met and defeated, and intrepid British sailors dominated the seas.   Queen Elizabeth is one of the most fascinating figures in history.   She was often harsh and cruel but courtiers followed her with adoration; poets celebrated her name in verse, and sailors went to their death with her name on their lips.

After R. Westall   *Rischgitz*

ANNOUNCING MARY'S DEATH TO ELIZABETH

Mary's death undoubtedly saved England from violent rebellion, since not only were the Protestants antagonistic to her persecutions, but most of the Catholics, including Philip, had counselled milder methods. The nation looked to Elizabeth for relief from social and religious sufferings and its hopes were realised.

After H. Fradelle   *Rischgitz*

THE EARL OF LEICESTER AND AMY ROBSART

The Earl of Leicester believed that he could persuade Elizabeth to marry him. He had, however, married Amy Robsart, who met with a mysterious death, and great suspicion fell upon Leicester since his ambition was generally known. Whether guilty or not, this event did not improve his marriage prospects with the queen, although he remained upon terms of scandalous intimacy with her. Elizabeth, however, never married.

From an old print   *Rischgitz*

MERRY ENGLAND IN ELIZABETHAN DAYS

This village green, with the manor house and church in the background, is a typical Elizabethan scene. In those days life was simpler than it is to-day and people were forced to make their own amusements. Dancing round the maypole was a favourite pastime. At a later date when the country was under the strict Puritan rule these simple, traditional amusements were suppressed, much to the anger of the people themselves.

From the picture by G E. Robertson   *Mansell*

CHRISTMAS REVELS IN TUDOR DAYS

Scenes of merriment such as that shown in the picture of Haddon Hall were typical of Christmas in Tudor times, when the villagers were entertained by the Lord of the Manor. In the gallery can be seen the minstrels.

From the picture by G E. Robertson   *Mansell*

READING THE BIBLE IN ELIZABETH'S DAY

Elizabeth and her Council hoped to establish a wide, tolerant Church, which would include every Englishman. But she was faced, on the one hand, with the Catholics, and, on the other, with the extreme Protestants who wished to carry the Reformation still further and abolish all semblances of the old faith. At one stage, the indiscriminate reading of the Bible was prohibited in order to attain at least outward conformity to the established church. Unfortunately the idea of establishing a tolerant Church was found to be impossible.

From the painting by Robert Herdman, A.R.A   *Spencer Arnold*

MARY, QUEEN OF SCOTS LEAVING FRANCE

Although Elizabeth had been declared lawful heir to the throne, her position was full of peril. Mary Stuart of Scotland had married the king of France and claimed the English throne through descent from Henry VII. Both France and Rome supported her claim. On the death of her husband, Mary was forced to return to Scotland to the great embarrassment of Elizabeth, who feared that she might enlist the help of a foreign power.

By permission of the Wellcome Historical Medical Museum

DEMONSTRATING THE MAGNET TO QUEEN ELIZABETH

William Gilbert is here seen demonstrating the use of the magnet to Queen Elizabeth. This invention, together with that of the mariner's compass, enabled long sea voyages to be made with a certainty of reaching a definite destination which, with only the help of the sun and the stars, they had never been sure of doing.

After Willsie   *Rischgitz*

JOHN KNOX PREACHING

Mary had quickly found Scotland far more radically Protestant, since the Reformation had been a movement carried out by the people in opposition to the government, instead of being a government measure only partially assented to by the people, as in England. John Knox, the most famous of a group of preachers who were unswervingly devoted to Protestantism in Scotland, is here seen preaching a violent sermon against Popery.

MARY AND RIZZIO

On her return as Queen of Scotland, Mary married Lord Darnley. Here we see her glancing with more than passing interest on her private secretary, Rizzio. In spite of the fact that Rizzio had actually recommended that the queen should marry Darnley, her attentions aroused the jealousy of her husband, who, with the aid of accomplices, seized him in her presence, and murdered him in an ante-chamber. The next year Darnley was murdered, and it was believed that Mary and the Earl of Bothwell, whom she soon married, were guilty of the crime. Though their complicity is by no means certain it seems more than likely to be true.

After T. Danby   *Rischgitz*

MARY ESCAPES FROM LOCH LEVEN CASTLE

By her actions Mary had aroused to anger all classes of her subjects. Soon there was a rebellion and after a fierce battle Bothwell was driven into flight and the queen was captured and imprisoned in a castle in the middle of Loch Leven. Here she was forced to abdicate and to agree to the coronation of her infant son as James VI of Scotland. Mary soon escaped and fled to England, appealing to Elizabeth to help her to regain the crown. How different was her eventual fate from the reception which she had been expecting !

After Robert Herdman   *Rischgitz*

THE HAPPIER DAYS OF MARY QUEEN OF SCOTS

Mary was a dangerous guest and Elizabeth considered her safer in prison. For nineteen years she remained a prisoner in England, and often her mind must have gone wandering back to those happy days in France.

After Millais   *Spencer Arnold*

THE HUGUENOTS

There would appear to be little doubt that Mary was implicated in Catholic plots to seize the reins of government. In fact, the Protestant faith was in danger throughout the Continent. France was torn by civil wars between the Catholics and the Huguenots, as the French Protestants were called, and a secret massacre was arranged. A white band was to distinguish the Catholics, and the Catholic girl is seen trying to tie a kerchief upon her Huguenot lover's arm, as they part on the eve of that fatal day, perhaps never to meet again.

After Clay   *Rischgitz*

THE EVE OF ST. BARTHOLOMEW'S DAY

In France, evil counsellors had induced the king to order a massacre of the Protestants. Here we see some of the Protestant courtiers fearful of the dreadful fate awaiting all but the few who managed to escape.

After E. Debat-Ponsan   *Rischgitz*

ST. BARTHOLOMEW'S DAY

On St. Bartholomew's Day thousands were slain. The Pope, misinformed in the matter, ordered a solemn thanksgiving for the slaughter, and struck a medal to commemorate it. When Philip II of Spain heard the news, he laughed outright. In 1570, the Pope excommunicated Elizabeth and released her subjects from their allegiance to her. Elizabeth and England were now in danger from the Catholic countries abroad.

From an old print

Rischgitz

A ROYAL PROGRESS

Travel was difficult in Elizabethan days and fraught with considerable dangers. Here we see the queen on a visit to Nonsuch Palace in Surrey accompanied by a retinue of armed retainers and courtiers. This palace was a favourite resort of Henry VIII. Later, the scene of the meeting between Elizabeth and Essex. See p. 210.

After Vertue

Rischgitz

ELIZABETH VISITS LORD HUNSDON

Scotland was in a state of turmoil and there were constant raids from over the border. Lord Hunsdon had done much to suppress these, and here we see Elizabeth on a state visit to thank him in person for his services.

From the picture by Sir J. Gilbert Rischgitz

ELIZABETH KNIGHTING DRAKE

Philip of Spain, on the death of Mary, had proposed marriage to Elizabeth, an offer which was rejected. He therefore prepared to invade England, but Drake, as he said, set out to "singe the Spanish King's beard." In the Gulf of Mexico he had captured more than a hundred vessels and had taken and plundered Nombre de Dios. He had brought back much treasure and, on his third voyage, sailed right round the world. He was knighted by the queen on board his ship, the *Golden Hind*, as she lay in the Thames at Deptford.

From the picture by R. Caton Woodville

THE DISCOVERY OF NEWFOUNDLAND

Newfoundland became England's first colony in 1583. Here we see Sir Humphrey Gilbert, who was Sir Walter Raleigh's step-brother, talking with the fishermen whom he found at work on the Grand Banks, and discussing with them his intention of hoisting the English flag at St. John's, and claiming it for Queen Elizabeth. Unfortunately, this gallant sailor was drowned on the return journey when his ship, the *Squirrel* was wrecked in a violent storm off the Azores, he having refused to leave his frigate and sail in one of his larger ships.

From the picture by Ernest Board

By permission of " Pictorial Education "

QUEEN ELIZABETH AND A GALLANT COURTIER

Raleigh came from Ireland determined to win the queen's favour. Here we see him spreading his cloak over a wet place to prevent Elizabeth from spoiling her delicate shoes. As he was a gracious courtier, a fine writer and a bold adventurer, it was not long before he became a great favourite with Queen Elizabeth.

After H. Fradelle
Rischgitz

"FAIN WOULD I CLIMB, BUT THAT I FEAR TO FALL"

Once Raleigh wrote the above words on a window-pane with the diamond ring which the queen had given him. Here we see Elizabeth pointing this out to her friend, Lady Paget. These words proved to be prophetic.

From the picture by A. K. Lawrence, A.R.A.
By permission of John Swain & Son, Ltd.

"IF THY MIND FAIL THEE, CLIMB NOT AT ALL"

Elizabeth, who had already been favourably impressed by Raleigh, added the above words to those of the young courtier. His heart did not fail, and he seized all his chances, eventually being knighted by the queen. But he lost his head during the reign of James I. This time fears he had expressed were destined to come true.

After Devis   *Rischgitz*

THE BABINGTON PLOT

There had been many plots against Elizabeth's life, but after the last of them, Babington's plot of 1586, Elizabeth was persuaded by Parliament and her ministers to allow the trial of her rival, the imprisoned Mary. The judges decided that she was guilty and Mary was condemned to death. Hating to execute her cousin, Elizabeth delayed signing the death warrant for two months. Finally she unwillingly signed the warrant.

Julius Schrader   *Rischgitz*

ELIZABETH SIGNING MARY'S DEATH WARRANT

At last Elizabeth signed the fatal document because she feared the plots against her to put Mary on the throne might prove successful. Moreover, the Protestants were crying out for the death of the Catholic Mary.

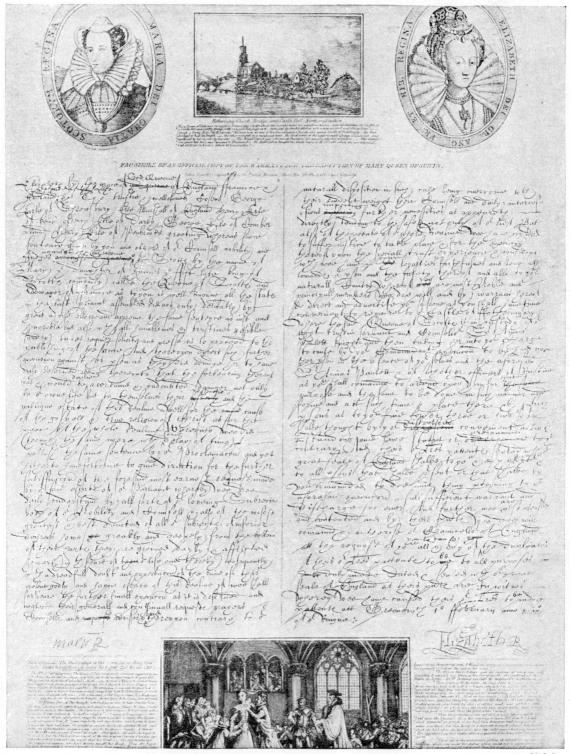

FACSIMILE OF AN OFFICIAL COPY OF THE WARRANT FOR THE EXECUTION OF MARY QUEEN OF SCOTS.

THE DEATH WARRANT OF MARY QUEEN OF SCOTS
Here we see a facsimile of the terrible document responsible for the death of Elizabeth's own cousin.

After the picture by R. Herdman   *Rischgitz*

MARY RECEIVES THE DEATH WARRANT

Elizabeth has been blamed for the execution of Mary, but in view of the obvious dangers to which she was submitted while her cousin remained alive, it is difficult to see an alternative. Undoubtedly, Mary was used as a tool in a number of plots of which she was innocent, but there was enough guilt to justify action. It was all very unfortunate, but the situation at home and abroad made Elizabeth's action inevitable.

After Serrur   *Rischgitz*

MARY'S LAST SUPPER

What were Mary's thoughts as she sat at supper for the last time with her faithful followers? Perhaps they were of her son in Scotland, who, in due course, was to be the inheritor of Elizabeth's policy.

After the picture by R. Herdman   *Rischgitz*

THE EXECUTION OF MARY QUEEN OF SCOTS

At the first blow the executioner missed his aim, and inflicted a deep wound on the side of the skull. No groan or cry escaped Mary's lips, and it was only after the third stroke that the head of the hapless Queen of Scots was held up to the gaze of the people, as the executioner cried, "So perish all Queen Elizabeth's enemies!"

After Smirke   *Rischgitz*

ELIZABETH INTERVIEWS HER FALLEN FAVOURITE

Courtiers grovelled and women flattered the imperious Elizabeth, but there was one man who refused to
cringe—her favourite, the Earl of Essex. Essex came to the court at an early age and through his charm
and brilliance reached a position second only to the crown. After his hopeless failure in Ireland, however, he
was forced to throw himself on the queen's mercy. His career ended and he was executed in 1601 for treason.

From the picture by J. Seymour Lucas, R.A.

By permission of the trustees of the late Sir Alfred Bird

"THE KING OF SPAIN'S NAVY IS ABROAD!"

Philip II of Spain was Elizabeth's implacable enemy, and this antagonism had been increased by the assistance which England had given to the Dutch in their war against Spanish tyranny. Here is Elizabeth making plans to fight Philip after she has heard that his fleet has left Spain and is probably on its way to invade England. The defeat of the Spanish Armada is probably the most outstanding victory in English history.

From the picture by Paul Hardy   *By permission of " Pictorial Education "*

BUILDING THE FAMOUS *ARK ROYAL*

The *Ark Royal*, on which the men in the picture are at work, was the flagship of the English fleet which sailed against the Spanish Armada in 1588. She carried heavy guns which fired " broadsides," not fore and aft like the guns of the Spanish ships. She could manœuvre round the galleons before the Spaniards could get near enough to grapple. The smaller English ships, being easier to handle, harried the "stately Spanish galleons" all round the English coast. In this they were assisted by a gale which split up the Spanish fleet.

QUEEN ELIZABETH AT TILBURY

Before the Spanish Armada arrived off the south coast of England, Queen Elizabeth went to Tilbury to review the troops which had gathered there to oppose a landing of the Spanish soldiers. Here she is seen on horse-back reviewing the men who were to crush the might of Spain. These soldiers were never called upon to grapple with the foe, for the galleons challenged by the English fleet in the Straits of Dover, suffered considerable damage. Finally, dispersed by flaming ships being set adrift among them, they fled north-wards followed by Drake and his men. A storm arose as the enemy rounded the Hebrides which destroyed the last remnants of the Spanish fleet. and for many days fragments of their vessels were cast by every tide upon the northern coasts of Scotland and Ireland.

After D. Maclise   *Rischgitz*

From the picture by J. Seymour Lucas, R.A.   *By permission of Arthur Tooth & Sons, Ltd.*

THE CALL TO ARMS

Here, the leading citizen of a port is reading the queen's proclamation calling all good men to the defence of England. Sudden news has come of the approach of the Spanish Armada, and ships and men must put to sea to beat off the invaders. There was a magnificent spirit among the English who believed they were unconquerable. A German seaman writing home said that they were rejoicing the Armada was at sea !

After the picture by Seymour Lucas   *Rischgitz*

THE MOST FAMOUS GAME IN BRITISH HISTORY

While Drake was playing bowls on Plymouth Hoe, a messenger, with a pale face and wild eyes, rushed up and cried, "Sirs! Gentlemen! the Armada is here!" "Gentlemen," Drake replied, "there is time to finish the match and beat the Spaniards, too." This was no mere boasting: he was certain it would be done.

After the picture by Seymour Lucas   *Rischgitz*

DRAKE ON THE *REVENGE*

While pursuing some vessels which proved to be merchantmen, Drake saw *Our Lady of the Rosary*, a galleon in the Spanish Armada. After a tussle, her commander struck his colours, and with his officers, was brought on board the *Revenge*. He said he would have surrendered to none but "el Draque" (the dragon).

From the picture by D. W. Brierly   *Rischgitz*

THE LOSS OF THE *REVENGE*

Sir Richard Grenville in the *Revenge* became cut off from the rest of the English fleet. Fifteen great Spanish warships attacked the solitary vessel and Grenville was mortally wounded. The Spaniards boarded the ship and carried away the dying captain to their flagship. Death was the only defeat he was prepared to admit.

From an old print   *Rischgitz*

LONDON BRIDGE IN ELIZABETHAN DAYS

There were houses and shops on the bridge in the time of Elizabeth, and the narrow arches of the bridge prevented ships going further up the river. This picturesque old bridge became out of date and was replaced.

John Claxton   Rischgitz

SPENSER READING "THE FAERIE QUEENE"

Spenser was one of the great Elizabethan poets. His most famous poem is "The Faerie Queene," which illustrates the chief virtues. Many of its scenes are coloured by Spenser's knowledge of Ireland where he held an official position, and Gloriana, the Faerie Queene, is based on Elizabeth herself.

Rischgitz

THE LIVING-ROOM IN SHAKESPEARE'S HOUSE

William Shakespeare was born at Stratford-on-Avon on April 24, 1564, and was destined to become the greatest Englishman in the world of letters. At eighteen he married a farmer's daughter, Anne Hathaway, whose lovely home can still be seen at Stratford. Soon after this he left Stratford to seek his fortune in London.

Rischgitz

WHERE SHAKESPEARE WENT TO SCHOOL
The Grammar School at Stratford-on-Avon which Shakespeare attended until the age of 14 years. This school, where he learned "small Latin and less Greek," gave him the usual education of Tudor times.

After the picture by T. Brooks   *Rischgitz*

SHAKESPEARE ACCUSED OF DEER STEALING

There is a story that Shakespeare was accused of deer stealing, and to escape the consequences of his crime, fled from Stratford, and arrived in London in 1585, and connected himself with one of the theatres there.

After the picture by E. Ender   *Rischgitz*

SHAKESPEARE READING TO ELIZABETH

Shakespeare in *Hamlet* says that players are "The abstract and brief chronicles of the time." He was more than this, since through his plays we are able to recapture the spirit of the Elizabethan age which is summed up in a couplet in *King John*: "This England never did, nor never shall, Lie at the proud foot of a conqueror."

THE GLOBE THEATRE

The theatre in which Shakespeare's plays were first performed was the " Globe," Bankside, near the Thames, which was built in 1599.   At this theatre, he appeared as an actor in many of his own plays, including *Hamlet*.

THE INTERIOR OF THE GLOBE THEATRE

There was no scenery in the Elizabethan theatre.   A notice-board told the spectators " This is a wood " ; " On the Seashore " ; " This is the English Army " ; and so on.   There were no actresses, female parts being taken by boys.   Usually a clown gave a performance between the acts, and there were a few musicians.

From an old print   *Mansell*

AN ELIZABETHAN WATER-MAN

In Shakespeare's England, the houses were crowded together and there was an inadequate supply of light. Drainage was very bad and such water supply as existed was of a very doubtful character. Polluted river water often led to an outbreak of plague, which was a common occurrence in England until Stuart times.

From an old print   *Mansell*

WHAT LACK YE? WHAT LACK YE?

Many were the things hawked through the streets of Elizabethan London. The vinegar-seller would find ready buyers among the city dwellers who constantly feared that scourge of Tudor and Stuart England — the Plague. Indeed, in Tudor times these hawkers largely took the place of shops, and the cries with which they shouted their wares have since become famous. To a certain extent they have continued to the present day.

221

AN ELIZABETHAN COAL SELLER

Even the coal seller hawked his heavy wares through the streets, though coal was not yet widely used as a household fuel on account of its unpleasant fumes. In ordinary dwelling-houses it was only just beginning to be possible in properly designed hearths with chimneys which allowed the fumes to escape. The majority of houses at this time were built of wood and, moreover, there was always a great danger of fire.

From an old print   *Rischgitz*

EFFECTIVE PUNISHMENTS

Nagging wives were not encouraged in Elizabethan days. Here is a wife (left) being taken to the market-place by her husband to be derided by the villagers. Drunken husbands also received their deserts by means of the drunkard's tub—a very uncomfortable contraption in which they were held up to public ridicule.

From an old print   *Rischgitz*

PRISONERS IN THE STOCKS

A fraudulent baker or butcher was forced to stand with hands or neck in the pillory or stocks, with his name writ large above him. More often than not, the gibes of the populace had the desired effect of curing them.

By permission of " The Illustrated London News "

AN ELIZABETHAN TENNIS COURT

Lawn Tennis was unknown in Elizabethan days, but the above game has several of the characteristics of the modern game. As yet, however, only the privileged few played games. Wrestling, fishing, fowling and archery were the most popular. This old form of tennis is still played to-day to a certain extent.

From an old print   *Mansell*

THE CRUEL SPORT OF BEAR-BAITING

Bear-baiting was a dangerous and cruel sport. The bear was tied to a stake and attacked by packs of mastiffs. The poor bear fought madly and hopelessly until he was overcome by the dogs. Cock-fighting was equally cruel, but very popular, though these barbarous sports were rightly hated by the strict-living puritans.

Valentine

HENRY VII's CHAPEL

During the Tudor period there was an enlightened interest in architecture, and the adornment of houses. The civil wars were ended, the power of the barons broken, and people felt safe to build without fear of senseless destruction. Henry VII's chapel is a beautiful example of Tudor architecture. In the ordinary houses there was a great increase in comfort, though what seem necessities now were luxuries in those days. Glass was fitted in the windows; carpets were put on the floors, and the walls were hung with beautiful tapestries.

B.P.—H   225

THE ORIGIN OF THE EAST INDIA COMPANY

English merchants were now striving to win markets in all parts of the world. To gain greater strength and protection, these merchants formed themselves into trading companies and obtained a charter from the Crown. The East India Company was the greatest of them all, and was responsible for laying the foundations of British influence in India which has survived to the present day to the advantage of both nationalities.

From the picture by Charles Soubre

Rischgitz

TOO LATE TO SAVE A LIFE

When the Earl of Essex was at the height of his popularity, Elizabeth gave him a ring with instructions to return it to her whenever he might be in trouble. Later, when in prison, he gave it to the Countess of Salisbury to give to Elizabeth, but she retained it, jealous of the queen's affections. On her death-bed she returned it to the queen, but by then it was too late to save the life of the Earl of Essex, who had been executed for treason.

After Smirke   *Rischgitz*

ELIZABETH APPOINTS HER SUCCESSOR

As her life draws to a close, Elizabeth appoints her successor. Too ill to go to bed, she lies on the floor propped up by pillows. James VI of Scotland, son of the tragic Mary Queen of Scots, was destined to become James I of England and the first of the ill-fated line of Stuart kings under whom the country was torn by civil strife, and of whom one was executed and one ignominiously driven from the throne.

From the picture by P. Delaroche   *Rischgitz*

THE PASSING OF A GREAT QUEEN

Elizabeth's reign had been a glorious one and is made for ever memorable by the distinguished men who flourished in it. Elizabeth herself had her fine qualities but she was coarse, capricious, and treacherous. But in spite of these faults her character was such as to inspire the greatest poets and the greatest adventurers that England has known before or since, for what other age has produced a Drake or a Shakespeare?

THE STUARTS
JAMES I, 1603-1625

JAMES I was the son of Mary Queen of Scots, and the great-great grandson of Henry VII. Previous to his accession he had been James VI of Scotland.

He came to the throne at a very difficult time. The despotism of the Tudors had been accepted because the country had been in need of a strong central government, but after the defeat of the Armada in 1588 this was no longer necessary. Moreover, the discoveries of new lands had led to a development of trade and the growth of a wealthy middle class—the class which was chiefly represented in Parliament. Also the general awakening of men's minds during the reign of Elizabeth had led to a growing tendency for the people to feel that they had a share in the government of the country. Consequently, it was extremely unfortunate that James was a strong believer in " the divine right of kings " ; in the idea that he was God's deputy on earth and answerable to God alone for his actions. It it is obvious that this was in direct opposition to the rapidly growing idea that the king ruled only by consent of Parliament. The clash of these two ideas was to lead to the death of Charles I, and to the Commonwealth under Cromwell.

RELIGIOUS TROUBLES

At the very start of his unfortunate reign, James antagonised both Scotland and the English Parliament. Parliament because it objected to free trade with Scotland, and Scotland because of his religious policy. James was an Anglican with the slogan " no bishop, no king," and the Scots hated the idea of having their Church controlled by bishops when they were Presbyterian.

But there were other religious difficulties. James, being an Anglican was between two fires —the Puritans on the one side and the Catholics the other. His refusal to give way over the Millenary Petition—the request on the part of the Puritans for a new prayer book—resulted in 300 Puritans being deprived of their livings because they refused to use the old one. The only result of this petition which was discussed at the Hampton Court Conference, was the authorised version of the Bible in 1611.

Early in his reign James made an attempt to conciliate the Catholics by remitting their fines for not attending church. The result was that large numbers of the Catholics stayed away and used their own form of worship. Parliament strongly disapproved, James became frightened, and the old fines were again strictly imposed. The immediate result was an attempt to blow up king and Parliament—the Gunpowder Plot. Previous to this there had been two other plots, the Bye Plot and the Main Plot, both attempts to get rid of the king and substitute one of more Catholic sympathies. Sir Walter Raleigh was implicated in the latter and imprisoned in the Tower, with the sentence of death hanging over him.

FINANCE

James' financial difficulties were as great as his religious ones. The finance of the country at the present day is entirely controlled by Parliament which pays an annual grant to the king. In the time of James it was controlled by the king, who had certain methods of raising money which were recognised by Parliament as being legitimate. He had the revenue from crown lands, from feudal dues ; from import and export taxes and from direct taxation on towns and country districts. But the revenue from these sources was not enough for James because the cost of government had considerably increased. The navy was bigger ; armies cost more to maintain and the value of money had decreased owing to the discovery of silver in South America. But above all James was extravagant. More money had to be raised from somewhere and to do this, James without the sanction of Parliament, levied " impositions " or further customs dues and introduced " monopolies " which were the rights given to private persons to deal in certain goods. In return for a monopoly a sum of money was paid to the king which he used himself.

QUARRELS WITH PARLIAMENT

These practices made Parliament extremely angry because the king now had sole control of the finance of the country and James' very

From an old print   *Rischgitz*

THE PARLIAMENT OF JAMES I

Now, by Act of Parliament, James became king of England, and although by his accession the two countries were united under one sovereign, each retained its own parliament, its own national church, and its own laws. In fact, the English parliament refused to grant free trade to Scotland and denied the people of that country the rights and privileges possessed by Englishmen. Not till many years later were England and Scotland one nation.

high-handed attitude to Parliament did not help matters. In 1614, he dissolved Parliament after it had sat for only seven weeks because it was opposed to him over the financial question. This was known as the " addled Parliament " because it did not pass a single law. For seven years after this James did without a Parliament altogether. Nevertheless the Parliamentary Party was becoming very conscious of its strength. In 1624 it impeached the Lord Chancellor him-

self, Sir Francis Bacon, for taking bribes. Bacon was a great lawyer and a great thinker, but there can be no doubt about his guilt.

James' advisers made him even more unpopular. Instead of trusting to Robert Cecil, the son of Lord Burghley, he was influenced by a favourite, George Villiers, Duke of Buckingham. Buckingham was a man of James' own age, amusing, good looking, conceited and arrogant, and generally hated throughout the country

After Marcus Cheeraerts   *Rischgit.*

THE SOMERSET HOUSE CONFERENCE

On the accession of James, hostilities with Spain officially ended, and in the picture we see the Spanish Ambassadors discussing terms with the English at the Somerset House Conference. Unofficial warfare between the seamen of both countries continued, however, until the Spaniards were finally driven from the seas.

because even lawyers and statesmen could only approach the king through him.

FOREIGN POLICY

James' foreign policy led to further trouble. His main idea was to keep the peace, but his policy of friendship with the Spaniards—who were hated by the nation—increased his unpopularity.

He made peace with Spain in 1604, but kept in alliance with France. In 1613, he married his daughter to Frederick the Elector Palatine of the Rhine, and he wished to marry his son, Henry, to a Spanish princess, and Charles to a French princess. Henry, however, died, and he transferred the idea of a Spanish marriage to Charles. He thought that if this could be brought about the Spaniards would restore his son-in-law, Frederick, to the Palatinate, from which he had been driven out in the Thirty Years War. In

1623 Charles and Buckingham visited Spain in an attempt to push on the marriage, but finding the Spaniards were not agreeable, he arranged for Charles to marry Henrietta Maria, the daughter of Louis XIII of France. This was quite pleasing to Parliament, who did not realise that James had secretly arranged with the French Minister, Richelieu, that the penal laws against the Catholics should be relaxed.

DEATH OF RALEIGH

It was James' friendship with the Spaniards which led to the execution of Raleigh, who desperate at being kept in the Tower, suggested that he should lead an expedition up the River Orinoco, where he believed there was gold. James agreed on condition that he avoided any trouble with the Spaniards. This was a very different attitude from that of Elizabeth, who allowed any buccaneering expedition which did not cause international trouble. It was also an impossible condition and Raleigh knew it, for the Spaniards considered that they had the sole right of exploiting that part of the world and would forcibly resist any interference on the part of the English. The inevitable fight took place, Raleigh's son was killed and he himself returned to England to be put to death on the old charge of high treason. Raleigh had been unpopular because of his complicity in the Main plot, but this was now forgotten and the country felt extremely indignant that he had been put to death merely to please the Spaniards.

SCOTLAND AND IRELAND

Though there was no official union between the countries, James was now the first king of England, Scotland, Ireland and Wales. Almost since birth he had been king of Scotland—and for this reason was looked upon by many people as a foreigner, but his desire for a real union with Scotland was not to be realised for another hundred years or so. The country was quickly awakening to the idea of parliamentary government. Nevertheless, he was, in fact, the first king of the two nations. By the beginning of his reign, Ireland, the most turbulent of all four countries, was conquered and the Plantation or Colonization of Ulster took place in 1609. This meant that the land was taken from the Irish and handed over to English and Scottish settlers.

COLONIES

One of the most important aspects of James' reign was the foundation of colonies in the new world. In the time of Elizabeth these lands had been opened though no definite settlements were made, but in the reign of James came the foundation of Virginia, for which Sir Walter Raleigh was responsible, then of Barbados and finally the settlements in the North. The Puritans who were dissatisfied with James' religious attitude left the country in search of new homes. The first to go were the Pilgrim Fathers, who sailed in the *Mayflower*, and these pioneers were followed by others. By the end of the Stuart period almost the whole east coast of North America had been settled and this period saw the beginnings of that great expansion which has resulted in the British Empire and the American nation.

from an old print   *Rischgitz*

THE GUNPOWDER PLOT CONSPIRATORS

When James became king, the Roman Catholics hoped for a restoration of their cause since he was the son of the ill-fated Mary Stuart. But they were disappointed and a few of them led by Robert Catesby, a Warwickshire squire, began to plot against him. They planned to blow up the House of Lords when the king went there to open Parliament. Guy Fawkes, a Catholic Yorkshireman, was entrusted with this task.

Rischgitz

THE WARNING LETTER

"My lord, out of the love I bear to some of your friends, I have a care of your preservation. Therefore I would advise you, as you tender your life, to devise some excuse to shift of your attendance at this Parliament, for God and man hath concurred to punish the wickedness of this time. And think not slightly of this advertisement, but retire yourself into your country where you may expect the event in safety, for though there be no appearance of any stir, yet I say they shall receive a terrible blow this Parliament, and yet they shall not see who hurts them. This counsel is not to be contemned, because it may do you good and can do you no harm, for the danger is passed as soon as you have burnt the letter : and I hope God will give you the grace to make good use of it, to whose holy protection I commend you." To the Right Honourable the Lord Mounteagle.

Rischgitz

GUY FAWKES' LANTERN

The letter above was sent by one of the conspirators as a warning to a cousin who was a member of the House of Lords. The nobleman (Lord Mounteagle) carried the letter to the king, who ordered a search of the House. This letter was responsible for making known the dastardly plot ; for saving Parliament and the lives of its members from an atrocious and bloodthirsty scheme ; and for bringing the conspirators to justice and death.

From an old print   *Rischgitz*

THE ARREST OF GUY FAWKES
Guy Fawkes was discovered and seized with all preparations made for blowing up the Houses of Parliament.

From the picture by J. Ralston   *Rischgitz*

GUY FAWKES BEFORE JAMES I
After suffering with bravery much interrogation and torture, Guy Fawkes betrayed his fellow-conspirators.

From the picture by E. Crofts   *Rischgitz*

THE LAST STAND OF THE CONSPIRATORS

Most of the conspirators had already fled to the country when they heard that the plot had been discovered and that their identity was known. Catesby and his friends had made for Wales, but were overtaken by the Sheriff of Worcester, and at Holbeach House after a fierce fight were all either slain or captured.

From an old print   *Rischgitz*

THE LAST OF THE CONSPIRATORS

Those who were captured were eventually hanged, drawn and quartered. Executions were held in public and were enjoyed as a public entertainment by the populace. Cruelty was a common characteristic of the people.

From the picture by G. E. Butler, R.W.A.　　　　　　　　　　　*Copyright of the Corporation of Bristol*

PERSECUTION OF THE PURITANS

Not only did James persecute the Catholics, but also the growing body of Puritans. These people believed that the Bible was the sole link between God and man and that bishops and priests were unnecessary. Here a Puritan children's meeting is suddenly interrupted by the Lord of the Manor to the consternation of all.

From the picture by Stephen Bird　　　　　　　　　　　*By permission of the artist*

THE FIRST LANDING IN VIRGINIA

"No bishop, no king," replied James to the Puritans, and persecuted them as a dangerous political sect. Many of them left England to found a new home in Virginia where they could be free from this persecution. The early population of America was largely composed of these Puritans who went there to seek a new life.

From the picture by A. Wilde Parson   *Copyright of the Corporation of Bristol*

JOHN GUY SAILS FROM BRISTOL

Humphrey Gilbert had taken Newfoundland but did not colonise it. He we see John Guy setting out from Bristol in 1611 on a colonising expedition. From now on there was a great expansion of colonies.

After Professor William Rothenstein   *From a panel in St. Stephen's Hall*

AT THE COURT OF THE MOGHUL EMPEROR

India in the seventeenth century was under the sway of powerful Moghul emperors. The English who had founded a trading post at Surat in 1612 were anxious to keep friendly. Here we see an ambassador from King James paying his respects to the Moghul emperor. England had to keep on friendly terms with the native rulers if she were to increase her trade. Moreover, the French and Dutch were also endeavouring to gain a footing in India, and commercial rivalry led to frequent conflicts between them and the English.

From Visscher's Maps of London   *Rischgitz*

LONDON BRIDGE IN 1616

This interesting picture shows the extent to which London had grown since we first saw the Roman city on page 36. The population, however, is still concentrated in a small area. For hundreds of years London was confined to what is now the City, and what is to-day Greater London either did not exist at all, or existed only in the form of country villages. One of these villages can be seen in the background of the picture.

From the picture by G. Merry

A MARKET IN

This picture shows a typical market-place in a country town in the seventeenth century. On the left is a fine gentleman, perhaps the Lord of the Manor and his lady, whose train is carried by a black slave from Virginia, or by a Moorish lad from Spain. The multiplicity of the articles for sale illustrates the increase in trade, especially with the Americans and the Far East. It may be noted that it was still the custom for men to

STUART TIMES

carry swords. There can also be seen the simpler dress of a merchant in contrast with the finery of the more highly-born gentleman. In the centre is a man undergoing his punishment in the pillory for some misdemeanour he has committed. Note also the market cross, the architecture of the church, and of the house with its oak beams and small windows. The horse and carriage was, of course, the usual method of conveyance.

After Gustave Alaux   *G.P.A.*

THE DEPARTURE OF THE *MAYFLOWER*

In 1620, one hundred and two men, women, and children, set sail from Plymouth in the gallant little *Mayflower* to seek religious liberty in the New World.   The Pilgrim Fathers, as they were called, preferred permanent exile from the land of their birth than submission to a religion which they detested.   The *Mayflower* was the first of many ships taking the Puritans out to where they could live without persecution for their religious beliefs.

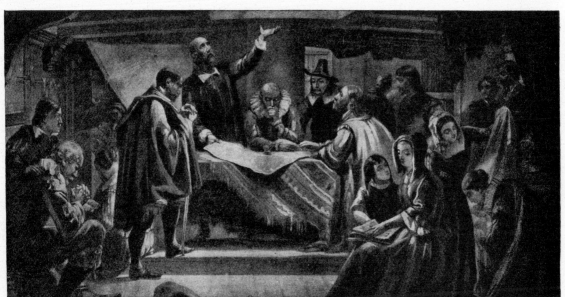

After Edwin White   *Rischgitz*

SIGNING THE COMPACT IN THE *MAYFLOWER*

In the cabin of the *Mayflower*, this band of pilgrims met together to sign a solemn compact to preserve the religious liberties which had caused them to emigrate. Their bravery in doing so merits great admiration.

After H. Boughton   *From the painting in the Mappin Art Gallery, Sheffield*

THE LANDING IN THE NEW WORLD

After a perilous voyage the Pilgrim Fathers landed at Cape Cod, and founded a colony which in after years grew into the United States. Unfortunately, however, religious liberty deteriorated into extreme intolerance. In spite of the hardiness of the life there, these early colonists prospered and grew in numbers as the religious dissenters continued to leave England where, under the rule of the Stuarts, they were consistently persecuted.

From an old print   *Rischgitz*

JAMES I FEASTING THE SPANISH AMBASSADOR

James, in spite of the opposition of Parliament and the people, wished to marry his son Charles to the daughter of the king of Spain. Here, as a part of his plan, we see him entertaining the Spanish Ambassador. But popular opinion was so much against the idea of a Catholic marriage that the Spanish Ambassador, who was then living in the Bishop of Ely's house in Holborn, was obliged to have a guard of soldiers to protect him from the violence of the mob. After considerable dispute between king and Parliament the marriage treaty was broken off. Charles, who had gone with the Duke of Buckingham on a journey to Madrid to see the Infanta, returned to England amid rejoicing that he had been prevented from making a Catholic alliance. Buckingham is said to have saved his country.

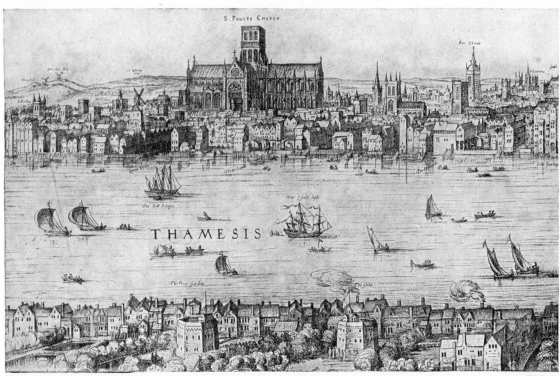

From Visscher's Maps of London   *Rischgitz*

LONDON BEFORE THE GREAT FIRE

In the background can be seen old St. Paul's (notice the windmill) and Bow Church, while in the foreground is the Globe Theatre and the Bear Garden. The Globe had been a famous theatre since Shakespeare's time. Much of London's prosperity was then, as it is now, dependent on the shipping which comes up the Thames.

CHARLES I, 1625-1649

JAMES had left England in a thoroughly unsettled state when he died and his son, Charles was not the type of man to improve matters. Charles was good looking, brave and dignified ; but he was also obstinate and determined to be an absolute monarch. Like his father he believed in the divine right of kings. He had married Henrietta Maria of France who, being a Catholic and of rather an interfering nature, was not liked in the country.

He came to the throne with the treasury empty and a war with Spain in progress. To get money it was necessary to come to an agreement with Parliament, but though he called three in four years, he quarrelled with, and dissolved, each one in turn. In 1629 he decided to govern without Parliament altogether.

CHARLES AND PARLIAMENT

The Duke of Buckingham was now Charles' adviser and the first Parliament of 1625 refused to vote enough money for the Spanish war, knowing how incompetently it was being carried on by the king and the duke. The religious question was another source of trouble with this parliament. Charles' sympathies were with the Arminian or High Church Anglican party, which had recently come into prominence, with William Laud as its leader. Parliament was frightened that this high church party would permit the growth of Roman Catholicism and demanded that the laws against the Catholics should be more strictly enforced. So Charles dissolved his first Parliament.

The king, badly in need of money, called his second parliament in 1626 which immediately attacked Buckingham, blaming him for the disastrous failure of the attack on Cadiz. Parliament was also furious that English ships should have been lent to the French to put down a rising of Protestants at La Rochelle. Parliament, under Sir John Eliot, started the impeachment of Buckingham, and refused to supply the king with money until he was dismissed. Charles consequently dissolved his second Parliament.

But Charles, being involved in a war with France, had to have money even more than before, so in 1629 he called his third Parliament. Sir John Eliot immediately drew up the " Petition of Right," stating that the king should not levy taxes without the consent of Parliament ; that he should not compel men to make forced loans of money ; that no man should be punished without fair trial ; and that he should not rule by martial law. To this Charles unwillingly agreed and he was at last granted the money he required.

Soon after this, Buckingham was murdered but the king's policy remained unchanged. He continued the quarrel with Parliament over the question of the appointment of Arminian bishops, and despite the " Petition of Right " continued to levy taxes without sanction from Parliament. There was a stormy scene in the House when Charles ordered its dissolution. The members held the Speaker in his chair while Sir John Eliot declared that no one should pay taxes to the king which were not sanctioned and condemned all those who were of the Arminian party. Parliament then dissolved and Eliot was thrown into prison, where he eventually died.

CHARLES' PERSONAL GOVERNMENT

Now followed the period of Charles' personal government. During this period his advisers were Thomas Wentworth, afterwards Lord Strafford—and William Laud, Archbishop of Canterbury and leader of the Arminians. Laud tried to enforce this doctrine on the Puritans through the High Commission Court and the Star Chamber. The Puritans hated him because they thought he had sympathies with the Catholics. In point of fact he hated the Pope as much as he hated the Puritans. He was an able and sincere man, but bigoted and intolerant. Charles' other adviser was Thomas Wentworth, Earl of Strafford, a friend of Laud's, and a man of the same type who had been brought back from Ireland which he had been ruling with a rod of iron.

During Charles' personal government the religious and parliamentary quarrels became worse and worse. Charles, as ever, being in need of money revived a number of old methods of levying taxes among which was " ship money." In the time of Elizabeth and before, it had been customary, when the country was in danger, to make the coastal counties build ships or to pay for their building. Charles called upon them to

Rischgitz

THE MARRIAGE OF CHARLES I

Shortly after his accession, Charles married Henrietta Maria, a French Catholic princess. The majority of English people hated her for her religion, and her extravagant habits soon got the king into trouble.

do this in time of peace, and later upon all the counties, both coastal and inland, to do so. It was tremendously unpopular, and a certain John Hampden refused to pay. When the case was tried, however, the judges came to a decision in favour of the king, and the payment of ship money went on.

RELIGIOUS AND PARLIAMENTARY QUARRELS

Laud was continuing to harry the Puritans, large numbers of whom were leaving the country, and going to the North American colonies rather than suffer this persecution. He deprived of his living every clergyman who would not use the Prayer Book and when in 1634 a Puritan clergyman named Prynne was sentenced to have his ears cut off for including in a book some words against the queen, and when again in 1637 Prynne and two others were fined £5,000 each, put in prison for life and had their ears cut off, for writing an attack against the church, public indignation reached its height.

In 1637, Laud made his fatal mistake. He ordered the new Prayer Book to be used in Scotland. There was a riot in St. Giles' Cathedral, Edinburgh, and the people immediately issued the National Covenant promising to defend their religion against the new innovations. A short time later the Scottish Church did away with the bishops and the established church, and re-established Presbyterianism.

Charles failed to raise a satisfactory army to enforce his wishes, and for a time agreed that the Scots should settle these matters for themselves. He recalled Strafford from Ireland, and called the short Parliament of 1640. But Parliament, led by Pym, refused to vote Charles the necessary money for the war unless he settled Parliament's own grievances. Charles immediately dissolved this Parliament.

War was now not far off. In the next Parliament (the Long Parliament) Laud was imprisoned and Strafford sentenced to death by a Bill of Attainder. Ship money and other taxes were declared illegal, the Star Chamber and High Commission Court were abolished and the Triennial Act was passed by which Parliament should meet every three years and the King should not dissolve it without its consent.

But Charles still had an opportunity of settling matters peaceably. The Grand Remonstrance, drawn up by Pym, stating all Charles' illegal acts and suggesting a plan of Church reform, was only passed by eleven votes. This narrow margin was due to the fact that there was a strong Anglican party in Parliament with whom Charles might have sided. But when on January 4, 1647, Charles went to Parliament intending to arrest five of its leaders, though he found " the birds flown," as he put it, war was inevitable.

THE CIVIL WAR

Roughly, the Parliamentary side was made up of the middle class traders ; the kings of the nobility and the peasants. The Irish Catholics and Scottish Presbyterians were possible allies of either side. Parliament was supported by the country roughly east of a line from Hull to Plymouth and most of the large towns where trade was carried on. The king by the north, then a country district with a small population, and the west. Parliament was in possession of very much greater financial resources, though this was off-set to a certain extent by the Royalist cavalry, an extremely important factor in the wars of those times.

The Civil War was chiefly a religious and partly a political war. It was a case of the Anglicans against the Puritans, and the government of the king against the government of Parliament. But even the political issue was largely a religious question, as it arose out of the " divine right of kings."

Charles started by marching south from the Midlands, the Earl of Essex tried to stop him at Edgehill and, after an indecisive battle, he pushed on to Oxford which he made his headquarters.

In 1643 the king's generals had conquered the

After Goodall   *Rischgitz*

THE HAPPIER DAYS OF CHARLES I

Charles I's reign is so overshadowed by tragedy that his happy days are seldom remembered. This picture shows him enjoying a day on the river with his family. Behind the Queen sits the little princess royal, Mary, who afterwards married the Prince of Orange and bore a son who became William III. Behind her is Charles, Prince of Wales, and heir to the throne, but fated to spend many years of his life in poverty and exile. The history of the Stuart period is marked by a conflict between the wishes of the king and the country.

After Edouard Gelli   *Mansell*

CHARLES IN VAN DYCK'S STUDIO

Van Dyck was a Flemish artist. Charles I heard of his fame and invited him to England. Our picture shows him standing, with palette and brushes, beside King Charles, while the queen and the court gaze in admiration at the portrait. Charles treated him kindly, granting him a pension and conferring a knighthood on him. The Civil War had deprived him of his living and he died at Blackfriars in reduced circumstances in 1641.

North and West, and Parliament, seeing no chance of immediate victory, enlisted the help of the Scots by the " Solemn League and Covenant." By this they promised to make England Presbyterian in return for help against the king. Charles sent his nephew, Prince Rupert, to stop them coming south. Both armies met at Marston Moor where the Royalists, in spite of a magnificent cavalry charge by Rupert, were defeated by the Puritans, under Cromwell, who had proved himself the best soldier on the Parliamentary side.

VICTORY FOR PARLIAMENT

Cromwell persuaded Parliament to reorganise the army which was known as the " New Model." Pay and discipline were improved, and by the " Self-Denying Ordinance " all members of the army had to resign their posts. This meant that incompetent generals like Essex were replaced by more efficient men. Sir Thomas Fairfax became the new commander-in-chief.

The New Model Army met the king at Naseby where the Royalist forces were routed. In 1646 the king gave himself up to the Scots who, in turn, handed him over to the English on finding that he would not introduce Presbyterianism into England.

There was now a quarrel within the Parlia-

mentary party between the " Independents " and the Presbyterians. The Independents disliked the narrowness of the latter and wanted a freer form of religion ; they belonged chiefly to the army and the Presbyterians to Parliament. Cromwell soon won the day for the Independents, and with what was left of Parliament (known as the Rump) a High Court of Justice was set up to try the king. He was sentenced to death and beheaded in 1649. The country was declared a Commonwealth to be ruled without a king or House of Lords.

At this time there were two controlling forces in the country—the army and the Rump government. The Rump was the remnant of the last government, now purged of the Royalists and Presbyterians. It was unpopular in the country because it closed the theatres—which the Puritans considered immoral—and suppressed the people's amusements generally ; because it was unable to lighten the taxation owing to the necessity for keeping a strong army and navy ; and because it was in no way representative of the country and reintroduced the High Commission Court, fearing that in its persecution of the royalists it would not get juries to convict. In spite of a few reforms it was thoroughly unsatisfactory. The army, therefore, powerful as it was already, was soon to become the real ruler of the country, with Cromwell at its head.

Many people look upon Cromwell as being one of the greatest Englishmen who has ever lived, but to form any judgment of a man it is necessary to decide by what standard the man is to be judged —whether by his personal character or by his lasting achievements.

As we shall see later, for reasons which admittedly were beyond his control, Cromwell's regime proved to be only a temporary one and it follows, then, that if he were a great man his greatness must lie in his personal character. About the fact that it did so there can be little doubt.

He was the son of a country squire and a man who loved the country and zealously attended church even in the worst of weather. He was a Puritan with the simple unaffected outlook of his sect, hating pomp and show and living a quiet, orderly life. When the Civil War broke out he threw himself wholeheartedly into the Parliamentary cause feeling that " God had raised him up to do so," and it was largely due to his energy and efficiency that Parliament proved successful.

While he ruled the country during the commonwealth he struggled to the best of his ability to do so constitutionally, but he failed because his position had come to him by force, and by force he had to rule. He never succeeded in settling the country, but he died an honest, God-fearing, sincere man, who had devoted his life to a cause he believed to be right.

After Hannah   *Mansell*

THE MAN WHO DISCOVERED THE CIRCULATION OF THE BLOOD

William Harvey, physician, first of James I and then of Charles I, is explaining to Charles how the blood circulates in the human body. His discovery was of the greatest importance, and was the gateway to a whole field of other discoveries that have aided suffering humanity and have led to the marvels of modern medicine.

From an old print.   Rischgitz

SCENES IN THE LIFE OF A STUART GENTLEWOMAN

These pictures illustrate the ideal behaviour of a lady not only in Stuart but in all times : to be modest and gracious ; comely but not gaudy ; and to have the motto "Grace my guide and glory my goal."

From an old print   Rischgitz

SCENES IN THE LIFE OF A STUART GENTLEMAN

The Stuart gentleman was to have his thoughts in the skies and his feet on the earth; to be modest;
well disposed towards his neighbours, and by the perfection of his conduct, find the way to heaven.

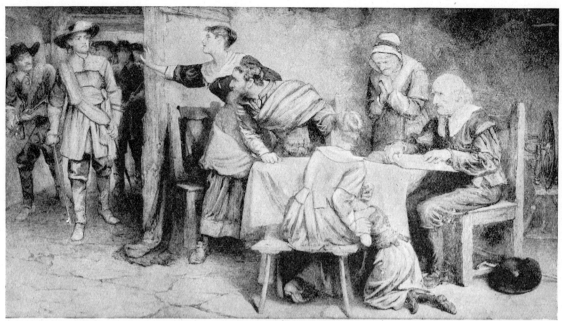

After W. H. Weatherhead   *By permission of the Oldham Art Gallery*

THE COVENANTERS

A Scottish peasant family is disturbed in the act of prayer by the king's officers, who have come to arrest these humble folk because they have sworn to uphold the Covenant, and worship God in the way of their forefathers. The Covenanters defied persecution and rose in rebellion against the oppressive government.

After E. H. Wehnert   *Victoria and Albert Museum*

GEORGE FOX PREACHING IN A TAVERN

Quakerism was the outcome of the teaching of George Fox and John Bunyan, who taught that contact with God could only come through the direct personal inspiration of each Christian unaided by priest or bishop. The Quakers were peaceful folk who led simple and sincere lives, with no wish to interfere with their neighbours.

After P. Caton Woodville　　　　　　　　　　　　　　*By permission of " The Illustrated London News "*

THE FOUNDING OF MADRAS

The East India Company became anxious in 1638 to secure a better footing on the east coast of India, and sent out Francis Day to select a better site for their headquarters. He purchased from the Rajah of Chandrajiri a piece of land and built on it Fort St. George. Thus was founded the city of Madras. In 1758 it was besieged by the French but was relieved by the timely arrival of the British fleet. Since that time it has been free from any serious attack. It is now the chief seaport on the east coast of India.

After P. Delaroche   *Mansell*

EARL STRAFFORD ON THE WAY TO EXECUTION

Charles attempted to govern without Parliament, and in this he was assisted by the Earl of Strafford and Archbishop Laud.   Strafford had proved a very efficient Lord Lieutenant of Ireland, and had trained a military force there which the Commons feared might be brought over to assist the king.   As a result he was impeached.

From an old print   *Rischgitz*

THE EXECUTION OF STRAFFORD

Strafford and Laud were arrested, and in the top picture we see the former on the way to execution, with the hands of Laud blessing him as he passed.   Laud was executed four years later.   So ended the king's advisers. Charles had promised Strafford his protection, but when he was in danger Charles did nothing to help him.

254

From the picture by J. S. Rouen   *By permission of Mrs. S. Rouen and The Gresham Committee*

CHARLES DEMANDS THE FIVE MEMBERS

With Strafford and Laud out of the way, Parliament was determined to curtail the personal power of the king. With this in view, in 1641, they drew up the famous Grand Remonstrance, which was a recital of all the abuses of Charles' personal government. It was only by a small majority that the Bill was passed in the Commons, but Charles would have been wise to abide by the decision. Instead of which, he appeared before the House with an armed force to arrest five of its leading members. Thus he issued a direct challenge to the right of Parliament to freedom of debate, and thereby threw away a good deal of the support which he had gained by his assent to the Grand Remonstrance. This was one of Charles' very foolish actions which a wise man would never have contemplated. It hastened on the outbreak of the Civil War which was to result in the Cromwellian régime and the death of the king. Charles paid for his rash folly with his life.

From the picture by J. Seymour Lucas   *By permission of the Wolverhampton Art Gallery*

THE FLIGHT OF THE FIVE MEMBERS

The five members had been warned of his approach, however, and here we see them escaping before the fatal policy of the king could be put into effect.   Though they escaped, the results of Charles' action were momentous.

From a fresco in the Peers Corridor, Houses of Parliament   *Rischgitz*

RAISING THE ROYAL STANDARD AT NOTTINGHAM

Charles' action made civil war inevitable, and Charles fled to Nottingham to raise the Royal Standard against the Parliamentary forces—the first step to the scaffold; though at first the Royalists had the upper hand.

HULL ORDERED TO SURRENDER BY CHARLES I

On April 23, 1642, Charles came before the fortress of Hull and ordered it to surrender. But Sir John Hotham, acting on instructions of Parliament, barred it against him. Charles appointed the Earl of Newcastle Governor of Hull in place of Hotham, but he was not recognised. The Commons had, in effect, deposed the king.

CHARLES I ON THE EVE OF EDGEHILL

Taking England as a whole, the south-eastern half, with London, was against the king, and the south-western half with most of the north was for him. Just below Edgehill in Warwickshire, Charles and the Earl of Essex (leading the Parliamentarians) fought the first but inconclusive battle of the Civil War. Lack of discipline affected both sides and night fell on a drawn battle. The moral advantage, however, rested with the king.

From the picture by Ernest Crofts, R.A.   Copyright of the Corporation of Bristol

THE SIEGE OF DONNINGTON CASTLE

Before the end of May, 1644, the Parliamentarians were masters of all the south and east of Berkshire except Donnington Castle. In the face of great difficulty, Col. John Bays defied the enemy who demanded his surrender. "I am entrusted," said he, "by his majesty's express command and have not yet learned to obey any other than my sovereign." But eventually, as seen in the picture, he was forced to surrender. Charles meanwhile was besieged in Oxford where he remained until June 3, when he made a successful escape to Worcester.

THE AMBUSH

In the background can be seen a Royalist caravan about to be ambushed by the Parliamentarians. On the king's side were a majority of the nobility, the clergy, and the country gentlemen. Not all the country, however, took sides. A great many preferred either to remain neutral or to leave the country until such time as its affairs had become settled, one way or another. John Evelyn, the famous diarist, was one of them.

THE PRISONERS

On the side of Parliament were the shopkeepers, small farmers and landowners, with a number of men of high rank; as a rule they were Puritans. Cromwell said: "I raised such men as had the fear of God before them, as made some conscience of what they did." They were nicknamed "Roundheads" because, despising the ringlets of the "Cavaliers" they cut their own hair short. Here we see a captured cavalier.

From the picture by Ernest Crofts, R.A., in the Diploma Gallery, Royal Academy

Mansell

TO THE RESCUE

The Roundheads have attacked and fired the country house of a cavalier. Prince Rupert, a nephew of Charles, was the leader of the cavaliers, and here we see a troop of Rupert's Horse riding furiously up the hill to the rescue. The picture shows how cavalier horsemen were dressed and armed in the Civil War, with leather coats and steel body-armour, carrying swords and muskets. The high boots and iron casques are also characteristic.

260

From the picture by J. Seymour Lucas, R.A., in the Diploma Gallery, Royal Academy

Mansell

NEWS FROM THE FRONT

A Royalist soldier, at considerable peril, has just broken through the enemy's lines and delivered a despatch from his captain to the commanding officer at headquarters. The messenger waits to carry back orders. Notice the heavy-jointed armour and metal helmet worn by the cavalier officers of that day.

From the picture by W. Dendy Sadler

By permission of the Manchester Corporation

THE CAPTURED ROUNDHEAD

In this picture we see a party of cavaliers belonging to one of the king's regiments, who have captured a Roundhead and have taken him to an inn and bound him to a chair. The sobriety of his dress makes a striking contrast to the gay be-ribboned uniform of his captors. He will suffer much chaffing, but no actual cruelty, since this usual aspect of war was singularly lacking throughout the Civil War.

From the picture by W. F. Yeames
By permission of the Corporation of Liverpool

"AND WHEN DID YOU LAST SEE YOUR FATHER?"

On the reply of a child hangs the safety of his father. In the picture the mother is seen waiting anxiously while her little son formulates his reply. How she must be longing to prompt him with a suitable reply—if only he would say "I do not know!" But even his stern questioners are affected by his youth.

Autotype Fine Art Co.
From the picture by R. Beavis

CARRYING STORES TO ELIZABETH CASTLE, JERSEY, DURING THE CIVIL WAR

In the great struggle between king and Parliament, Guernsey supported the Parliamentarians, but Jersey was divided. After some heavy fighting, however, Elizabeth Castle was captured for the Royalists, and it was from here that Charles II, in 1649, signed the declaration of his claims to the English throne.

From the picture by Ernest Crofts   Rischgitz

THE BATTLE OF MARSTON MOOR

Events had gone badly for Charles, since by the end of 1643, Gloucester and the West, London and the lower Thames valley, were in the hands of the Roundheads. Then the Scots decided to join the Parliamentarians and in 1644 joined them before York. At Long Marston, eight miles west of York, the Royalists were completely defeated and thus lost the north of England. The scene represents the preparations before the battle.

From the picture by Charles Landseer   Rischgitz

THE SACKING OF BASING HOUSE

The Earl of Worcester's Castle of Raglan and the Marquis of Winchester's Basing House were strongholds of Romanism and Royalism during the war. Their fall was long-delayed, but here we see Basing House being sacked by the Roundheads who have already discovered the family plate, but are greedy for further spoil.

From the picture by G. D. Leslie

Rischgitz

THE DEFENCE OF LATHOM HOUSE

One of the houses which held out against the Parliamentarians was Lathom House, defended by Charlotte de la Frémouille, Countess of Derby, for eighteen weeks. Prince Rupert relieved the siege of Lathom House, and hung it with the Parliamentary banners which he had captured after the battle of Bolton before riding on to the siege of York and the disastrous battle of Marston Moor. The combat lasted from sunset until ten o'clock at night ; but in that short space of time four thousand one hundred and fifty were killed and many wounded.

From the picture by Egg in the Diploma Gallery, Royal Academy   *Mansell*

CROMWELL BEFORE NASEBY

Cromwell, after Edgehill, at which battle he had fought, realised the weakness of undisciplined forces and proceeded to organise his regiment of '' Ironsides,'' and afterwards, with Fairfax, the new model army of '' God-fearing men.''   Here we see Cromwell praying in his tent before the Battle of Naseby which was to decide '' what the liberties and laws of England, and what the king's power and prerogative should hereafter be.''

From the picture by Landseer   *Rischgitz*

CROMWELL AT THE BATTLE OF NASEBY

On Saturday, June 14, 1645, Cromwell's '' Ironsides,'' who '' trusted in God and kept their powder dry,'' gained the victory of Naseby. After the fight, papers were picked up on the battlefield which proved that Charles was planning to bring foreign forces to England to save his cause.   A selection from these letters was printed and published by the Parliament and did much finally to turn the tide of popular feeling against the king.

From the picture by J. Payne   *Rischgitz*

SOVEREIGN OF THE SEAS

In 1634, in a time of perfect peace, a tax called " Ship-money " was instituted in order to equip a fleet. The coastal towns paid up with a good grace, but inland, bitter resentment was felt. In 1635 the *Sovereign of the Seas* was built, one of the noblest ships ever floated. Ship money was an old tax which was revived by the king.

From the picture by P. Delaroche   *Rischgitz*

CHARLES I IN THE GUARDROOM

After Naseby, Cromwell and the army made overtures to the king, but Charles was plotting even when discussing peace. No agreement could be arrived at between the king and his people. He was arrested by the Parliamentary forces and imprisoned, first at Hurst Castle in Hampshire, and afterwards brought to London, and here we see him in the guardroom being submitted to many indignities by the common soldiers.

From the picture by W. Fisk   *Rischgitz*

THE TRIAL OF CHARLES I IN WESTMINSTER HALL, 1649

On January 20, 1649, Charles was tried in Westminster Hall on a charge of high treason. A week later the judges pronounced sentence of death on "Charles Stuart, King of England," as a "tyrant, traitor, murderer and public enemy"; "Convicted, attainted and condemned of High Treason and other high Crimes."

From the painting by Sir John Gilbert, R.A.   *Mappin Art Gallery, Sheffield*

CHARLES LEAVING WESTMINSTER HALL AFTER SENTENCE OF DEATH

Charles' duplicity had been his ruin, and in spite of the efforts of Prince Charles, his son, then a refugee in France, nothing could now save the king. The fight for despotic monarchy had been fought and lost.

From the picture by W. Fisk   *Rischgitz*

CROMWELL'S FAMILY INTERCEDING FOR THE LIFE OF CHARLES I

But there were those, even members of Cromwell's own family, who revolted against the execution of their king, however unwise he may have been. But to such pleadings Cromwell turned a deaf ear. He could not go against the verdict of one hundred and fifty Commissioners even had he been willing. In any case the death of the king had now become for Cromwell an act of justice that had to be accomplished.

From the picture by Blackburn   *Rischgitz*

CHARLES I ON THE MORNING OF THE EXECUTION

On the last sad morning, Charles is seen with his young children and William Juxon, Bishop of London, who has come to offer consolation of religion to the doomed king. Many a loyal subject would have willingly changed places with Charles, who went to his execution with the most kingly dignity and bravery.

From the picture by Ernest Crofts, R.A.   *Arnold*

CHARLES I ON THE WAY TO EXECUTION

On January 30, 1649, Charles walked through St. James's Park to Whitehall, where he was to be executed. With him is the Bishop of London. Behind the tree are two cavaliers who have bared their heads, heedless of the angry looks of the soldiers. In spite of the Parliamentary victory Charles still had many supporters.

From the picture by Ernest Crofts, R.A.

By permission of the Royal United Service Museum

THE EXECUTION OF CHARLES I

The Civil War started in 1642 and ended with the death of Charles on the scaffold in front of the Palace of Whitehall on a cold winter day in 1649. "A great shudder ran through the crowd that saw the deed, then came a shriek, and all immediately dispersed." Nothing in Charles's life was truly kingly except the leaving it. The idea that there was divinity in kingship still persisted and many people were horrified at what had been done.

THE COMMONWEALTH
1649-1660

THE Irish Catholics had been becoming more and more Royalist in sympathy and were hated by the Puritans because they were Catholics. In 1649 Cromwell took an army across and brutally put down any resistance. In an endeavour to establish Protestantism members of the army were given the estates of the Irish Catholics and Royalists. Though Cromwell did give some sort of peace and prosperity to the country his methods were so harsh that the " Curse of Cromwell " is spoken of to this day.

THE ROYALIST RISING

The Scottish Presbyterians also were now Royalist in sympathy because the " Solemn League and Covenant " by which England was to become Presbyterian had not been fulfilled owing to the supremacy of the army which was Independent. The Scots declared the Prince of Wales, King Charles II. Cromwell, now head of the army in place of Fairfax, invaded Scotland in 1650 and defeated the Presbyterians at Dunbar. Charles II invaded England the next year hoping to gain many Royalist recruits, but the English were tired of fighting. His plan did not succeed and he was defeated at Worcester. Cromwell referred to this victory as " the crowning mercy," meaning that now all three kingdoms were brought under the English Parliament there would be an end of fighting.

THE RULE OF CROMWELL

After Cromwell had put down Ireland and the Royalist movement in Scotland, he was more powerful than ever. He proceeded to denounce the Rump for starting the war with the Dutch who were Protestants, and for its not being representative of the country. He thought that it ought to dissolve itself and when it did not do so he went down to the House with a band of soldiers and expelled the members.

Cromwell had no wish, however, either to rule by military force or by himself as dictator without a Parliament, but he was in difficulties about what form the constitution should take. First of all he tried what is known as the " Bare-bones Parliament." This was an assembly of strong Puritans named after a fanatic named Barbon, but it proved unpractical and Cromwell soon got rid of it. The army now drew up the " Instrument of Government " which stated that the Protector should call a Parliament once every three years; that it should not be dissolved until it had sat for five months; that it should have the power of electing a new Protector at his death ; that religious toleration should be granted to all but Papists and Anglicans ; and that members should be elected from all four countries. To all this Cromwell agreed, but the Parliament which met in 1654 showed that it was opposed to religious toleration; refused to grant supplies to the army ; wished to reduce its numbers ; and 100 members refused to observe the " Instrument of Government." These members were at once excluded and five months later Parliament was dissolved.

For the next eighteen months Cromwell did without a Parliament, and to keep control of the country which was in a very unsettled condition, he appointed twelve major-generals to rule by martial law and put down any attempt at revolution, and to enforce the Puritan code of morals.

The country was now at war with Spain and to raise money Cromwell again called Parliament. This did away with the major-generals, voted the money and presented him with the " Humble Petition and Advice " establishing a second chamber and offering him the title of king. Cromwell refused the latter, knowing that it would not be tolerated by the army. But he failed to work in agreement with this Parliament and dissolved it in 1658. He died seven months later worn out by hard work.

His son Richard was elected Protector in succession but he was a weak man without his father's ability. General Monk, who was in charge of the army in Scotland, seeing the army quarrelling and no satisfactory government to take office, came south to London, and declared for a government to be freely elected by the country. This assembled in 1660 and, amid general rejoicing, immediately requested Charles II to assume the crown.

CROMWELL IN WHITEHALL

Although Cromwell had signed the death warrant and had refused to listen to the pleadings of his family, he was much upset by the execution of the king. Tradition declares that he went secretly to see the beheaded corpse. He looked steadfastly at it and sighed out the words '' Cruel necessity ! '' This picture shows him looking with troubled face at a portrait of the king. He was a godly man who hated mere acts of violence.

The only really satisfactory aspect of Cromwell's period of power was his foreign policy—to help Protestant countries in Europe and to develop the colonies.

THE NAVIGATION ACT

The Navigation Act of 1651 had laid down that only British ships should trade with British possessions. The Dutch, who had for a long time been the chief shipping nation of the world, were angry at this interference with their trade and the rivalry of the British. War broke out in 1652 and, thanks to the brilliant work of Admiral Blake, who cut off the enemies' food supply, the Dutch were forced to come to an agreement about the Navigation Act two years later.

Cromwell made treaties with Sweden and Denmark and allied himself with Portugal, thereby considerably benefiting English trade. In 1655 the island of Jamaica was taken from the Spanish and when Spain declared war Cromwell allied England with France which, though a Catholic country, was now tolerating the Protestants. This alliance resulted in the French capturing Dunkirk, which had been Spanish, and handing it over to England as a reward for her help. England was now very much respected abroad. Her army was small, but of first class efficiency ; her navy under Blake extremely powerful. It was this respect from other countries which was the only permanent achievement Cromwell managed to make.

CROMWELL'S FAILURE

Throughout his period of power, Cromwell wished to rule constitutionally but was forced by circumstances to be a dictator. His wish for a settled form of government was impossible because it was necessary to keep the Royalist Party in subjection which he could not do with a freely elected government; in fact he was in much the same position as Charles I. Like Charles he was in perpetual conflict with the Parliament which existed during his Protectorate, but unlike Charles he was strong enough and able enough to rule the country in spite of this. His trouble lay in the necessity for ruling by the sword, a method which could not endure after his death. He must have known the instability of this system and his whole policy at home was to discover a workable constitution. In this he failed and was bound to fail unless he accepted the crown, and the nation, if they were to have a king, would have preferred someone with more claim to the throne than military power. At his death the inevitable happened ; the country was without a leader. The only solution was to recall Charles II.

THE QUARREL CONTINUES

In spite of the Civil War two antagonistic parties had continued to exist : the Parliamentarians on the one hand and the king's supporters on the other, the quarrel between them being largely one of religion, Anglican versus Puritan.

During his life Cromwell, by his strong rule, kept the Royalists in suppression, but after his death there was no one to succeed him strong enough to continue to do so. The Puritans were without a leader ; the Royalists wanted the return of the king. The restoration of the monarchy was a return to the same state of affairs as had existed before the Civil War ; the pendulum had only swung back again in favour of the Royalists.

The quarrel between king and Parliament, Anglican and Puritan was so deep-rooted and so evenly balanced that there was no possible settlement except as a compromise. Neither party, however, was prepared to agree to this and it was many years before religious toleration came to this country and before the relationship between king and Parliament was finally settled. The Stuart kings might have alleviated the trouble, but Cromwell, having no constitutional position, was forced to rely on the sword—the one thing which was certain to fail.

From the picture by Lucy   *Rischgitz*

CROMWELL PREVENTED FROM EMIGRATING

Cromwell was a child of destiny. According to tradition he and his cousin, John Hampden, embarked on a vessel in the Thames for New England in 1637. But it is said that they were prevented from sailing by the king's orders. They were to remain to teach a despotic sovereign a lesson which neither he nor England were ever to forget. It was ironic that Charles kept in England the man who was to take his throne from him.

From the picture by Ernest Crofts

Rischgitz

CROMWELL AT BOOTHAM BAR, YORK

In June, 1650, Charles II landed in Scotland where he had already been proclaimed king. Cromwell, with a large force marched against him, and on arriving at York, the magistrates removed the royal arms from Bootham Bar and replaced them with those of the State. The army continued north, met the king's forces at Dunbar on September 3, and a battle fought lasting one hour; resulting in a victory for Cromwell. Ten thousand prisoners were taken and three thousand slain. He also captured much baggage and guns.

From a contemporary satirical print   Rischgitz

CROMWELL'S CAR

This satirical contemporary print represents the Royalists' conception of the rule of Cromwell. The devil is driving the car, and all that is dear to the Royalist cause is being driven over by the chariot which is drawn by two animals which are spreading the fire of desolation. Justice is slaughtered, Truth imprisoned in a dungeon, while, in the background, a pair of wolves ravage a flock of sheep. In the scales wielded by the figure of Cromwell the feathers of a deceptive liberty weigh heavier than the symbols of Church and State.

From the picture by Cope   *Rischgitz*

DEATH OF PRINCESS ELIZABETH AT CARISBROOKE, 1650

Princess Elizabeth was the second daughter of Charles I and was present at the last sad meeting before his execution. She was afterwards imprisoned, and on the landing of Charles II in Scotland, Parliament ordered her to be moved to Carisbrooke Castle, where she died of fever soon after her arrival. Such was the sad end of yet another member of the unfortunate and ill-starred Stuart family.

From the picture by J. A. Houston, R S A.

Preston Corporation Art Gallery

THE SECRETING OF THE REGALIA OF SCOTLAND

In times of civil war, the opposing forces live upon the land and such booty as each can capture. The Scottish royal regalia would have proved a valuable prize to Cromwell's forces, but in 1652 a faithful Scot secreted it in the vaults of a church. The previous year during General Monk's campaign the royal robes and the national records had been captured at Stirling and sent to London as part of the victorious trophies of his expedition.

277

From the picture by Ward   *Rischgiz*

PRINCE CHARLES ESCAPING AFTER WORCESTER

In Scotland, Prince Charles was looked upon as the legitimate sovereign by a strong and influential party, but at the Battle of Worcester in 1650, he was defeated by Cromwell. After many escapes he succeeded in getting out of the country. In this picture Charles is seen disguised as a servant of Miss Lane, a royalist supporter, who is riding pillion, on the way to Bristol. This incident took place shortly after he had spent the night hidden in an oak-tree at Boscobel. The story of his escape to France is one of the most exciting in history.

Rischgitz

DEFEAT OF THE DUTCH FLEET BY ADMIRAL BLAKE

By the Navigation Act of 1651, the importation or exportation of any goods except in English ships was prohibited. This led to war with Holland, and in 1653, Admiral Blake finally defeated the Dutch who were thereafter compelled to salute the English flag wherever they saw it. The definitive battle of this campaign was fought first off Cape La Hogue, where a fleet of more than seventy English ships met the Dutch Navy.

From the picture by B. West
Mansell

CROMWELL DISSOLVING THE LONG PARLIAMENT

Disgusted at the inefficiency of the existing Parliament, Cromwell called in his musketeers, and pointing to the mace he cried, " What shall we do with this bauble ? Here, take it away ! " and gave it to a musketeer. The Commons were turned out and Cromwell seized the records and ordered the doors to be locked.

From the picture by Maguiro
Mansell

CROMWELL REFUSING THE CROWN

In 1657 the members of Cromwell's second Parliament drew up what was called the Petition and Advice, in which, among other requests, Cromwell was asked to take the title of king. He agreed to all clauses, but refused the Crown. He said that he could only accept it doubtingly, which would not be of faith and if it were not of faith it would be a sin. The secretary writing at the table is John Milton.

Mansell

CROMWELL REBUKED BY HIS DAUGHTER

Walter Scott in his novel of "Woodstock" makes Cromwell say: "I would I had any creature, were it but a dog, that followed me because it loved me, not for what it could make of me." Even his daughter found cause to rebuke him. Her name was Elizabeth Claypole and she was her father's favourite. At this time she was slowly dying of a painful disease, and her distress added to the burdens already borne by the Protector.

After the picture by F. Newenham   *Rischgitz*

CROMWELL DICTATING TO HIS SECRETARY, MILTON

John Milton, the famous Puritan poet, became Cromwell's secretary. Here we see the Protector dictating a letter to the Duke of Savoy, demanding that he shall cease his persecution of Protestants in Piedmont.

After the picture by Boughton   *Rischgitz*

THE MEETING OF MILTON AND MARVELL

Andrew Marvell was another Puritan poet, and here we see his first meeting with Milton, to whom he was afterwards to become assistant secretary. In the reign of Charles II, Marvell wrote against the excesses of the court. Marvell is the most famous of a group of fine lyric writers who lived about this time.

After the picture by David Neal   *Copyright B.P.C*

CROMWELL AND MILTON

As a relaxation of the arduous duties of government, Cromwell is here seen listening to Milton playing the organ. Milton was a great music-lover, and there are many references to it in his works which, in beauty, rank equal to those of Shakespeare; the very sound of his verse has been compared to that of an organ.

After the picture by M. Munkacsy   *New York Public Library*

MILTON DICTATING "PARADISE LOST"

" Paradise Lost," Milton's greatest poem, was commenced about 1658, and here he is seen dictating it to his daughters. It deals with the " Fall of Man." In later years he wrote " Paradise Regained " which tells the story of the Temptation in the Wilderness. Two other famous poems of his are "Comus" and "Lycidas."

After the picture by Lucy   *Rischgitz*

CROMWELL AND HIS FAMILY AT HAMPTON COURT
Milton is here seen playing to Cromwell and his family.   The poet's life had been clouded by his unfortunate marriage to Mary Powell, and in 1650 he lost the use of his left eye, and two years later he was quite blind.

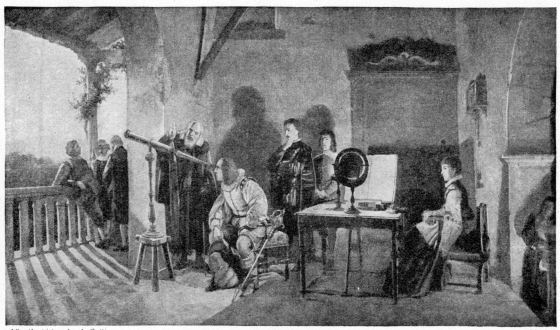

After the picture by A. Gatti   *Mansell*

MILTON VISITS GALILEO
The Papacy had declared that the earth was flat.   Galileo disproved this theory, and for his pains he was subjected to the cruelty of the Inquisition.   While touring the Continent, Milton visited Galileo in prison.

After the picture by D. W. Wynfield　　　　　　　　　　　　　　　　　　　　　　*Rischgitz*

DEATH OF CROMWELL

Cromwell had lived in busy times, had borne the weight of heavy state affairs, and had often gone in fear of his life. In September, 1658, he was ill of the gout and ague, and when he received news of the death of his favourite daughter, he sank, never to raise his head again. Before his death, he appointed his son Richard to succeed him. His last prayer was : Lord, though a miserable and wretched creature, I am in covenant with Thee through Thy grace, and may and will come to Thee for Thy people. Thou hast made me a mean instrument to do them some good, and Thee service. Many of them set too high a value upon me, though others would be glad of my death. Lord, however Thou disposest of me, continue, and go on to do good for them. Teach those who look too much upon Thy instruments, to depend more upon Thyself, and pardon such as desire to trample upon the dust of a poor worm, for they are Thy people, too."

After the fresco by E. M. Ward in the Houses of Parliament　　　　　　　　　　　　　　*Rischgitz*

MONK DECLARING FOR A FREE PARLIAMENT

On the death of Cromwell, General Monk, then commander-in-chief in Scotland, marched into England with the determination of calling a new Parliament which should be free and representative of the real political feeling of the people. Richard Cromwell was too weak to govern, and after nine months he gracefully retired. Monk now expressed his determination to arrange for the restoration to England of Charles II.

THE RESTORATION

ON May 26, 1660, amid general rejoicing Charles landed at Dover where he was met by General Monk and the Mayor of the town who presented him with a " very rich Bible " which Charles insincerely said was " the thing that he loved above all things in the world." The people were delighted that the harsh rule of the Puritans was over and Pepys in his diary tells how the streets were thronged with happy faces and decked with flags. Few events can have been received with so much enthusiasm and so much subsequent disappointment.

Before landing in England Charles had issued the Declaration of Breda promising arrears of pay to the army, a general pardon to those concerned in the revolution, security of possession for those who gained land under the Commonwealth and liberty of conscience to all Protestants; but like so many of Charles's promises these were not destined to be fulfilled. The army was disbanded except for a few regiments ; lands were returned to their original owners ; many who had been concerned in the revolution were imprisoned and thirteen of those concerned in the trial of Charles I were executed ; freedom of conscience was not granted to all Protestants.

Charles soon made himself unpopular both in Scotland and Ireland. The union which had been set up under Cromwell was ignored and both countries again had their own Parliaments. Bishops were again imposed upon the Scottish Presbyterians much to their disgust, and in Ireland estates were taken from the natives and given to the Protestants who had been loyal to the crown, which annoyed the Irish.

RELIGIOUS TROUBLES

The religious difficulties were as great as ever and Charles, being at heart a Catholic, was a most unsuitable person to deal with them. Clarendon was now Charles's adviser and his policy was to have the Church and the State identified and this national Church broad enough in its view to embrace all shades of opinion. Unfortunately this was not possible because the bishops who were the backbone of the Anglican Church were intolerable to the Puritans. The religious settlement, when it did come, was widely different from this policy of Clarendon's. The Act of Uniformity of 1662 made the revised Prayer Book compulsory and every clergyman was forced to take an oath that he would conform to it. Many refused to do so and were deprived of their livings. Other religious acts passed between 1661-1665 are known as the Clarendon Code. By the Corporation Act all mayors and magistrates had to conform to the Church of England ; by the Licensing Act no book could be printed without the sanction of the government ; by the Conventicle Act not more than four people were to meet together for worship unless it were that of the Church of England; the Five Miles Act forbade those clergymen who had been deprived of their livings to go within five miles of the parish where they had originally held office. The Puritans were again as badly off as they had been before the Revolution.

Parliament, meanwhile, had no intention of allowing Charles to return to the despotism of his father. The High Commission Court and Star Chamber—courts which were used for the king's own purposes—were abolished and the second Triennial Act of 1664 ensured that Parliament should meet every three years.

THE PLAGUE

In 1665 the Great Plague broke out. Plagues had not been uncommon in London where the streets were narrow and dirty, but never had there been one like this. No less than one-fifth of the population of London succumbed to it— chiefly the poor who were unable to leave the town like the richer people. The plague was followed, in 1666, by the fire which, although it did great damage, did at least purge the city of infection. It is nothing short of a tragedy that the ensuing opportunity to rebuild London on a finer scale was not accepted. If Sir Christopher Wren had had his way the city of London would be a very different place to-day.

During this time the country was again at war with the Dutch over the Navigation Act and in 1666 the Dutch fleet took the opportunity given them by the plague and the fire to sail up the Medway and do considerable damage.

RICHARD CROMWELL

Few men or women can ever have wished to govern a country less than Richard Cromwell. After his retirement he went abroad, but during the reign of Charles II he returned to England and lived peacefully until his death. He was a very weak and worldly man whose election to the position of Protector was more a matter of routine than any feeling on the part of his nominators that he was a suitable successor.

Clarendon, who was already extremely unpopular with the Puritan section of the community, was blamed for this outrage on English pride and after the war was somewhat ignominiously concluded by the Treaty of Breda, the outcry against him was so great that he was forced to go into exile. Clarendon had served the crown faithfully and well all his life and his betrayal by Charles is equalled only by the betrayal of Strafford by his father.

THE CABAL

Charles now formed the Cabal, a group of five ministers, two of whom were Roman Catholics, and so named after the first letters of the names of each of its members—Clifford, Arlington, Buckingham, Ashley (later Lord Shaftesbury) and Lauderdale. The Cabal really marks the beginning of the modern Cabinet though there are great differences between the two. The Cabinet to-day is composed of men with the same opinions : if one disagrees with the others he resigns. Moreover, the modern Cabinet works in conjunction with Parliament, the Cabal did not.

With this ministry Charles started on his schemes to make himself independent of Parliament. Louis XIV had invaded the Spanish Netherlands and to resist this danger from a Catholic power the three Protestant states, England, Sweden and Denmark, joined together in the Triple Alliance. In 1670 this alliance was broken by Charles's two secret Treaties of Dover. His object in signing these was to get money which would make him independent of Parliament and to make England a Catholic country. These treaties provided that England would make war on Holland and would become converted to Catholicism. Charles was to get £300,000 for the first clause and £200,000 for the second. Meanwhile he secured a grant of £800,000 from Parliament to help the Triple Alliance !

Charles, now wishing to gain the support of as big a section of the country as he could, issued the Declaration of Indulgence exempting all Nonconformists and Roman Catholics from the penalties of the Act of Uniformity and the Clarendon Code. But the country was becoming suspicious about the Treaty of Dover and many people thought that the Declaration of Indulgence was an attempt to encourage the Catholics, so Charles agreed to the Test Act, by which anyone holding a position in the

Church or State had to conform to the Church of England. The two Catholic members of the Cabal — Clifford and Arlington — immediately resigned and Charles made Danby, a stout Anglican, his chief minister. Danby made peace with the Dutch—a popular move because war with another Protestant country was not liked — and arranged the marriage between Mary, daughter of James, Duke of York, to the Protestant William of Orange.

WHIGS AND TORIES

Parliament was now sharply divided. There were two parties : the Country Party headed by Shaftesbury, a former member of the Cabal, and the Court Party under the leadership of Danby whose object was to increase the king's influence there. Later these two parties were to be known as Whigs and Tories.

The country was still uneasy and an event of 1678 created a panic. A certain man named Titus Oates invented the story of a plot to murder the king and put the Catholic James, Duke of York, on the throne. This " Popish Plot " was furthered by Shaftesbury whose object was to exclude James from the throne. The nation was thoroughly alarmed and the Catholics were persecuted right and left. Charles now behaved with extreme shrewdness. He knew that the whole story was false but he did not oppose the popular outcry knowing that that would draw suspicion on himself ; on the contrary he even went so far as to allow Titus Oates to be installed in Whitehall with a pension. Charles saw that if " he gave them line enough," as he put it, the violence of the Whigs would cause a Royalist reaction.

The Whig Party in Parliament now devoted all its attention to the Exclusion Bill by which the Duke of York should be barred from the throne and the Duke of Monmouth, an illegitimate son of Charles, should become the heir. This Bill was passed by the Commons but rejected by the Lords. But as Charles had forseen, the Whigs were going too far and a Royalist reaction set in. An example of this change is to be found in *Absolom and Achitophel*, a brilliant satire on Shaftesbury and his party. Charles now seized his opportunity and ruled without Parliament. Shaftesbury was forced to leave the country. Some of the more violent Whigs started the " Rye House Plot," an attempt to murder the king, but it was discovered and two of the Whig leaders executed.

From an old print

RETURN OF THE EXILE

While Cromwell was in power Charles had been living on the Continent making abortive negotiations with various foreign powers. None of them proved successful. Here we see him sailing from Holland to England.

Shortly after this the king died ; just before the end he was formally admitted to the Roman Catholic Church.

CHARLES AND THE COUNTRY

Charles II was a shrewd, intelligent man but he used his shrewdness and intelligence for his own ends and not for the country. He was prepared to sell the nation to the French to get more power for himself but he was able to see when his plans were failing and change his tune accordingly. Though he was loose-living and pleasure-seeking he was intensely interested in science, literature and architecture. During his reign the Royal Society was founded ; Wren designed some of the most beautiful buildings in the country and literature flourished immensely. Indeed the literature of the Restoration period is particularly interesting, being a perfect mirror of the time. On the one hand are the writings of the Puritans, Milton and Bunyan. Both were intensely serious in purpose and to compare them with the non-Puritan writers shows what an immense gap there is between the outlook of the two sects. The majority of the Restoration dramatists and poets reflect the laxity and frivolity of the court ; they also reflect the French influence in England—due to the fact that Charles had spent much of his life in France.

The Restoration was popular in England because it put an end to the despotic rule of Cromwell which closed the theatres, suppressed the people's amusements and was altogether too strict. The morality of the court under Charles may have been shocking but the people generally were freer and happier than they had been during the Commonwealth.

In spite of his double dealing in political affairs Charles had managed to keep his popularity to the end. He succeeded in this owing to the violence of the Whigs who, if they had not gone to such extremes, finishing with the Rye House Plot, might have got the support of the whole of the country.

The country, however, was not yet in a properly settled state. Charles, like all the Stuarts, was of Catholic sympathies and desired to be an absolute monarch. Throughout the whole Stuart period it was these two characteristics which caused the perpetual friction between king and Parliament. Charles, by his tact, had not allowed matters to come to a head, but when James came to the throne after him the trouble was no nearer settlement and was liable to break out again any moment. The snake had been scotched not killed.

THE REIGN OF CHARLES II

In life and manners it is difficult to imagine a greater contrast than between the rule of Cromwell and the reign of Charles II. We see on the one hand the serious, godly Cromwell, listening to the great moralist and thinker, Milton; on the other we see Charles, witty and amusing, desporting himself with gay, charming Nell Gwynn. Such examples are typical of the difference of the two periods; of the rule of the Puritans, simple, serious and earnest; of the rule of the restored Monarchy, gay, brilliant and licentious. Such a contrast between two outlooks exists in every age and in every country, but perhaps it has never been so clearly marked as during the Commonwealth and the Restoration.

But what is often overlooked in the Restoration period is the development of science. This was a subject in which Charles himself was interested and consequently it became a fashionable pastime. But apart from the court amateurs, great discoveries were being made by the genuine men of science. Harvey had discovered the circulation of blood in the human body; Newton discovered the law of gravitation; and in 1662 the Royal Society was founded, having as its object the advancement of science.

Such are the diversities of interests during the Restoration period that it is not possible to sum them up in a short space. It marks the second great peak of English culture. It was witty and frivolous, sincere and earnest; it was licentious and learned; sometimes beautiful, sometimes sordid; a time of uncertainty and doubt, a time of progress and discovery. The character of the king himself was as varied as the time in which he lived.

After Benjamin West   *Rischgitz*

CHARLES II ARRIVING AT DOVER

In 1660 the son of Charles I was invited to return to England and take the throne. He landed at Dover where he was met by General Monk and the mayor of the town. The country received him with great enthusiasm. Pepys says in his famous diary that the ways were strewed with flowers and the streets hung with tapestry.

After Stothard   *Rischgitz*

CHARLES RECEIVING THE DUCHESS OF ORLEANS

The Duchess of Orleans was the youngest daughter of Charles I. During the Civil War she had to flee from the country in disguise to Paris, where she became very influential at the Court of Louis XIV and where she married the Duke of Orleans. In 1670 she came to England and obtained Charles' signature to the secret Treaty of Dover. The young Duchess is here seen greeting her brother after an absence of many years.

SOLOMON EAGLE'S WARNING TO LONDONERS

The plague, which was probably brought to London by some Dutch sailors, broke out in 1665. The people of that time were very superstitious and when preachers started telling them that the judgment of God had come upon the city, they were readily believed. Here is a picture of one of the preachers named Solomon Eagle telling the plague-stricken people that God had brought all this down on them as a punishment for their wickedness.

A SCENE DURING THE GREAT PLAGUE

It is not easy for us in the twentieth century to imagine the full horror of the plague. Here is a picture depicting one of the many thousands of dreadful situations that must have arisen. A man returns home to find his wife lying unconscious and dying. He is horrified; his lamp drops from his hand. What is he to do? Is he to flee from the house and avoid the infection, or is he to take the nobler but fatal course of staying with her until the end? There is a wonderful account of this terrible year written by Daniel Defoe, the author of *Robinson Crusoe*, telling us of all the superstition, heroism and cowardice that actually took place.

From the picture by F. W. Topham

THE GREAT PLAGUE STRUCK YOUNG AND OLD

The people who were afflicted by the plague put crosses on their doors with the words "Lord, have mercy upon us," as a warning to others that they were infected. This picture shows a young child being taken out from such a house through the window, the rescuers being unwilling to enter for fear of infection. Her clothes have been left behind lest they, too, carry with them the fatal germs of disease.

From a contemporary engraving *Rischgitz*

THE DEAD CART

So many people died from the plague that it was impossible to give them all a decent burial.   A cart would go round accompanied by the tolling of a bell and the mournful cry " Bring out your dead."   The bodies were collected in this cart, and thrown into a pit which served as a common grave.   These plague pits can be traced even to-day as grim reminders of the times when sanitation had no place in the lives of the people.

293

From the picture by J. R. Burgess　　　　　　　　*By permission of " Pictorial Education "*

THE GREAT FIRE OF LONDON

After the plague a great fire broke out and burned for four days, spreading quickly in the narrow streets and wooden houses. Though it caused great damage it effected the destruction of all infection left from the plague. Many people escaped from their burning houses, with their possessions, into boats on the Thames. The fire was only checked by the courage of the king in destroying the houses in the path of the flames. He himself toiled with his men, becoming so blackened with smoke, that he was unrecognised by the people.

These Engins,(which are the best)to quinch great Fires, are

JOHN KEELING

Made by John Keeling in Black Fryers (after many years Experience) Who also maketh all other sorts of Engin.

From a contemporary engraving

FIRE ENGINES OF THE SEVENTEENTH CENTURY

A contrast to modern times ! The fire engine of the seventeenth century was nothing more than a tank on wheels from which the water was pumped by hand. In spite of the advertisement of John Keeling, shown in this picture, these fire engines proved themselves to be of very little use against the ravages of the Great Fire.

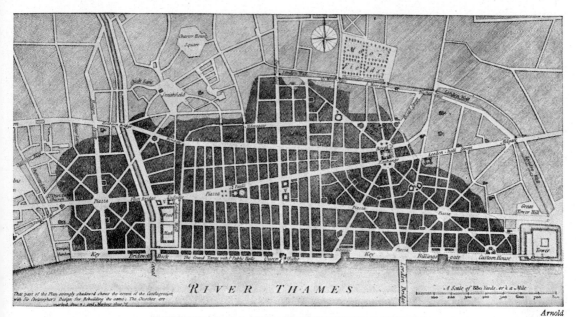

RIVER THAMES

Arnold

WREN'S PLAN FOR REBUILDING LONDON

After the Fire, Wren got out a plan for rebuilding London, with great wide streets and noble buildings. Unfortunately this plan came to nothing as there was not sufficient money, and the owners of houses which had been destroyed, immediately built them again on the same sites. However, he did rebuild a large number of very beautiful churches which may be seen to-day, their graceful spires rising above the other buildings.

From the picture by Paul Hardy   *By permission of " Pictorial Education "*

REBUILDING ST. PAUL'S

With most of London St. Paul's was destroyed by the great fire.   Before this Wren had got out plans for rebuilding it and now came his opportunity of doing so.   When Wren died he was buried in his own magnificent cathedral, and on his tomb are the words : '' If you seek his monument look around you.''   Here is King Charles, who took a great interest in the arts, personally examining the work of rebuilding.   Wren suffered much from enemies during his 49 years' task, and when eighty six years old, was ignominiously dismissed his post.

INTERIOR OF ST. PAUL'S

A view of the interior of new St. Paul's looking towards the altar and showing the fine choir stalls which were designed by Grinling Gibbons and the great dome ornamented with mosaics. Above the arches runs the "whispering gallery," so named because the slightest sound carries from one side of the cathedral to the other. In his old age Wren was carried once a year to look upon this wonderful masterpiece of his art. He also built no less than fifty-two churches in London, and the Monument commemorating the Great Fire.

"A NEW WHIP FOR THE DUTCH"

Here is a naval architect showing the latest model of a new type of ship to be used against the Dutch. Bending over the model is John Evelyn the diarist. On his right is Samuel Pepys, also famous for his diary, and a great naval administrator. On the extreme right is the English sailor the Earl of Sandwich.

THE DISGRACE OF THE EARL OF CLARENDON

Edward Hyde, the Earl of Clarendon, loyally supported the crown all his life, and all his life suffered by doing so. He was driven into exile during the civil wars but returned again to serve Charles II after the Restoration. Charles, however, to keep his popularity with the country dismissed him from office. He was impeached by Parliament and forced into exile. He is remembered chiefly for the "Clarendon Code" and his legal writings.

From the picture by A. Forestier   *By permission of the " Illustrated London News "*

FIRST APPEARANCE OF WOMEN ON THE STAGE

During the Commonwealth the theatres were closed by the Puritans who considered them immoral.
Before this no women ever acted on the stage—their parts being taken by boys.   With the Restoration the
theatres were opened and became very popular and for the first time women became actresses.

From the picture by S. Harding   *Rischgitz*

CHARLES RECEIVES THE FIRST PINEAPPLE

The first mention of pineapples in England is to be found in the diary of John Evelyn who speaks of tasting one at the table of Charles II. This picture shows the royal gardener, Mr. Rose, presenting to the king the first pineapple grown in England. After this they were grown in private gardens until the extension of cultivation in the West Indies and other places made it unnecessary to grow them in this country.

From the picture by Charles Landseer   *Rischgitz*

TOASTING NELL GWYNN IN A TAVERN

Nell Gwynn is one of the most romantic characters in history. She was born in extreme poverty and spent much of her early life selling oranges in the theatres. Then she became an actress and at once captivated the town by her gaiety, charm and graceful dancing, and even made friends among the nobility.

From the picture by E. M. Ward   *Rischgitz*

CHARLES II AND NELL GWYNN

Nell Gwynn ultimately became the king's favourite. He gave her a house and kept her in fine style. From that time on she was one of his most loyal friends and had considerable influence over him. Through her, old regular soldiers were given a pension, and are known to this day as the Chelsea pensioners. Legend says that the Hospital which now shelters these men was intended as a palace for Nell, but that she begged the king to give it instead to the soldiers who had been wounded during his Restoration.

THE NIGHT WATCH

It was only in comparatively recent years that Sir Robert Peel started the police force as we know it to-day. Before that there were only a few watchmen and bands of armed men to keep what Edward I called the " watch and ward." This picture shows such a band of night watchmen as they were in the time of Charles II. These night watchmen were very necessary as there were no lights in the towns at that time and rogues could prowl at will in the dark, narrow streets. Most people stayed indoors after sundown for fear of attack and robbery.

From the picture by R. Caton Woodville   *By permission of " The Illustrated London News "*

A TREATY WITH A NATIVE PRINCE

English colonies spread rapidly during the whole of the Stuart period.   This picture shows a trading agreement being reached with a native prince on the Gold Coast.   This country was the cause of much hostility between the English and Dutch who both had trading stations there.   All the English ports were destroyed by the Dutch in the war of 1664-65.   In 1672 Charles granted a charter to the Royal African Company to trade there.

From the picture by Frith

CLAUDE DUVAL—THE

The roads of the seventeenth century were infested with robbers who used to hold up the travellers' coaches in lonely parts of the country. One of the most famous places frequented by these lawless bands, was Hounslow Heath, and very few travellers crossed this lonely tract without being stopped and despoiled of all their goods. Some of these highwaymen, as they were called, used to behave with elaborate courtesy, taking their victims' money with a bow. Perhaps the most famous of these was Claude Duval, a Frenchman who had been in the service of the Duke of Richmond. He was renowned as much for his gallantry to ladies as

Rischgitz

GALLANT HIGHWAYMAN

for his robberies. He was hanged at Tyburn and buried in Covent Garden Church. His epitaph reads :
"Here lies Duval ; Reader, if male thou art,
Look to thy purse : if female, to thy heart."
The picture shows the highwayman forcing one of his fair victims to dance a minuet to a tune played by
one of his men whilst the rest of the band rifle the money boxes. It is said he ended such dances by stealing
a kiss from the unfortunate lady. Samuel Butler has written a satirical ode to the "Most Renowned Du Val."

From an old print

Rischgitz

TITUS OATES—THE BOGUS ANTI-PAPIST
Titus Oates, the originator of the bogus Popish Plot, undergoing his yearly punishment in the stocks.

After the picture by Sir G. Harvey　　　　　　　　　　　　　　　　　　　　*Rischgitz*

THE COVENANTERS' COMMUNION

The Covenanters were the English and Scottish Presbyterians who bound themselves by a covenant to defend their own simple faith.　They were persecuted in the time of Charles II because they refused to acknowledge the authority of the bishops.　Rather than submit to authority they carried on their services in the open air.

After the picture by A. Johnstone　　　　　　　　　　　　　　　　　　　　*Rischgitz*

THE COVENANTERS' MARRIAGE

Here we see the simple marriage ceremony of the Covenanters being performed out on the Scottish hills to avoid any interference by their persecutors.　They hated any show of pomp in their religion believing that simplicity was nearest to godliness.　They were a sincere and brave group of people whose religious beliefs and practices have survived all attacks and are still a powerful influence at the present time.

From the picture by Sir George Harvey, R.S.A.   *Spencer Arnold*

BATTLE OF DRUMCLOG

The Covenanters' resistance to the reimposition of bishops upon them gradually developed into open rebellion. Eventually a Royalist force under John Graham of Claverhouse was sent against them and the two forces met at the Battle of Drumclog. The Covenanters had a considerable advantage in position and the Royalist forces had to await the attack. The Covenanters made a sudden charge and their determination and ferocity were responsible for the complete rout of the Royalists. This, however, was the only success they had.

From an old engraving   *Rischgitz*

PENN RECEIVING THE CHARTER OF PENNSYLVANIA

One of the many North American colonies founded during this period was Pennsylvania. It took its name from a certain William Penn, a Quaker. The Quakers were a new sect who refused to take oaths or to fight, but lived hard-working and virtuous lives. King Charles is seen handing over the royal charter for the foundation of the colony.

From the picture by E. M. Ward

Autotype Fine Art Company

DEATH OF CHARLES II

Charles died suddenly in 1685. By his shrewdness and tact he had managed to keep his popularity to the end. He had always been suspected of having sympathies with the Roman Catholics and at his death these suspicions were proved to be correct as he was received into the Roman Church just before he finally passed away.

JAMES II TO WILLIAM AND MARY

WHEN James II came to the throne in 1685 the country was quiet. Parliament being largely Tory granted him an allowance for life. James, though a Roman Catholic, showed that he had no intention of interfering with the Church of England and when he kept Charles's Tory ministers everything seemed to be satisfactory.

MONMOUTH'S REBELLION

Unfortunately the Whigs, having no influence in Parliament, resorted to war. A rebellion was raised in the west country by the Duke of Monmouth who gathered round him an army of almost unarmed country people. A pitched battle was fought at Sedgemoor with the king's troops and Monmouth was hopelessly defeated. He was taken prisoner and quickly executed. Then followed what are known as the " Bloody Assizes." Judge Jeffreys, with most incredible

brutality, sentenced to death or slavery all those who were thought to have been concerned with the rebellion. The whole country was revolted at his savagery.

THE KING AND HIS MINISTERS

James, having crushed this rebellion, now thought himself powerful enough to follow out his own policy. Being a Catholic he was angry that those of his own religion could not hold office in the State and he was determined to repeal the Test Act which prevented them from doing so. James dissolved Parliament when it refused to do so and dismissed his Tory ministers. He now claimed the power to suspend the Test Act, and when the judges, either through bribery or intimidation, came to a decision in his favour he proceeded to do so, giving posts to Catholics in the army, in the legal profession and at Oxford and Cambridge. Moreover, he issued the Declaration of Indulgence suspending the laws against the Catholics and Dissenters. James, however, misjudged the strength of the opposition and when he ordered the Declaration to be read in all the churches there was a storm of protest. Very few of the clergy obeyed and when seven bishops, headed by Sancroft, Archbishop of Canterbury, protested against this order, James had them brought up for trial. At this there was tremendous excitement in the country and almost universal thanksgiving when the bishops were acquitted.

WILLIAM AND MARY

James had been tolerated chiefly because he was an old man and it was thought that his daughter Mary, a Protestant, would succeed him. But when he had a son, who, it was thought, would be brought up a Catholic, the Whigs and Tories joined forces and requested William, Prince of Orange, and his wife Mary to accept the crown.

William was in a difficult position. His own country, Holland, was in danger from the French and though he badly needed the support of England he was frightened to take an army across when Louis was on the warpath. However, he took the risk and James himself made things safe for him by refusing any help from the French.

JAMES FLEES THE COUNTRY

James was now in a hopeless position. His policy of giving commissions in the army to Catholics led to internal strife between the Catholics and Protestants. Churchill, the future Duke of Marlborough, and other leaders deserted, and with the army in confusion he could not risk a battle. After a few days of futile parleying he was allowed to flee from the country

From the picture by S. Pettie   *By permission of The Manchester Corporation*

MONMOUTH PLEADS FOR HIS LIFE

Monmouth was captured after his rebel army had been hopelessly defeated at Sedgemoor, and hoping to save himself, he wrote an abject letter to King James blaming others for what he had done and pleading for an interview. This James granted, but he refused to allow Monmouth's plea for mercy. Monmouth then offered to become a Roman Catholic, but James' priests declared that he was not sincere and he was executed in 1685.

From the picture by E. M. Ward   *Mappin Art Gallery, Sheffield*

BULLYING JUDGE JEFFREYS

The rebels of Monmouth's rebellion were tried by Judge Jeffreys who behaved with barbaric cruelty. In this he was encouraged by the king. Men were condemned to death or to slavery abroad without a proper hearing and the roads in the West Country were lined with gallows. People who had no sympathy with the rebels were horrified at the cruelty of the "Bloody Assizes." By encouraging this persecution James sacrificed what popularity had previously been his. He was later arrested and thrown into the Tower, where he died.

after he had been captured at the first attempt. William and Mary, after some discussion, were proclaimed joint sovereigns.

THE BEGINNINGS OF THE CONSTITUTION

The Stuart kings had antagonised the country by their Catholic sympathies and Parliament by their struggles for independent and personal government. The accession of William and Mary marks the end of this dual conflict : Since that time no English king has either been a Catholic or been able to rule without the consent of Parliament. With the end of the Stuarts comes the beginning of the English constitution as we know it to-day. The Stuarts had tried to prolong the existence of an outworn system of government and had failed.

PARLIAMENT SAFEGUARDS ITSELF

Early in the reign of William and Mary Parliament made its own position safe. In 1689 it passed the Bill of Rights enacting that the crown had no power to suspend laws as James had done and that no Roman Catholic should be allowed to come to the throne. Then followed the Toleration Act by which all Protestants might worship in their own way. This Act marks the beginning of complete religious toleration which exists to-day. In 1701 the Act of Settlement was passed settling that if William and his sister-in-law Anne died without heirs the throne should go to Sofia, Electress of Hanover, the grand-daughter of James I. It is by this law that the present king owes his right to the throne. Another most important action of

From an old Dutch print   *Rischgitz*

SEVEN BISHOPS CONVEYED TO THE TOWER

In 1689 James ordered the Declaration of Indulgence to be read in all the churches suspending the law which prevented Roman Catholics and Dissenters from holding official positions in the Church or State. Very few of the clergy obeyed. When Sancroft, Archbishop of Canterbury, and six other bishops petitioned the king against this order James immediately had them arrested and taken to the Tower to await trial for seditious libel.

Parliament was to vote money to the king for one year only so that it was impossible for him to dispense with Parliament.

Meanwhile the Irish Catholics revolted against the Protestant rule of William, wishing to keep James on the throne. The Protestants made a magnificent defence, particularly at Londonderry where they were besieged for some weeks. James brought a French army over to assist in the revolution but William, seeing how serious the position was, crossed with an English army and defeated the rebels at the Battle of the Boyne. The Irish Catholics were reduced to subjection and the revolution crushed.

THE PRESBYTERIAN CHURCH

The Scots, on the whole, tolerated the reign of William. A few of the extremists rose in revolt but were defeated by John Graham, Viscount Dundee. The rule of the bishops was ended and the Scottish Church made Presbyterian—which it has continued ever since. Some of the Highland clans still preferred the rule of James, they rose in revolt and won the Battle of Killiecrankie but their leader was killed and they were almost exterminated at the massacre of Glencoe. By this terrible act William forfeited his popularity among the Scots, amongst whom were many Jacobites, or supporters of James.

PEACE WITH FRANCE

For nearly twenty years of his life William had been opposed to the French who had been a perpetual source of danger to Holland and the other small Protestant states. Commercial jealousy had previously led to wars between England and Holland but now the two countries combined and were at war with France almost continuously from 1689-1697—resisting Louis XIV's plans to put James back on the English throne. William commanded the combined English, Dutch, Spanish and Austrian forces in the Netherlands and though he had no brilliant success he managed to check the progress of the French. The English were much more successful at sea, winning a magnificent victory at La Hogue. An indecisive peace, known as the Peace of Ryswick, was made in 1697 between William and Louis, ending the first French war.

BEGINNING OF THE NATIONAL DEBT

The French war had been very costly and to meet the expense incurred the national debt was started. Previous to this time, when king or Parliament needed money, it was borrowed and paid back in full out of the revenue. The loans to Parliament were now so great that the total amount could not easily be repaid and the interest on the money was paid instead. This meant that though it would have been difficult for the State to repay everyone who had loaned money yet the private man could get his capital back if he wished, and meanwhile he was drawing an income from it. This system is in operation to-day.

After the war Louis had agreed to acknowledge William to be king of England, but when James died in 1701, Louis went back on his word and recognised his son as king. At this the English were furious, and William declared war, but the situation was changed by his death in 1702.

Much that was good had been done in William's reign. The relation between king and Parliament was settled ; the finance of the country was put on a sound basis and there was more toleration, both religious and civil, than there had been before. But William was not popular ; many people still believed that a king should only be king by hereditary right and wished to see James or his descendant back on the throne. These " Jacobites " continued to be a real danger until 1745. Moreover William had antagonised the Irish Catholics by his persecution and many of the Scots by the massacre of Glencoe.

THE STATESMANSHIP OF WILLIAM

William's great merit lay in his ability as a diplomat. For many years he had held Louis at bay by a clever system of alliances and his control of the allies in the French war was masterly. The policy which he pursued all his life of keeping a check on French ambitions met with success—after his death—by the Treaty of Utrecht.

From the picture by J. R. Herbert Rischgitz

TRIAL OF THE SEVEN BISHOPS

James had issued the Declaration of Indulgence to put the Catholics in responsible positions. The country was strongly Protestant in feeling ; the petition of the bishops was extremely popular and great indignation was felt at their arrest. The very sentinels at the Tower asked the blessing of the men they were guarding, and during the trial the excitement was intense. When they were acquitted there was universal thanksgiving, and that night William and Mary were asked to take the throne, as the young prince was regarded as a Catholic.

From the picture by Northcote   *Rischgitz*

WILLIAM III LANDING AT TORBAY

William accepted the invitation to take the English throne and on November 5 he landed at Torbay. It was a dangerous venture as Holland, his own country, was in danger from the French. However, when like General Monk, he called a free Parliament, the country rallied round him and he was able to secure the crown.

From the picture by E. M. Ward   *By permission of the Tate Gallery*

JAMES II RECEIVING THE NEWS OF WILLIAM'S LANDING

When James received the news that William had landed at Torbay his army was in a state of confusion. The Catholics were quarrelling, and the future Duke of Marlborough, John Churchill, deserted at the critical moment. With his army in confusion he could not give battle and by publicly repudiating any protection from France he lost his only opportunity of keeping the crown. After a few days of futile parleying with William he fled.

JAMES II THROWING THE GREAT SEAL OF ENGLAND INTO THE THAMES NEAR WHITEHALL

James had sent his wife and child out of the country and he himself fled on November 11, 1688. He left at 3 a.m. by coach for Millbank, crossed the river by wherry and landed at Vauxhall. On his way across he threw into the water the Great Seal which was used for stamping the king's assent on all important documents. From Vauxhall James went on to Sheerness where a vessel was awaiting him. He was unable to leave because of a gale, and some sailors rowed out, plundered the ship, robbed James and his friends and took him to an inn in Rochester where he was recognised and forced to return to London. The people were touched and received him joyously. He spent the night at Whitehall but was removed to Rochester by the order of William.

After Dodd   *Rischgitz*

From the picture by A. C. Low   *Copyright : Louis Wolff & Co., Ltd.*

JAMES II ESCAPES

James' first attempt at escape had been a failure and he was now in the power of William. William, however, saw that no good purpose would be served by keeping James in the country and very wisely he allowed him to escape a second time. It is probable that if James had not fled the revolution would not have been " bloodless."

After Northcote   *Rischgitz*

THE FRENCH KING WELCOMES JAMES

On his second escape James went straight to the French court where he was greeted by Louis XIV who, after a time, allowed him a French army to raise a rebellion in Ireland.   This failed and he returned to France. He was offered French help to secure the Polish throne, but he refused knowing that it would debar him from attaining the English crown.   James never gave up the hope of being restored to his throne.

After Northcote   *Rischgitz*

CROWN OFFERED TO WILLIAM AND MARY, 1688

There was much discussion in Parliament as to who should be recognised as sovereign—William or Mary. The Tories who believed in hereditary right wanted either a regency in James's name or Mary to be queen with William as prince consort.   This proved impracticable, and William and Mary were given the crown jointly.

From an old engraving   *Rischgitz*

CORONATION PROCESSION OF WILLIAM AND MARY

William and Mary were finally crowned as joint sovereigns with the executive power in the hands of William. The final settlement by Parliament ensured that William would have to govern constitutionally and that no king of England could be a Roman Catholic. The scene shown here really marks the first stage in the development of the form of monarchy as we have it to-day, and the growth of religious toleration in the people.

After B. West   *Rischgitz*

WILLIAM III AT THE BATTLE OF THE BOYNE

In 1690 James went to Ireland with a French army to help the Irish Catholics who had been in rebellion. William now crossed with an English army, and defeated James at the Battle of the Boyne. James in his younger days in France had shown himself to be a thoroughly brave and competent soldier, but now his courage seemed to have deserted him. After this defeat the Irish Catholics were persecuted even more than they had been by Cromwell.

From a contemporary engraving   *Rischgitz*

FLIGHT OF JAMES II FROM IRELAND

James' failure at the Battle of the Boyne and his flight from Ireland, meant the end of any hopes he might have of regaining the English throne. The result of the Irish Rebellion and the defeat of the French was the persecution of the Irish Catholics and the safety of Protestantism in England. William was wounded during the encounter.

From the fresco by George Harcourt, R.A.   *By permission of the artist and the Gresham Committee*

FOUNDING OF THE BANK OF ENGLAND

This picture shows the founding of the Bank of England in 1694. It owes its origin to a Scot, William Paterson, and the Whig Chancellor of the Exchequer, Charles Montague. The foundation of the Bank of England marked a new departure in finance. Previously, money lent to the government had been paid back out of the revenue. Now the capital was kept (this formed the National Debt) and the interest repaid.

From the picture by R. Caton Woodville　　　　　　　　*By permission of " The Illustrated London News "*

EXPLORATION OF AUSTRALIA

William Dampier was a trader and buccaneer. He made many amazing voyages of discovery in the South Seas, and in 1699 he was sent out by the Admiralty in the *Roebuck* for the purpose of exploring round Australia. This picture shows him talking to the Australian aborigines and taking a great interest in their native weapon, the boomerang, of which little or nothing was known at that time. For a long time Australia, though rich in natural resources, remained undeveloped. It was regarded as a place of punishment rather than a source of revenue.

From the picture by Eyre Crowe   *Rischgitz*

POPE'S INTRODUCTION TO DRYDEN

John Dryden for many years of his life was acknowledged to be the greatest English poet. In 1687 a small boy of twelve was taken to see the great man at his favourite haunt in Wills Coffee House. He was Alexander Pope, Dryden's successor in greatness. Dryden is seen standing in the centre ; Pope is the small boy on the right.

After Maclise   *Rischgitz*

PETER THE GREAT AT DEPTFORD

Peter the Great was Tsar of Russia, 1672-1725. From his youth he had been passionately fond of anything to do with ships, and when, in 1697, the Russian embassy set out to persuade the Western Powers to help hem in a war against Turkey, Peter the Great went with it as a volunteer sailorman. When the embassy came to England Peter spent the greater part of his time at Deptford studying shipbuilding.

QUEEN ANNE

1702-1714

QUEEN ANNE came to the throne in 1702. She was a good-natured lady with little or no political influence. Her favourite at court was the Duchess of Marlborough whose husband, the Duke, proved to be a sound statesman and one of the most brilliant generals this country has ever had. Having great influence both at court and in Parliament he was able to carry on William's policy of aggression against the French and in 1702 started the long war of the Spanish succession.

WAR OF THE SPANISH SUCCESSION

Louis XIV wished to establish his grandson Philip as King of Spain when the old line of kings had died out. England and many of the European powers were frightened that this alliance between France and Spain would prove so powerful that Louis would be able to do as he liked, and to prevent this they supported the claims of the Archduke Charles of Austria.

The war was first fought in the Netherlands where Marlborough had great difficulty in controlling the petty quarrels of his allies, and in obtaining sufficient supplies of food from home. His first great success came in 1704. Up till then the war had been confined to the Netherlands but in that year Louis marched through Bavaria intending to invade Austria. Marlborough quickly moved across Europe and gained a magnificent victory at Blenheim. Returning again to the Netherlands, Marlborough followed up this success with victories at Oudenarde and Malplaquet. Meanwhile Gibraltar was captured.

By 1709 Marlborough and the allies had control of the war. Louis was in a bad way and was prepared to make peace but the Whigs who were in power at home refused to do so unless Louis sent his army to expel Philip from Spain—which was the one thing he was not prepared to do. Consequently the war dragged on for four more years.

The country was tired of this useless war and angry with the Whig Government for prolonging it. The queen no longer favoured the Duchess of Marlborough and the Whig Party with Marlborough himself fell from power. The Tories who succeeded in office brought home the victorious Duke, and after carrying on the war inefficiently for three years made the Treaty of Utrecht.

By this Treaty Philip was to be recognised as king of Spain but the crowns of France and Spain were not to be united in one person; Louis was to recognise the Protestant succession and expel the Pretender; England was to retain Hudson's Bay, Nova Scotia, Newfoundland, St. Christopher, Gibraltar and Minorca; the "Asiento" contract stipulated that England might carry on the slave trade with Spanish South America, sending one ship a year.

The war had achieved its object—to stop the growth of French power and prevent the ensuing Catholic supremacy which would mean a return of the Stuarts to England; England had secured colonies and the basis of trade with the Spanish colonies in South America. She had got what she wanted and Lord Bolingbroke, who negotiated the treaty, showed his wisdom by treating Louis with not undue severity. If the Whigs had remained in office, Marlborough had reached Paris and the French utterly crushed there could have been no real basis for a settlement. To crush a nation means in the long run a tremendous growth of national spirit within that nation and the desire for revenge.

UNION WITH SCOTLAND

Meanwhile an event of great national importance had taken place; in 1707 the union between England and Scotland was finally effected. Though the Scots were Presbyterians they were also largely Jacobite in sympathy, and when they passed the Act of Security stating that Anne's successor should not be king of Scotland the two nations were heading for complete separation and being of very different political persuasions this was dangerous to England. When the Act of Union was put forward it was reluctantly accepted by the Scots because they badly needed free trade with England.

After 1707 the Scots kept their own Presbyterian Church, but the two nations had but one Parliament, they also kept their own system of laws but gained the right to trade with English colonies. Though the union was not popular at first it was of incalculable benefit to both countries. It gave to Scotland the increase in trade she needed and security to England.

GROWTH OF PARTY GOVERNMENT

The system of party government as we know it to-day developed considerably in the reign of Anne. The Whig and Tory Parties had started originally as opponents of James II and his supporters. The two parties continued to exist in opposition to each other but over different questions. The Tory Party was, for the most part, composed of the landed gentry and the Church : the Whigs of the middle-class traders. The Tories tended to be high church in outlook and the Whigs low church—the difference being due to the old quarrel between Anglicans and Puritans. The Tories were vastly superior in numbers but they had not the unity of purpose or the organisation of the Whigs who, being traders, were centralised in the towns while the Tories were spread over the country. The policy of the Whigs was infinitely more tolerant than that of the Tories because, being a minority party, they were not in a position to persecute like the Tories who came into power in 1711.

The first thing the Tories did was to pass an Act that no person could sit in Parliament unless he drew an income of £300 per year from the land, which meant that the Tory influence in Parliament was enormous. Having done this they started to persecute the Dissenters, passing the Occasional Conformity Bill, enacting that anyone who had conformed to the Anglican Church and held an official position as a result should pay a heavy fine if he attended a place of Nonconformist worship. The Schism Act which followed this was even worse ; Dissenters were not allowed to educate their own children but were compelled to hand them over to persons approved by the Anglican Church. The object of the Tories was to get round the Toleration Act and exterminate all those who were not of the Anglican Church. If the Tory Party had not split up at the death of Anne the result might have been another civil war.

But in spite of this persecution the fact that the Whig and Tory parties were more or less evenly balanced led to a growth of free thinking and free speech since the majority of people were protected by one or other of the two parties. The value of an official opposition which is so great to-day is shown at this period for the first time. If one section of the community is free to express its own ideas a compromise may often be reached with other sections ; but if it is suppressed it will probably resort to force like the Whigs in the time of Shaftesbury.

Another development during the beginning of the eighteenth century which was to prove of vital importance to this country was the growth of sea power. The fact that England controlled the sea had been a vital factor in the French wars—and the defeat of the French policy had been an absolute necessity to the safety of this country. Moreover, this supremacy at sea enabled England to develop trade abroad—particularly with India and her colonies—and it was trading which produced England's future greatness.

THE EAST INDIA COMPANY

The East India Company had originally been founded by Elizabeth, when it was given exclusive rights of trading, and any interlopers were liable to forfeit their cargoes. There was great competition with other countries—particularly the Dutch—and it was not until about one hundred years after its foundation that it was able to enjoy its monopoly. After the Restoration, the company profited enormously and attracted many private traders. In 1694, Parliament gave all English subjects the right to trade with India, and two years later a new company was formed with the old company holding a controlling interest. But what is particularly interesting is that the East India Company did not limit its activities to trading but acquired territory and exercised both civil and criminal jurisdiction. It laid the foundation not only of a very profitable trade but of what is now British India.

Throughout the reigns of William and of Anne a great stabilisation of the country took place. The religious difficulties of the Stuarts, though not settled, were nothing like as acute as they had been. There was little friction between the Crown and Parliament ; Scotland was economically united to England at last ; the European situation ceased to be dangerous after the Treaty of Utrecht. But above all a spirit of tolerance was coming over the country which was largely due to the enormous increase in trading and the financial prosperity of the country. The English were becoming " a nation of shopkeepers."

From the picture by H. M. Paget   *Spencer Arnold*

ANNE HEARS THAT SHE IS QUEEN

Bishop Burnet announces the news of her accession to Queen Anne in 1702. Burnet had originally been in favour with Charles II, but for various reasons he fell from grace, and during the reign of James II became a naturalised Dutchman. He was popular with William III as he had persuaded his wife Mary to leave all political power to her husband. He proved an excellent bishop and died in 1715. He is most famous for his *History of my Own Time*. Seated beside the Queen is Sarah, Duchess of Marlborough. She had a tremendous influence over Anne. They addressed each other as "Mrs. Freeman" and "Mrs. Morley."

After l'Evèque   *Rischgitz*

THE DUKE OF MARLBOROUGH AT THE BATTLE OF BLENHEIM

In 1704 the French attacked Austria, one of the allied powers.   Marlborough quickly moved his troops from the Netherlands and met the French at Blenheim.   The battle which followed resulted in one of the most famous of English victories, and the saving of Austria.   Blenheim Palace near Oxford was given to Marlborough to commemorate this victory.   Blenheim Palace is still the magnificent home of the Marlborough family.

From a contemporary print   *Rischgitz*

THE ATTACK ON GIBRALTAR

Gibraltar was first captured by the British in 1704 during the war of the Spanish Succession, and the British flag hoisted in the queen's name by Sir George Rooke.   The attempt at recapture by the Spanish and French was foiled by the magnificent defence of Sir John Leake.   During the following years many attempts were made by negotiations and force of arms to regain it, but Gibraltar has remained British from that day to this.

After E. Blair Leighton   *Spencer Arnold*

THE FALL OF THE MARLBOROUGHS

The Duchess of Marlborough had for a long time been a great favourite of the queen, but when Anne began to tire of the duchess's domineering ways, the duke saw that it was time for his wife to deliver up the gold keys of her office, which she had so often refused to do. Marlborough secured them from her and brought them to the queen, who " received them with far greater pleasure than if they had been the spoils of the army." Such was the end of the Marlboroughs' supremacy at Court where they had been the dominant personalities.

From the picture by Crowe — Kischgitz

DANIEL DEFOE—A LOVER OF LIBERTY

Daniel Defoe, best known for his story of Robinson Crusoe, and his journal of the Plague, was a Dissenter who also wrote religious pamphlets. A satire on the High Churchman's attitude to Nonconformists, led to him being imprisoned and put in the pillory. People took his side and his punishment became something of a triumph.

After H. M. Paget — Spencer Arnold

A SCENE IN A LONDON COFFEE HOUSE

The coffee houses became extremely popular at the beginning of the nineteenth century. It was to them that the members of the fashionable, literary or artistic world would go to gossip, to discuss current affairs or the latest poem that had been written. One of the most famous was Wills, where it is on record that the poet Dryden had a special seat reserved for him. The coffee house occupied much the same place in society then as the club does now

After Huck   *Kischgitz*

THE UNION OF ENGLAND AND SCOTLAND

This picture shows Queen Anne putting her signature to the Act of Union of 1707, which brought England and Scotland under one government. This and the victory over the French were the features of Anne's reign. The union meant greater political security for England, and for Scotland free trade with England and her colonies.

From an old print   *Kischgitz*

PUBLIC REJOICING FOLLOWING PEACE OF UTRECHT

Queen Anne ordered the Peace of Utrecht to be celebrated by a public thanksgiving. Both Houses of Parliament went on a solemn procession to St. Paul's. Here we see the 4,000 " Charity Children " placed upon stands in the Strand, which extended 600 feet in length, to sing hymns in honour of Her Majesty's presence. This peace ended the war of Spanish Succession and gave England Gibraltar, Nova Scotia and Newfoundland.

After H. M. Paget   *Spencer Arnold*

ANNE ON HER DEATHBED APPOINTING SHREWSBURY LORD TREASURER

In 1714, Bolingbroke had been plotting to control the country through a Jacobite Cabinet and had Lord Oxford dismissed as a preliminary step. On June 27, the queen attended a meeting of the Council over the question of Oxford's successor, and on retiring she was struck with a fatal illness. She just had time before she died, however, to appoint the Whig Duke of Shrewsbury and thus thwart Bolingbroke's plan. The evil legacy of the Stuarts was still troubling England and was to continue to do so until 1745.

GEORGE I

1715-1727

At the end of Anne's reign, Bolingbroke and some of the more violent Tories had been plotting, either to restore the Stuarts to the throne, or to put the country under Jacobite control. The sudden death of Anne, however, upset Bolingbroke's plans, and George I was able to come peaceably to the throne. As a result of his intrigues, Bolingbroke had to leave the country, the Tories were unpopular on account of their Jacobite sympathies, and a long period of Whig ascendancy followed. George I was brought to the throne because, being a Protestant, he was more acceptable than the Old Pretender, who was a Catholic. His right of ascendancy lay in the fact that he was descended from James I through Sophia Dorothea, the younger daughter of Elizabeth, daughter of James I. He was a German who knew little of the English language and less of the English system of government. Consequently he was forced to leave matters of state almost entirely to his ministers. This had far-reaching consequences. It meant that Parliament had at last got rid of the domination of the king—one of the causes of upheaval under the Stuarts—and that never again, with the one exception of George III, was an English king ever to attempt to gain personal control of the government of the country.

THE KING'S INFLUENCE WANES

George I was a somewhat gross, stupid man, brought up in the profligacy of a German Court. As he left the government of the country almost entirely in the hands of his Whig ministers, and as the country prospered under these ministers, he could not be called a bad king, though personally he was probably one of the least attractive monarchs who has sat on the English throne. Under him, or more accurately, under the Whigs, England went through a period of prosperity which was one of the greatest in her history : there was a great boom in trade ; colonies were developed and extended, and peace abroad led to greater and greater financial security.

But there were still troubles to be settled.

The union between England and Scotland was still unpopular, and many of the Scots felt that the restoration of the Stuarts might lead to a renewal of their independence ; consequently there was a strong Jacobite element in Scotland. In England, there was a minority of Roman Catholics who were prepared to go to any length to restore the Stuarts, but the vast majority of Tories who had some Jacobite sympathies were law-abiding country squires and had no desire to see another civil war.

THE JACOBITE RISING

Thus, the Jacobite rising of 1715 was serious in Scotland, but it did not spread in England beyond a small Jacobite force which was hopelessly defeated at Preston. In Scotland, the Royalist troops gained an indecisive victory at Sheriffmuir which was enough to put a check on the rebellion. The Old Pretender, son of James II, had not arrived in Scotland early enough and he had little of the personal charm or power of leadership necessary to attract the country to him.

As a result of the 1715 rebellion, the Septennial Act was passed. Before this, Parliament could remain in power for three years without an election (the Triennial Act), but it was felt that an election at this troubled time would be dangerous to the safety of the country, and the period was lengthened to seven years and remained so until 1911.

TROUBLES AT HOME AND ABROAD

There were dangers abroad as well as at home. For some years Spanish power had been on the wane, but now there was a revival which led to ambitions to regain possessions in the Mediterranean—ambitions which conflicted with British interests there. At the same time, Charles II of Sweden, a lifelong enemy of the Hanoverians, and considered to be the future Jacobite leader, was an ally of Spain.

The defeat of the Spanish at Cape Passaro coincided with the death of Charles and the position ceased to be dangerous.

Meanwhile, the country was badly shaken at

home. Stories of fabulous wealth in the South Seas led to the prices of shares in the South Sea Company rising to enormous heights. Bogus companies were started and the gullible public embarked on an orgy of speculation. The inevitable crash came, thousands of people, rich and poor, were ruined, and it was rumoured that the government was involved in the crash. The ensuing panic was an opportunity for the Jacobites to seize power, but the genius of Sir Robert Walpole prevented this, and he restored the country to sanity and to financial prosperity. Walpole was the one man who had foretold what the so-called South Sea Bubble would lead to, and consequently he was trusted to take office when others were discredited. He was a financial genius who had made a personal fortune out of the Bubble by selling his shares when everyone else was buying.

RISE OF WALPOLE

But Walpole was to do much more than bring about a return of financial credit. His whole policy was based on the need for keeping the Jacobites in check. He saw that though the Whig Party was in power, the Tories were numerically much stronger. The Tories were for the most part country gentlemen with Jacobite sympathies who were content enough with the régime of the House of Hanover so long as they were not interfered with. Walpole realised that a foreign war would mean increased taxes for the majority of Tories, and this would make them unsettled and rouse their Jacobite sympathies from being negative to positive. Consequently his policy was based upon peace abroad in order to build up prosperity at home and to keep satisfied even those with Jacobite tendencies. This policy succeeded, and the country under Walpole prospered exceedingly. There were no disruptions, and the land-owning Tories became gradually more and more satisfied with the conditions under the Hanoverians and less and less inclined in any way to break the peace.

PARTY GOVERNMENT : THE CABINET

The development of party government has already been seen—how the Whig and the Tory Parties came into existence over the Exclusion Bill ; how other issues sprang up and the original one gradually disappeared and the two parties remained in existence. The other aspect of the modern constitution which came into being during this period was the Cabinet. Party government was important because it meant freedom of speech for the opposition, but the Cabinet is no less important.

The modern Cabinet is composed of men whose general policy is that of the majority in the House of Commons. Their purpose is to deal quickly with situations as they arise. Quick action cannot be obtained from a large body like the Commons, so the Cabinet is deputed to carry out the executive work, but it is answerable to Parliament for what it does. If one man in the Cabinet disagrees with another he usually resigns ; if there is general disagreement, the whole Cabinet resigns and a general election takes place.

The Cabal of Charles II had been a form of Cabinet but its members were not necessarily united and it was not answerable to Parliament. Walpole was head of the Government—a position known later as Prime Minister—and he had other ministers to help him with the executive work of Parliament. It was necessary for Walpole to adhere closely to his policy of keeping the Jacobites in check, and to do this he excluded all those who were not of the same mind as himself. Walpole's Cabinet is therefore a development of the Cabal along modern lines.

THE CONSTITUTION

The constitution of the country was now very similar to what it is to-day. There was party government—the Whigs in power and the Tories in opposition ; there was the Prime Minister, though he was not yet known by that name ; there was a House of Commons representing the country and the House of Lords representing the peerage and acting as a check on the Commons ; lastly there was the king who had previously contended with Parliament for power but who now, by his nature and nationality, was content to leave matters in the hands of his ministers, thereby approximating to the present position, where the king acts in an advisory capacity, rarely using his power of refusing to put his signature to an Act of Parliament.

The constitution under George I had not been made consciously on any political theory but had come about purely through circumstances. It was an accident of birth and character which made George I leave matters entirely to his ministers and reverse the policy of the Stuart kings ; it was the need for suppressing Jacobitism that made Walpole compose his Cabinet of men

After the picture by A. Allard   *Rischgitz*

THE ARRIVAL OF GEORGE I AT ST. JAMES'S

In spite of the plotting against the House of Hanover by Bolingbroke and the more violent Tories, George I came peaceably to the throne in 1715. He was a gross, immoral man who spoke little English, as a consequence of which he was content to leave the governing of the country to his ministers. The lack of interest of the king in English affairs led to a strengthening of the power of Parliament and especially of the Cabinet.

with the same opinions as himself; the fact that some men wished James II to come to the throne and some did not, which led to the beginning of party government.

LITERATURE AND ARCHITECTURE

In the early Hanoverian period there was a great development in literature. Pope followed in the footsteps of Dryden; the novel became popular with the works of Fielding, Richardson and Smollett; Dr. Johnson was universally admired for his poetry, criticism and philosophy; the essays of Addison and Steele were widely read for their humorous descriptions of life.

Architecture flourished, too; all over England can be seen beautiful examples of the simple style which developed under Queen Anne and the Georges. Houses were larger and more comfortable but they were also of beautiful design—a contrast to the Victorians who built spacious houses, but who ruined them with too much ornament and decoration. In both literature and architecture the Georgian period is famous for its common sense, which made for simplicity as opposed to the imaginative and complex methods of a later period.

Prosperity at this time meant prosperity for the aristocracy and landed gentlemen who were free from taxes; and for the trading classes who had peace to trade abroad. It did not mean prosperity for the poor who were hardly taken into account at all. In England, to-day, every section of the community is able to make its grievances heard, but in the eighteenth century the only people represented in Parliament were the Whigs and Tories, who were all men of substance. The poor had no say at all in the government of the country.

THE JACOBITE RISING OF 1715

This illustration reproduced in miniature shows the whole progress of the Jacobite rising in 1715. One of the reasons why the rising failed was the lack of any spirited leadership by the Old Pretender.

After the picture by E. M. Osborn   *Rischgitz*

THE EARL WHO ESCAPED DRESSED AS A WOMAN
The Earl of Nithsdale was one of the Jacobite leaders in the rising of 1715. He was taken prisoner at Preston and from thence conveyed to London. His wife pleaded before the king for his pardon, but it was refused. Through his wife's devotion and skill he was eventually able to escape from the Tower dressed as a woman. The Earl and his wife lived the rest of their lives at the Pretender's Court at Rome.

From the picture by E. M. Ward Mansell

THE SOUTH SEA BUBBLE

The South Sea Bubble was a fever for speculating in bogus companies pretending to trade in the South Seas. The bubble burst in 1720 and thousands of people were ruined. Even the government was involved. Here we see a street market, before the crash, with the brokers buying and selling to people of all classes.

From the picture by F. Hayman, R.A. National Portrait Gallery

THE FIRST PRIME MINISTER VISITS A PAINTER

Sir Robert Walpole, Earl of Oxford, was the younger son of a country squire. He inherited his father's estate and became a prominent member of the Whig Party. He restored national confidence after the South Sea Bubble, and for twenty years was the chief statesman in the country, being the first Prime Minister.

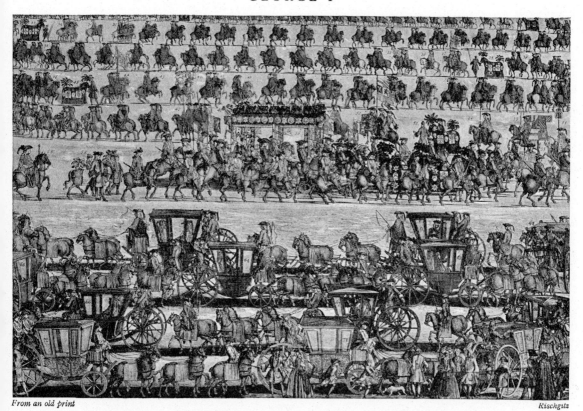

From an old print   *Rischgitz*

FUNERAL PROCESSION OF THE DUKE OF MARLBOROUGH

The Duke of Marlborough, through the influence of his wife, had been a great favourite of Queen Anne. In the queen's later years the Marlboroughs fell from favour and left the country, but at her death Marlborough returned to take up his old position in the army, though he did not again enter public life. He died in 1722.

THE SPANISH BESIEGE GIBRALTAR

In 1727 the Spanish made an attempt to regain Gibraltar which they had lost in 1704. The Spanish commander Count de las Torres, boasted that he would drive the heretics into the sea in six weeks. His bombardment lasted for four months, and even then was unsuccessful as English men-of-war in the harbour were able to obtain supplies of food from the African coast. Gibraltar has remained a stronghold of Britain ever since.

From an old print   *Rischgitz*

Providing for and employing all the Poor in Gr. Britain

From an old print   *Rischgitz*

A WORKHOUSE SCENE IN 1720

The picture shows an illustrated playing card of the eighteenth century depicting a scene in the workhouse which was provided by the parochial authority for the relief of orphans, the poor, the aged and infirm.

From the picture by Frith   *Wolverhampton Museum*

THE REJECTED POET

Alexander Pope was the greatest poet of his time.   He was a small man, slightly deformed, which may account for his embittered nature.   Lady Mary Montague was a prominent figure at Court and for a time a friend of Pope's.   A quarrel took place, the reason for which is not certain, but there is a story in existence that when Pope made a declaration of love, Lady Montague slighted him by bursting into laughter. Pope made many enemies for himself by his attacks on contemporary writers in his satiric poem, the *Dunciad*.

GEORGE II
1727-1760

ON June 14, 1727, a horseman arrived at Richmond Lodge and demanded to see the master of the house. On being refused permission he marched straight into his room where he was sleeping. " I am Sir Robert Walpole," said the messenger, " and I have the honour to announce to your Majesty that your Royal Father, King George I, died at Osnaburg on Saturday last." " Dat is one big lie " roared his sacred majesty King George II. But Sir Robert Walpole stated the truth, and from that day until three and thirty years later, George II ruled over England.

George II was in many respects not unlike his father. His English was little better ; his chief interest lay in Hanover, not in England ; his morals were what was expected from a German Court. He was extremely brave : he fought at Oudenarde and Dettingen with courage equal to any of his soldiers, but he was a man of small intellect, and during his life he owed much to his wife, Caroline of Ansbach.

THE END OF WALPOLE'S PEACE POLICY

George had quarrelled with his father who excluded him from St. James and all court ceremonies. He had moved to Leicester House and there he did all he could to oppose his father's ministers. Consequently, it seemed probable, that on his accession he would dismiss Walpole and the Whig ministers to whom he had been opposed. Queen Caroline, however, used her influence, and Walpole continued in office. Walpole continued in his policy of peace abroad and prosperity at home by keeping the House of Commons under his control. This was done by excluding all those who were not of the same opinion as himself, and by the judicious use of bribes. Bribery was a common practice at that time. Walpole must not be condemned for his belief that the " end justified the means " because that was the normal procedure of the time, and without it the country may not have enjoyed the peace and prosperity which Walpole's administration brought.

Walpole's peace policy continued until 1739, but before that time the merchant classes had been clamouring for a war with Spain to increase their trading rights in South America. These rights had been claimed since the time of Drake, but had been limited by the Asiento Treaty, which allowed only one ship a year to trade there. An incident arose in 1739 when an English sea captain named Jenkins was supposed to have had his ears torn off by the Spaniards. This aroused such a popular frenzy that Walpole gave way and the country started on the War of Jenkins' Ear. A long period of peace usually means inefficiency in war when it does come. This is what happened in 1739 : the war was carried on so badly that Walpole was blamed for incompetence and at last fell from power in 1742.

Before this date, the War of Jenkins' Ear had led to the War of the Austrian Succession. Charles II of Austria had died without a son, and he wanted his daughter, Maria Theresa, to succeed him. Spain, France and Prussia thought that this would be a good opportunity for attacking Austria, and England joined in to support Maria Theresa. In 1743, George II led his troops to victory at Dettingen—he was the last English king to fight personally in a war—but two years later his son, the Duke of Cumberland, was defeated at Fontenoy and peace was made in 1748.

THE SECOND JACOBITE RISING

Meanwhile, there was trouble at home. The Jacobites took the opportunity of the war abroad, as Walpole had foreseen, to rise in rebellion in 1745. Charles Edward Stuart, the young Pretender, a dashing and popular young man, landed in Scotland, where the Highlanders rallied round him. He took up his quarters in Edinburgh and marched to Prestonpans. The Royalist troops were all abroad and the hastily gathered force which was sent against him proved no match for the warlike Highlanders, and was defeated. After this victory, Charles invaded England, marching as far south as Derbyshire, but as he gained few new recruits

From the picture by Hogarth and Sir James Thornhill   *Rischgitz*

THE HOUSE OF COMMONS IN THE EIGHTEENTH CENTURY

A scene in the House of Commons during Sir Robert Walpole's administration, which lasted from 1721-1742. The three figures in the foreground are, from left to right, Sir Robert Walpole himself, the Rt. Hon. Arthur Onslow, Speaker in the House, and Sidney Godolphin who had been a minister since the time of Marlborough. In the dress of this period the men cropped their hair and wore large powdered wigs like the modern barrister. Walpole's sound policy during his twenty-one years in office brought great prosperity to the country.

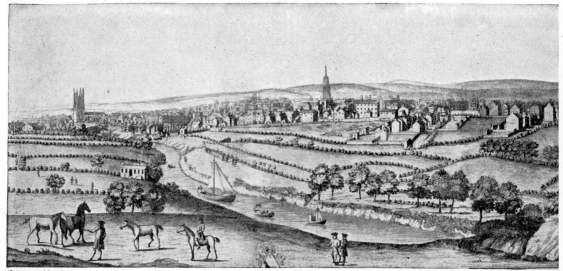

From an old print   *Rischgitz*

MANCHESTER AND SALFORD AS THEY WERE IN 1730

Before the invention of machinery the north was a sparsely populated region given over to agriculture. Even in those days, however, Manchester was a large town, having a population of about 30,000 people. It is interesting to note that in spite of its size, it did not send a representative to Parliament until 1832.

he decided to return to Scotland. The weary army managed to stave off the British attack at Falkirk, but the Prince of Wales, the Duke of Cumberland, with an army of regulars, defeated the rebels at Culloden, the last battle to be fought on English soil. Cumberland's behaviour at this battle was so brutal that he has since been known as " the Butcher." The rising was now crushed, the Young Pretender fled to the Continent and Jacobitism was finished for ever. As a result of the 1745 rebellion, the Scottish clans were disbanded, though a few of the fiercer Highlanders formed new regiments, some of which exist to this day. The disbanding of the clans was really an advantage to Scotland. It was impossible to have a peaceful country half of which was run by separate leaders with strong fighting organisations under them. The whole of Scotland came under one law, and peace and order was the result.

WALPOLE'S SUCCESSORS

After the fall of Walpole, the country was governed by Henry Pelham and his brother, the Duke of Newcastle. Nothing very much was done at this period; there was an interval between the leadership of Walpole and the future leadership of Pitt. Pitt had been in opposition to Walpole as one of the discontented Whigs known as " the Patriots." His oratory against

Walpole was one of the causes of that minister's downfall, but he was not at first given even a subordinate position under the new ministry of the Pelhams, owing to the antagonism of the king, whom Pitt had offended by his slighting remarks about Hanover. However, he was eventually given the post of Paymaster-General, and he showed himself so honest in this capacity, that he gained the favour both of the king and the country. He continued to make his influence felt in Parliament and to gain the esteem of the country until 1757 when he formed a joint ministry with Newcastle.

PITT AND THE SEVEN YEARS WAR

The year before Pitt took office as head of the government, the Seven Years War had broken out. It had its origin in colonial conflicts between England and France. The French were attempting to join their two colonies, Canada and Louisiana, by a chain of forts which would have meant the shutting up of the English colonies between the Allegheny Mountains and the sea. There was a similar territorial conflict in India, and in 1756 the Nabob of Bengal, an ally of the French, captured the British settlement of Calcutta. War between England and France was now inevitable. The war spread throughout Europe; England and Prussia were ranged against Austria, Russia and France.

Under Pitt the war was carried on brilliantly.

He subsidised Frederick the Great of Prussia to the extent of £700,000, so that he, with the help of British troops, was able to carry on the war on the Continent. Without his help, and without the subsidy which made it possible, England would have had the impossible task of fighting against a united Europe. In India, Clive won the Battle of Plassey, defeating the huge army of the Nabob with a small force, and conquering the province of Bengal. In America, General Wolfe captured Quebec after his famous exploit of scaling the heights of Abraham. In spite of early disasters the war was going well for the British.

JOHN WESLEY

At home there had been a great religious revival, due to the enthusiasm and brilliance of John Wesley. The period of peaceful prosperity under Walpole had led to a deadening of men's religious feelings and Wesley, to counteract this, had started groups of people all over the country who made piety and charity the chief interests of their lives. Because of the orderliness of their lives, these groups were known as Methodists. The movement grew. Wesley and the great preacher Whitefield started religious meetings up and down the country. The Established Church disliked these revivalist meetings, and Wesley, who was a Church of England clergyman, had to give up his original idea of keeping his movement within the Church. Nevertheless, Methodism and Wesleyanism grew steadily and became a great influence in nineteenth-century England.

The two great events of George II's reign, apart from the work of Wesley, were the fall of Walpole and the rise of Pitt. These two men stood for directly opposed policies. Walpole, as we have seen, kept England out of war and built up a magnificent trade at home. Pitt, on the other hand, had an imperialistic policy and was a brilliant and popular war minister.

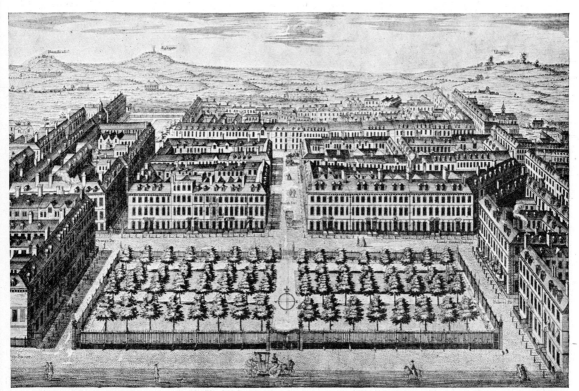

From the picture by Sutton Nicholls　　　　　　　　　　　　　　　　　　　　　　*Rischgitz*

LONDON IN THE EARLY EIGHTEENTH CENTURY

Red Lion Square, in Holborn, is to-day in the heart of London. This picture shows the same square as it was about 1730. At that time Holborn was on the edge of the country and Highgate and Hampstead were merely villages. To-day Greater London extends a considerable distance beyond these places which are now large, busy suburbs. Though small compared with to-day, London was then by far the largest town in the country.

From an old print   *Rischgitz*

A CRICKET MATCH IN 1743

There is mention of cricket being played as far back as the thirteenth century. In the time of Edward IV, the game was illegal and anyone playing it was liable to two years' imprisonment and a fine of ten pounds. It became popular in the eighteenth century, and in 1748 it was declared to be legal and a very manly game.

From the picture by Hogarth   *Rischgitz*

WATCHING A FIGHT IN A COCKPIT

Cockfighting has been known since ancient times. For centuries it was very popular in England and Henry VIII had his own cockpit at Whitehall. It has died out now because laws were passed against it on account of its cruelty. There were several varieties: most frequently two birds were matched against each other, but sometimes there was a " battle-royal " when a number of birds fought until only one, the winner, remained.

From the picture by Francis Wheatley, R.A.

Mansell

MY LADY GOES SHOPPING

The streets of London used to be very picturesque, quite different from those of to-day. Beggars, aristocrats, tradesmen and hawkers jostled together in the narrow, dirty streets, and thieves and rogues were common. Pedlars of goods took the place of shops, and here are two beautifully-dressed ladies purchasing sweet oranges.

From the picture by Francis Wheatley, R.A.

CHAIRS TO MEND !

England in the eighteenth century was the home of the individual craftsman who was responsible to no master and who, therefore, took a personal pride in his work. The coming of machinery had not yet put an end to individual work by the creation of mills and factories turning out mass-produced goods. Men and women would go through the streets crying out their wares just as the man to-day cries out coal! or milk! and many of these cries of London have become famous. This picture shows a chair-mender at work in the street. The private manufacture of goods in the home was known as the "domestic system."

344

From the picture by Francis Wheatley, R.A. Mansell

HOT GINGERBREAD FOR SALE !

Everyone to-day has seen men selling roasted chestnuts in the street. In the eighteenth century there were many men of the same type with all sorts of goods for sale. Here is a man with his barrow, going round selling his gingerbread to the maidens and children. London life was very different in those days because it was more leisurely. The wealthy people used to assemble in the coffee-houses, and discuss the news of the day.

From the picture by Robert Hillingford   *Spencer Arnold*

GEORGE II AT THE BATTLE OF DETTINGEN

During the war of the Austrian Succession, 1740-1748, when the English helped Maria Theresa of Austria against the Spanish and French, George II led the British army himself and won a victory at Dettingen in Germany. This was the last battle in which an English king fought in person and he did so with conspicuous bravery.

From the picture by J. Duncan   *Mansell*

THE SECOND JACOBITE REBELLION

While France and England were at war Bonnie Prince Charlie, son of James II who had been forced to give up the crown of England in 1688, made an attempt to win back the throne for himself. Prince Charlie raised his standard in Scotland, and met at first with considerable success, defeating the soldiers of George II at the Battle of Prestonpans. The picture shows his triumphant entry into Edinburgh after the victory.

From the picture by J. Duncan
Mansell

"BONNIE PRINCE CHARLIE" AND FLORA MACDONALD

The Prince then marched south, across the border. But the English did not support him and he returned to Scotland, and was defeated by "Butcher" Cumberland at the Battle of Culloden. He fled to the Hebrides where he was helped to escape by Flora MacDonald, chief of one of the Scottish clans.

From the picture by John Pettie, R.A.
Mansell

HIGHLAND SUPPORTERS OF THE PRINCE

The Young Pretender, as the Prince was known, got little help in his daring enterprise except from the fierce and warlike Highlanders. At first these were more than a match for the Royalist troops, terrifying them with their wild Gaelic cries, but after a time the regular soldiers found how to fight against them. The Government broke up the clan system as a result of the rebellion, but a few have remained to do magnificent service.

THE ART OF HAT-MAKING

Hats were originally made by felting, a process which St. Clement—now the patron saint of hat-making—is supposed to have originated. This picture shows the primitive methods used for making hats in the eighteenth century. It was not until 1888 that efficient hat-making machinery was imported from the United States.

BIRMINGHAM IN THE EIGHTEENTH CENTURY

Birmingham is mentioned in the Domesday Book as being an area of four miles with half a mile of woods, worth £203. It was strongly Parliamentarian in the Civil War, and was plundered and burned by Prince Rupert who levied a fine of £30,000 because it helped the Parliamentary cause. Later it was a hot-bed of dissenters who were frequently rioting. It first became an important manufacturing town at the end of the seventeenth century.

THE FATE OF A DANDY

Social life in the nineteenth century was more colourful than it is to-day. This scene in Temple Bar shows what was liable to happen to a man who gave himself airs. The crowd is being revenged on a dandy's elegance, and perhaps his insults, by hanging him up in a butcher's shop and seems highly amused at his position.

THE ENGLISH "GRETNA GREEN"

In the seventeenth and eighteenth centuries runaway marriages were solemnised in the Fleet Chapel inside the Fleet Prison. When marriages without banns were prohibited, any place near the prison was used for the celebration of such marriages. These unlicensed marriages were declared illegal by Act of Parliament in 1753. A young sailor and his sweetheart is seen alighting from a coach and a parson will solemnise the marriage.

After Maurer *Rischgitz*

THE HORSE GUARDS PARADE IN THE EIGHTEENTH CENTURY

The king arrives at the Horse Guards Parade, in St. James's Park, in a coach drawn by eight horses, accompanied by a guard of soldiers. A group of fine ladies and gentlemen are watching the procession, which forms an interesting comparison with to-day. The dress of the fashionable people at this time was extremely elegant.

From the picture by Hogarth *Rischgitz*

THE BUSTLE OF A COUNTRY INN YARD

Old inns were often built round a yard which was used for the arrival and departure of coaches, which this lively sketch by Hogarth portrays. English inns in the eighteenth century were famous for their hospitality to travellers weary from a long journey by coach. Inn yards have survived in many cases to the present day.

From an old print   Rischgitz
BY THE KING'S COMMAND
A Jubilee ball was held at Ranelagh on April 28, 1749. Ranelagh was built as a mansion with fine gardens by the earl of that name. In 1742 it was made into a proprietary place of entertainment and became very fashionable. The Chelsea Hospital at the present day occupies the original site and gardens.

From the picture by Bowles   Rischgitz
THE ARISTOCRACY AMUSE THEMSELVES
When Ranelagh became fashionable a building named the Rotunda was erected for holding balls and concerts. At the close of the eighteenth century Ranelagh ceased to be popular, and in 1803 the land was bought by the Chelsea Hospital. The old Ranelagh has disappeared, but there is a modern club of that name. Vauxhall Gardens and Ranelagh are mentioned as places of amusement in nineteenth century literature.

From the picture by Hogarth   *Mansell*

CANVASSING FOR VOTES

In the eighteenth century, when manners were rougher than to-day, canvassing was no easy task. Here is a typical scene outside an inn. The canvassers are at work, and in the distance a riot is in progress round the excise office. Excise was the great bone of contention in the time of Walpole, who nearly lost office over it.

From the picture by Hogarth   *Mansell*

RECORDING THEIR VOTES

In the eighteenth century only people who owned land to the value of forty shillings or more were allowed to vote, and villages which existed in name only sent one or more members to Parliament. An election was frequently a bloodthirsty affair. The hustings, or temporary erections where votes were recorded, were surrounded by people of all sorts who became more and more excited and frequently came to blows.

From the picture by Hogarth   *Rischgitz*

CHAIRING THE SUCCESSFUL CANDIDATE

Bribery and corruption were rampant in the eighteenth century, and no person could hope to be elected to the House of Commons unless he did his share. Here is a typical election scene; men drinking at the candidate's expense, free fighting and general frivolity hardly in keeping with such a serious occasion.

After the picture by Hogarth   *Rischgitz*

CELEBRATING THE ELECTION OF A MEMBER

When a member had been elected, fresh jollifications took place, still at the expense of the successful candidate. To-day, the election expenses of candidates are strictly regulated by law, and any candidate exceeding the amount allowed may forfeit his seat. But in those days, only the wealthy could become Members of Parliament. In fact politics had almost degenerated into contests for personal power and the gaining of generous pensions.

A CUSTOMS WHARF IN THE EIGHTEENTH CENTURY

This picture shows a busy scene at the wharf. The customs officers in their three-cornered hats, skirted coats, knee breeches and silk stockings are checking the goods unloaded from the ships and settling the customs due. At this time the customs were being defrauded of immense sums of money by the growth of smuggling. Walpole introduced an Excise Bill to levy the full tax on wine and tobacco from the warehouse. This Bill met with tremendous opposition and rather than risk the loss of office Walpole dropped the Bill.

From the painting by W. Hatherell   Spencer Arnold

THE GREAT PREACHER OF THE EIGHTEENTH CENTURY

John Wesley was the founder of the Methodist Church, which to-day numbers over 30,000,000 members in all parts of the world. With his brother Samuel, he travelled all over England for many years, preaching out of doors when clergymen refused to allow him to preach in their churches. Here we see a spell-bound congregation listening to him preaching from a market cross. Thus he led a great religious revival.

From the drawing by Paul Hardy

By permission of "Pictorial Education"

FIRST STEPS TO THE ELECTRICAL AGE

Benjamin Franklin, American diplomat, statesman and scientist, was the first man to prove that electricity and lightning were the same thing. He sent up a kite which had a piece of metal wire to catch the lightning and in his hand a piece of silk ribbon and a key to act as a circuit breaker. He found that the electric current passed down the twine which controlled the kite. This was the first lightning conductor. His brave experiment has given to the world the control of a force of incalculable power and value.

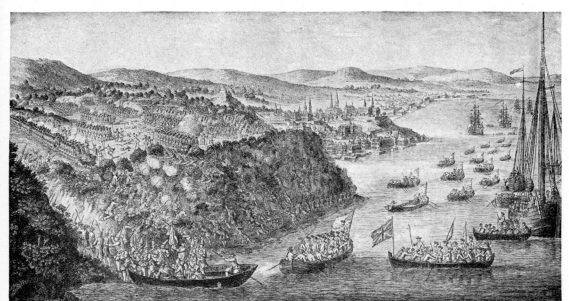

From an old print   *Spencer Arnold*

WOLFE CAPTURES QUEBEC

In 1759, when the Seven Years War was in progress, Pitt sent out a young general named Wolfe to capture Quebec, the capital of Canada, which was then French. His only possible method of attack was to take his troops up the River St. Lawrence and scale a dangerous narrow path up the Heights of Abraham.

From the picture by Benjamin Watt, P.R.A.   *By permission of the National Gallery of Canada*

DEATH OF WOLFE

Wolfe successfully brought his troops up the Heights of Abraham to the plain at the top where the French position was situated. He was twice wounded and was dying from a third bullet when someone near him exclaimed: "They run, see how they run!" "Who run?" demanded Wolfe. "The enemy," was the reply. The dying general gave a last order and then said "Now God be praised, I will die in peace." Thus Canada became a part of the British Empire. The French general also lost his life in this battle.

GEORGE III
1760—1820

GEORGE III was the grandson of George II. He was the first of the Hanoverian kings who had been brought up in England and could speak English fluently and was proud of being British. He was in some respects unlike his predecessors ; his domestic life was not tainted with the immorality of the German court, and he had a great desire to regain the personal power which George I and George II had allowed to slip from them. This love of power, as we shall see, was to result in very serious consequences.

George hated the Whigs, who were in office when he came to the throne, because it had been they who had restricted the authority of the crown during the previous reigns. Fortunately for the new king, the Whigs were not popular in the country, and therefore his dismissal of Pitt and Newcastle did not occasion a public outcry.

He particularly hated Pitt who, having won the Seven Years War, was something of a public hero. Pitt was, in fact, the only man capable of ruling the country—which was the very reason why George got rid of him ; he wanted to rule himself, unfettered by a powerful Prime Minister.

George now tried several ministries, but each one failed, and in desperation he was forced to recall Pitt, now the Earl of Chatham. The new Earl soon broke down through ill health and George put Lord North in office. North was just the sort of man he wanted, an easy-going, second-rate statesman who would not interfere with his plans. The position of the king as a personal monarch would now appear to be strong. He had broken his enemies, the Whigs, and got rid of Chatham whom he hated.

TROUBLE IN AMERICA

Meanwhile, however, trouble had arisen with the American Colonies. George considered, with good reason, that the colonists ought to help to pay some of the cost of the Seven Years War. Unfortunately, instead of putting the matter to the Americans in a diplomatic way, they were simply taxed without having any say in the matter. The tax in question was the stamp tax on legal documents, against which the colonists immediately raised a great outcry, asserting that they would not be taxed without being represented in the English Parliament. So great was the opposition that the stamp tax was repealed— only to be substituted a short time later by a tax on tea and certain other imported articles. Chatham, although seriously ill, attempted to persuade Parliament that the colonists had a good case, but his advice was not heeded. The first shipload of tea to arrive in America was flung overboard before it could be landed, and from that moment the relations between the American colonists and the Mother Country became steadily worse.

CHATHAM TRIES TO HELP

Both sides were behaving foolishly. The Americans ought to have paid some taxation, but they hated George and his ministers and a growing section was crying out for independence from England The English, for their part, were foolish arbitrarily to levy taxes without some form of consent from the Americans. The only man who took a sensible attitude was Chatham, and but for his illness and waning influence, the American colonies might have remained a part of the British Commonwealth of nations.

WAR BEGINS

In 1775, the Americans formed a Congress drawn from all thirteen states, raised an army, fought the English troops at Bunker Hill and declared their independence. The dying Chatham, in his last speech, urged Parliament to seek a compromise before it was too late to repair the damage which had already been done. He did not object to American freedom, but he had the vision of a great united British people—and if his vision had become a reality, as it might have done if he had been supported, the whole course of world history would have been changed.

In 1778 the Americans defeated General Burgoyne at Saratoga and forced him to surrender. France, Spain and Holland, seeing England's position weakened, joined in the war,

From the picture by Sir Joshua Reynolds   *Rischgitz*

GEORGE III—THE FIRST ENGLISH-BORN HANOVERIAN

George III was the first of the Hanoverians who was born and brought up in England. This fact and the domestic purity of his life—a contrast to his father's—made him well received at first. He was a very determined man who loved power and hated the Whigs who had taken it from him. He dismissed Newcastle and Pitt and chose as a minister Lord North, who let him do as he pleased. He reigned from 1760–1820. He married Charlotte of Mecklenburg-Strelitz in the second year of his reign who proved an excellent consort.

From an old print
Rischgitz

GEORGE III REVIEWING THE VOLUNTEERS

There was a vital need for an efficient army during the reign of George III. From 1775 to 1815 England was in danger of losing her Empire. First there was the American War of Independence, then war against France and Spain and later in the reign the struggle against the redoubtable Napoleon.

but thanks to the defence of Gibraltar by Eliott, the victory of Admiral Rodney in the West Indies and the work of Warren Hastings in India, these countries were kept at bay. But the Americans forced another English army to surrender at York Town and eventually peace was made in 1783, England recognising the independence of the United States of America.

At home, George was having trouble in forming a ministry, and after a period of coalition government under Charles James Fox, he put Chatham's son, William Pitt the Younger, in office, and in 1783 this appointment was ratified by the country at a general election. The younger Pitt continued in office until 1801, and, like Walpole, he brought about a period of stability and reconstruction. Under him the position of the Cabinet and the Prime Minister was better defined ; members of the Cabinet were no longer to be the puppets of the king. He effected a treaty with France which improved trade ; he brought about reform in the government of India and endeavoured to do the same at home. Pitt was popular with both the king and the country and in his term of office brought about financial stability and general goodwill.

THE FRENCH REVOLUTION

In 1789 there occurred an event which was to prove of world-wide importance. Many Frenchmen who had taken part in the war of American Independence had returned to France infused with the spirit of liberty which had inspired the American colonists. They saw their land as a new playground for the rich, while the poor were

exploited by both Church and State. So strong had the privileged classes become that they were almost entirely exempt from taxes, the middle-class traders and the poor having to bear the full burden. Parliament, such as it was, had not met for years, justice was the prerogative of the rich, and the king, Louis XVI, although well meaning, was much too weak to play the part of a despot successfully. To add to the discontent which already existed, the crops failed, and this proved fruitful ground for revolt. The king, in desperation, called Parliament together and attempted to right some of the wrongs, especially those of the middle classes. But he was not strong enough to resist the opposition of the aristocrats, who were not willing to lose any of their privileges.

THE DEATH OF LOUIS XVI

The middle classes led the first revolt, and there is no doubt that it was intended as a purely constitutional movement, and if their demands had been met, especially for representation in parliament, the terrible events which followed might have been avoided. The king did his best, but after repeated failures to keep his promises it was realised that more drastic steps were needed before the strength of the privileged classes could be broken. The king and his family were taken prisoners as a precautionary measure while reforms were being forced through the newly established Parliament. Foolishly, however, he attempted to escape, and when it was discovered that the court party had been intriguing with foreign powers to invade France and re-establish the old régime, the extremists decided upon the death of the Royal Family and many of the aristocrats.

THE RISE OF NAPOLEON

" Liberty, Equality and Fraternity " became the battle-cry of the revolutionists, and flushed with the success of their own movement, they saw visions of freeing the peoples of other countries from the shackles of the privileged classes. Thus an internal revolution became a fervid crusade, and was met by the invasion of France by Prussia and Austria. At this juncture, Napoleon Bonaparte rose to prominence in time to save the revolutionaries from inevitable defeat, for although they were doubtless splendid revolutionaries they were inexperienced in the art of warfare. It now became obvious that Napoleon was to prove a real danger in Europe, and Great Britain decided to join the Allies.

Until Nelson defeated the French Fleet at the Battle of Trafalgar in 1805, England was constantly in danger of invasion. But inland, Napoleon progressed from one success to another, and in 1808 was planning to place his brother on the Spanish throne. The Spanish resisted however, and the British sent a force to Spain to assist them. Arthur Wellesley, who was later created Duke of Wellington, was in charge of this campaign, called the Peninsular War, and carried it through to a brilliant conclusion.

THE FALL OF NAPOLEON

In 1812, Napoleon's invasion of Russia failed and he was menaced on one side by the Austrians, Prussians and Russians and by the English and Spanish on the other. He capitulated in 1814 and was banished to Elba. The following year he escaped, returned to France where his army rallied round him once again, and fought the

From the picture by Rossetti   *Mansell*

DR. JOHNSON IN THE MITRE TAVERN

Dr. Johnson started life as a poor man in Lichfield, but he soon built up a great reputation as a poet, scholar, critic, and talker. He was friendly with many great men and on one occasion was granted an audience by the king. Much of what he said and did was recorded by his friend and biographer, Boswell.

Allies, England and Prussia, at Waterloo. After one of the most famous battles in history he was defeated by the Duke of Wellington and the Prussians and banished to St. Helena. Europe and England were at last free from the Napoleonic scourge.

During this period England had been menaced, not only by the war with France and the danger of invasion, but by the spread of French revolutionary ideas.

Machinery was developing rapidly, and instead of articles being made by the individual craftsman in his home they were now manufactured in factories. The sudden development of large, ugly towns resulted in shocking conditions of living, poor pay and overwork. The French revolutionary slogan of " Liberty, Equality and Fraternity " had a great effect on the unfortunate industrial workers and they felt that they would gain much by following the example of the French and revolting against the yoke of their oppressors.

The parliamentary class, however, was horrified at the atrocities of the French Revolution—though at first they had been in sympathy with it—and, moreover, the workers' conditions, though they were terrible if judged by modern standards, were not nearly as bad as those of the French. Consequently, the revolutionary ideas gained no firm foothold.

George III died in 1820. For some years before his death he had been mad, and his son George, Prince of Wales, acted as his regent. During the reign of George III the country survived terrible dangers and saw a complete revolution of social life.

" THE INDUSTRIAL REVOLUTION "

The supremacy of the younger Pitt brought an end to the possibility of a crown despotism which George had at one time made seem possible ; the Cabinet and Prime Minister were now firmly established in the constitution ; the separation of America and England changed the history of the world ; England prevented the European domination of Napoleon and British India continued to develop. But perhaps most important of all was the change from the individual craftsman to the mass production of material— the industrial revolution which changed the country from agriculture to manufacture on a large scale. The conditions which resulted from this social revolution were terrible, but it was the very evil of these conditions which, in the

end, brought about the reform which made England a real democracy and a free country. The evils of the industrial system opened men's minds to the conditions of the poor which had never before been taken seriously into account ; and the benefits of better transport, cheaper living, a breaking down of social class and a vastly increased revenue to the country are incalculable.

MAIN EVENTS OF GEORGE'S REIGN

During the reign of the obstinate, foolish but determined king, George III, events of such importance took place that their results, not only in Europe, but throughout the whole known world, cannot possibly be full appraised.

First there was the French Revolution, shattering the old and accepted régime; spreading its visionary idea of " Liberty, Equality, and Fraternity " throughout Europe; and producing the figure of Napoleon Bonaparte—a modern Cæsar as he liked to think himself—a Cæsar, indeed, who might have ruled the world had it not been for Nelson and the power of the British Navy.

Then came the American revolt from England when the colonists, who had become a great nation, threw off the dominance of the country of their origin and became the United States of America. Who can imagine the course of world history if this had not happened; if Pitt had had his way and this vast, wonderful country had remained within the confederation of British nations?

It is possible to imagine that, if Napoleon had succeeded in defeating England, he would have been the virtual ruler of the world; that the British Empire might have been broken up; and that England would have been to-day only a second-rate power. On the other hand, it is also possible to imagine a British Empire including the U.S.A., a united power which no other nation in the world could have resisted.

History is crowded with things which " might have been," but perhaps never before have the possibilities been so enormous and never before so much depended on the actions of statesmen and generals. Thus we have the Battle of Trafalgar, the Battle of Waterloo, the defeat of the British in America, all changing the history of the world, not indirectly, but having an immediate and vast influence upon future happenings. We can see that upon these battles the future of mankind hung as if by a thread.

From the picture by A. Forestier

By permission of the "Illustrated London News"

THE GREAT ACTOR DAVID GARRICK

Here is Garrick, the great eighteenth century actor taking the part of Macbeth. It may be noted that the idea to-day of performing Shakespeare in modern dress is not new—Macbeth and Lady Macbeth are dressed in Georgian costume, the modern dress of that period. Garrick was one of Dr. Johnson's many friends. Note the arrangement of the orchestra and the candle illumination, also the candles suspended over the stage.

From the picture by Dorothy Stanley   *Tate Gallery*

HIS FIRST OFFENCE

The laws against criminals were very much harsher in the eighteenth century than they are to-day. Men could be hanged for stealing five shillings and it was a common sight to see as many as twenty men hanged at once. There were no special courts for children and no excuse for a first offender with the result that criminals became reckless on the principle that they might as well be—literally—hanged for a sheep as a lamb. Not till late in the nineteenth century was any successful attempt made to reform the criminal code.

After the picture by Rowlandson and Pugin   *Rischgitz*

CRIMINALS AT BOW STREET

Justice was meted out in a very summary manner in the eighteenth century. Here is the police court as it must have been seen by the magistrate Sir John Fielding who showed up so many of the injustices of his time in his brilliant novels, "Tom Jones," "Joseph Andrews," and others which are still read to-day.

After Gillray   *Rischgitz*

RELIEVING A POOR SOLDIER IN PRISON

Prisons in the eighteenth century were terrible places. The gaolers were not paid a salary but lived on what they could extract from the prisoners, which meant that the rich lived well and the poor were treated like animals. John Howard was a reformer who by his philanthropic efforts improved conditions considerably.

From the picture by Hogarth   *Rischgitz*

THE SQUALOR OF A WOMEN'S PRISON

This scene in Bridewell Prison gives a vivid picture of the dreadful state of prisons in the eighteenth century. Punishment was drastic and there was no attempt to reform prisoners and fit them for an honest life. Note the woman stealing articles of clothing from the richly dressed victim who is being threatened by the gaoler.

From the picture by Rowlandson   *Rischgitz*

POLICEMEN OF OTHER DAYS

While the aristocracy were walking in the Mall, talking in a coffee house or attending a ball, the underworld was indulging in unchecked crime. Both London and the provinces were infested with footpads and highwaymen while the inns were used as headquarters for thieves. The only organised police force to maintain law and order were the watchmen, seen above, and the Bow Street runners started by Fielding.

From an old print

Rischgitz

AN EIGHTEENTH CENTURY POLICEMAN

Here is a night watchman on his rounds. Note the sentry-like box in which he shelters. These men were known as '' Charlies ''—possibly after Charles I who had reorganised the police force—such as it was— in 1640. They paraded the streets crying the hour and the weather, but there is no doubt that many were in league with the robbers. It was in 1829 that Sir Robert Peel started what is now the modern police force

From the picture by G. Merry

SOCIETY IN

This was a typical scene towards the end of the eighteenth century. A fine lady, with a handsome escort, is leaving a mercer's shop where she has been buying some finery of the latest fashion. The tradesman is seeing them off his premises and rubbing his hands at doing a good piece of business. Milady is about to step into a chair which would be carried by several flunkeys and which was the usual method of going a short distance. Farther down the street a carriage is waiting outside the jeweller's shop; a smart young beau going to some assignation on horseback, and a handsome young officer of smart appearance is waiting outside

GEORGIAN TIMES

the house opposite. Near him is a porter and a street pedlar, crying out her wares. In the centre of the street is a poor boy, badly dressed, with no shoes on his feet, forming one of those contrasts typical of the times. We must assume that the time is a fine summer's evening since the lady is dressed in evening clothes and wears feathers and jewels in her hair. Later the lamps will be lit over the doorways and link boys will light their masters through the streets. Having reached their destination, the boys will extinguish their torches in the metal cones that can be seen on either side of the arch over the entrance to the house on the left.

From the picture by A. Forestier

A STRANGE MACHINE

By permission of the "Illustrated London News"

In 1769 Cugnot produced a form of steam car in France, but the first which was in any way efficient was designed by Richard Trevethick in 1802. Twenty-two years later a number of these steam cars were made and they ran as a passenger service from Cheltenham to Gloucester at an average speed of 10—14 m.p.h.

After Marcus Stone by James Scott

A SMALL BOY MAKES A GREAT DISCOVERY

The power of steam had been known as far back as 130 B.C. but it had been put to no real use. Steam engines were made in the early eighteenth century but it was left to James Watt to make them practicable. Here he is in his humble home, discovering how steam condenses. The first of his many great experiments. At the age of nineteen, James came to London to be apprenticed to a scientific instrument maker.

From the picture by Paul Hardy   *By permission of " Pictorial Education "*

JAMES WATT AT WORK ON THE STEAM ENGINE

In 1763 James Watt was an instrument maker at Glasgow and while employed by the University to repair a steam engine he was struck by the great loss of steam involved in it. His remedy for this was the first of his great inventions which made the steam engine satisfactory and him to be a great engineer. It was not until 1769, however, that Watt's inventions were specified in his first patent. His experiments had taken most of his private resources, but Dr. John Roebuck, founder of the Carron Ironworks, agreed to finance him.

From an old print

Rischgitz

A NEW FASHION IN CARRIAGES

Fashions at the end of the eighteenth century became more and more extravagant. Here is a picture of what the artist thought might happen any day—a carriage designed to deliver a lady straight to her drawing-room without the trouble of walking upstairs. It is to be hoped the elaborate apparatus for controlling the carriage will prove adequate to the double weight, and that the amazed onlookers will not behold the embarrassment of so great a lady by any misadventure. The lady's head-dress is no less magnificent than her carriage!

From the picture by R. Caton Woodville.   By permission of the "Illustrated London News"

A GREAT ADVENTURER

James Cook was born of humble parents in 1728. In 1755, after he had been at sea for some time, he joined the Navy and did some pioneer work in Newfoundland and Labrador. In 1768 he was appointed to lead an expedition for making researches in the South Pacific and the great continent thought to exist there. On this voyage he sailed round New Zealand, charting and surveying the coast, and discovered the straits between the two islands. His discoveries proved to be of the greatest possible value to navigation.

From the picture by Paul Hardy   *By permission of "Pictorial Education"*

COOK FACES THE AUSTRALIAN ABORIGINES

Cook sailed from New Zealand to Australia, landing at Botany Bay on April 28, 1770. The natives showed no fear as he approached the shore, but took up their spears in a threatening attitude. Not even musket shots alarmed them. Though he landed several times Cook was unable to have any friendly communication. They were very much braver than the natives Columbus discovered, who were terrified at the sound of a gun. Captain Cook's discoveries brought many new lands under the British flag.

From an old print   *Mansell*

DEATH OF CAPTAIN COOK

Cook made two other voyages apart from this one to Australia and New Zealand, the first to discover once and for all if there was a southern continent, and the second to find the North West Passage. On this latter voyage he met his death in a scuffle with the natives at Hawaii. So died a great and brave Englishman.

From the picture by Paul Hardy   *By permission of "Pictorial Education"*

SETTLERS IN CANADA

During the reign of George III there were many new Canadian settlers, who lived a rough life hunting for furs and cultivating the land. Some of them were loyalists from the United States and some were Englishmen who, with no employment at home, had set out to start a new life in a great but undeveloped country.

From the picture by N. Percy Moran

THE BOSTON TEA PARTY

The North American colonists objected to being taxed without being represented in the English Parliament.
When a tax was put on tea and the first shipload of tea arrived, a number of them dressed up as Red Indians,
boarded a ship anchored in Boston Harbour and flung the tea overboard as a protest against the tax. England
treated the American mediators in the conflict which ensued, with such intolerance that war became inevitable.

From the picture by F. Darley   *Rischgitz*

THE FIRST BLOW FOR LIBERTY

After the incident of the Boston Tea Party the British Government passed penal acts against Massachusetts, the state where it had occurred. This led to an outbreak of hostilities at Lexington where the colonists struck their first blow for liberty and where thousands of Americans now make an annual pilgrimage.

From an old print   *Rischgitz*

STRUGGLE ON CONCORD BRIDGE

The skirmish at Concord Bridge was one of the first of the war. The British were defeated, and retired to Boston where they were besieged by the colonists. It is interesting to note that after this fight the Americans stated their loyalty and claimed that, as they were fired on first, their action was one of self-defence. To-day a granite obelisk marks the spot where the first British soldiers fell beneath the American fire.

After the picture by Trumbull   *Rischgitz*

BATTLE OF BUNKER HILL

After preliminary skirmishes between the Loyalists and Independents the first serious battle took place at Bunker Hill. The British were on the whole successful, though they lost one-third of their troops. This picture shows the death of the American general, Joseph Warren. The war had now begun in bitter earnest.

After the picture by Trumbull   *Rischgitz*

THE FOUNDATION OF THE U.S.A.

The year following the Battle of Bunker Hill a Congress, or form of Parliament, representing the thirteen American States, met together and issued the " Declaration of Independence " stating that they were no longer subjects of the king and that they were a free nation. The signing of this declaration brought into existence a great new nation—the United States of America—though it was not yet recognised by the British.

From the picture by E. Leutze   *Rischgitz*

AN AMERICAN HERO

George Washington, a brilliant general and a fine man, was Commander-in-Chief of the American forces. In 1776 he was being forced to retreat south from New York, the English objective being Philadelphia—but he suddenly crossed the Delaware River, attacked the English in the rear and defeated them at Trenton.

From the picture by M. August Couder   *Rischgitz*

THE BRITISH LOSE AMERICA

In 1778 a British army under General Burgoyne had been forced to surrender at Saratoga and when again in 1781 a second army surrendered at York Town, the end of the war had really come. Here is General Washington himself giving orders for the last assault on the town. After the British defeat hostilities ceased and a preliminary peace was made in 1782. It was not until the next year that a definite treaty was signed.

From the picture by John Singleton Copley   *Rischgitz*

CHATHAM'S LAST APPEAL

The Earl of Chatham had always opposed the war with America because he wanted to see a great united nation, which could stand up to the rest of the world. He had been stricken by illness for some time but in 1779 he staggered into the House of Lords, a dying man, and made his last passionate appeal for peace and understanding with the Americans. But his appeal was in vain, the war went on and the British lost America.

From an old print   *Rischgitz*

A TURNPIKE FOR DISSENTERS

This is a cartoon advocating the repeal of the Test Act which barred the way to all religious dissenters holding any official position whatever in the State. It depicts the Pope wearing the triple crown asking John Bull to allow him to pass through to the church on the hill. The turnpike is used as a symbol of the barrier to office because the turnpike system was a great nuisance to travellers on the English roads. It was introduced to pay for the upkeep of roads which, until a comparatively recent date, were in a shocking condition. These turnpikes were very unpopular then.

After A. Barraud and J. Hoyter   *Rischgitz*

THE LAST GREAT IRISH PARLIAMENT

During the latter part of the eighteenth century Ireland had been asking for independence from England, and in 1782 this was granted. The Irish Parliament which met under the leadership of Grattan, though it was Protestant, relieved some harsh laws against the Catholics, but in 1800 Ireland was united with England.

After Wheatley *Rischgitz*

THE GORDON RIOTS

In 1779 a certain Lord George Gordon made himself head of a Protestant association which objected to acts passed for the relief of the Catholics. The following year he headed a mob to Westminster to present a petition against these acts. The ensuing riot, in which great damage was done, was named after him.

After John Copley *Rischgitz*

THE SIEGE OF GIBRALTAR

When England was fighting against America in the War of Independence, France and Spain joined in against her. Spain had lost Gibraltar in the time of Marlborough and she now made another attempt to regain it. Eliott, the English general, put up a magnificent resistance, however, with only a small garrison against tremendous odds, and Gibraltar, the key to the Mediterranean, remained an English possession and has done so ever since. Its importance lies in the fact that it guards the British trade route to the East.

From the picture by John Copley Rischgitz

THE DEFENCE OF JERSEY

During the American War of Independence the French attacked Jersey in 1779 and 1781. The successful defence of the island against the second attack was largely due to the bravery of young Major Pierson, who, like Wolfe at Quebec, fell at the moment of victory. Jersey was one of the Norman possessions of William I.

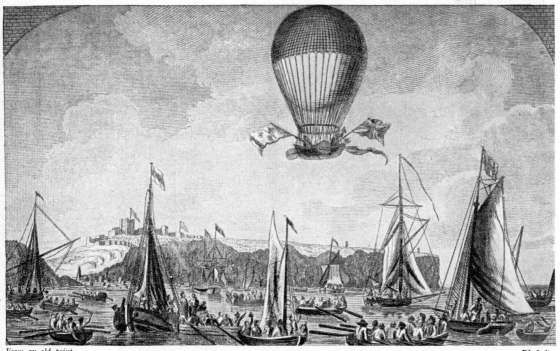

From an old print Rischgitz

THE INFANCY OF FLYING

The first man to fly was a Frenchman, Pilâtre de Rozier who went up in a balloon on October 15, 1783, and this first flight was quickly followed by others. Here we see Blanchard on his flight across the Channel from Dover in 1785. The number of ships, filled with spectators, gives some idea of the excitement caused by Blanchard's flight. The use of the balloon was, however, very limited as it could not be steered.

After Bowles   *Rischgitz*

WHITSUNTIDE JOLLIFICATIONS

A typical holiday seen in the eighteenth century, showing a crowd of jolly people off to have a good time. Judging by the dust flying from the coach wheels it is travelling at a great rate. Nevertheless, one lady is making her poor dog run alongside. Notice the unfortunate beggar at the roadside appealing for alms.

From an old print   *Rischgitz*

BOXING WITH BARE FISTS IN 1788

The prize fighters, or professional bruisers, fought without gloves and aristocrats placed very large bets on the fight results. Boxing became increasingly popular during the eighteenth and nineteenth centuries and was not confined to the professional fighters. Young bucks took it up and often, under the tuition of a professional, became extremely competent. These amateurs used gloves or "mufflers" which had been introduced by Jack Broughton. Fighting with bare fists was eventually stopped by law because of the dreadful and often fatal injuries received by the combatants.

From the picture by Morland   *Rischgitz*

THE SMUGGLERS' RETREAT

Smuggling, chiefly in wine, spirits and tobacco, was a very common practice indeed in the eighteenth and nineteenth centuries, though not everyone regarded it as a crime. Adam Smith, a great free trader, speaks of the smuggler as a man who would have been an excellent citizen " had not the laws of the country made that a crime which nature never meant to be so." Here is a picture of smugglers landing their contraband cargo at some lonely spot and then transferring it to a wagon which will take it away to be sold.

SPINNING AND WINDING WOOL

Before the coming of machinery, spinning, weaving and other manufacturing processes were done in the home. With the swift development of machinery in the late eighteenth and nineteenth centuries, however, large factories sprang up in the northern districts where coal and iron were easily procurable. Men moved from their old homes in the country to work in these factories ; large manufacturing towns grew swiftly and workers had to live in dirty, ill-ventilated dwellings. At first conditions were terrible, but reforms in the end were gradually made.

From the picture by W. Hincks   *Rischgitz*

From the caricature by Bunbury   *Rischgitz*

THE SMOKING CLUB

Bunbury was an excellent caricaturist who lived in the latter part of the eighteenth century and the beginning of the nineteenth. Unlike Rowlandson and Gillray he did not make use of political subjects, but kept to the social aspects of life. He here makes fun of the habit of smoking, which had grown steadily to its present-day proportions since tobacco had first been introduced into England by Raleigh in Tudor times.

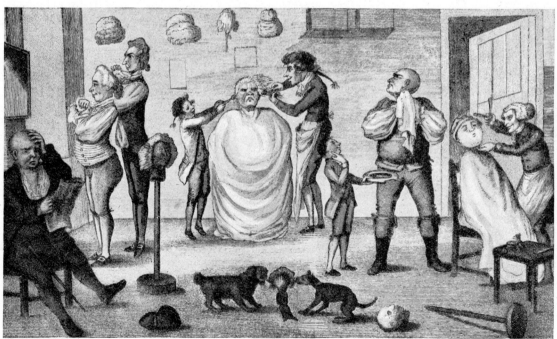

From the caricature by Bunbury   *Rischgitz*

THE BARBER'S SHOP

This is one of Bunbury's most famous works, and depicts the crude method of shaving customary at the beginning of the nineteenth century. The figure standing in the right centre has been cut by the barber and the small boy at his side is pointing out the place so that he may staunch the blood.

After J. Zoffany *Rischgitz*

WELCOMING THE NEW GOVERNOR-GENERAL

Bengal first came under the control of the East India Company in 1765, though trading settlements had existed there for many years before that time. Clive's victory at Plassey confirmed British authority there, and Warren Hastings stabilised this by forming a civil rather than a military government. This picture shows an Indian embassy setting out to meet Lord Cornwallis, Warren Hastings' successor.

From the picture by Mather Brown *Rischgitz*

TWO ROYAL HOSTAGES

Lord Cornwallis was Governor-General of Bengal from 1786 to 1792. He was an excellent administrator and introduced many reforms. His work was interrupted by a quarrel with an Indian leader named Tippoo Sahib. Cornwallis took personal charge of the war against him, which was ended by a treaty in 1792 putting half Tippoo Sahib's territory into British hands and forcing him to give up his two sons as hostages.

From an old print   *Rischgitz*

TRIAL OF A GREAT ADMINISTRATOR

Warren Hastings had for many years carried on the administration of Bengal, increasing British territory and trade. He was in a particularly difficult position as the French, jealous of British power in India, were perpetually raising trouble. Also, he had many enemies at home, who succeeded in having him impeached by Parliament on charges of bribery and maladministration. He was triumphantly acquitted in 1785.

From the picture by Karl Anton Hicker.   *Rischgitz*

A GREAT STATESMAN ADDRESSES THE HOUSE OF COMMONS

Here is William Pitt, the younger, speaking before Canning, Wilberforce, Sheridan, Charles James Fox and others in St. Stephen's Chapel. A Royal Palace occupied the site of the present Houses of Parliament but in 1547 it was considerably damaged by fire and ceased to be used as such. St. Stephen's Chapel was used by Parliament until 1834 when the whole building, except for Westminster Hall, was burnt down.

From the caricature by Gillray   Rischgitz

THE POOR MAN GOES HUNGRY

In 1775, the foreign wars, the duty on imported corn, and the poor harvest at home raised the price of bread to a prohibitive rate. Meat and other foodstuffs were equally expensive, and low wages for the working man made it very difficult for him to obtain adequate nourishment for himself and his children. We see here the exhorbitant prices of food contrasted with the low rates at which a man was paid.

From the picture by Val Prinsep in the Diploma Gallery, Royal Academy   *Mansell*

THE SPIRIT OF FREEDOM

The French people, ground down by the Church, the nobility and the Crown, and encouraged by the success of the Americans' struggle for freedom, rose against their oppressors in 1789 with the cry '' Liberty, Equality and Fraternity.'' The revolution might have been a purely constitutional one, but the stupidity of Louis XVI turned it from a struggle for freedom to a reign of terror, brutality and bloodshed throughout the land.

From the picture by P. Delaroche By permission of the Corporation of Liverpool

THE MAN OF POWER

From the chaos of the French Revolution, rose a man of genius, Napoleon Bonaparte, who started as an army officer, became First Consul and ended as Emperor of France. Under his generalship France, without an ally, fought and almost defeated the whole of Europe. In 1800 he led his victorious army across the Alps by the St. Bernard Pass—then only a wagon track—and defeated the Austrians at Marengo. Napoleon led the French armies on many other campaigns—in Italy, in Egypt and in Russia. In spite of his brilliant generalship he eventually met defeat, chiefly because he was unable to break English power at sea.

From the picture by Alexander Johnson   *By permission of the Ferens Art Gallery, Hull*

RECRUITING SAILORS IN THE EIGHTEENTH CENTURY

One of the greatest evils of the eighteenth century was the method of recruiting seamen for the Navy. An armed force would come ashore, forcibly seize all the likely men they could find and carry them off to serve their king and country under harsh discipline and for small pay. The Press Gang, as this force was called, was a source of much misery and was dreaded in all seaport towns wherever it appeared. In this picture a young countryman is being torn away from his bride as they cross the square after the ceremony.

From the picture by G. Joy

Mansell

NELSON'S FIRST FAREWELL TO HIS MOTHER

Horatio Nelson, the son of a Norfolk rector, was born in 1758. His mother was a relation of Sir Robert Walpole and it was through her brother, Captain Suckling, that Nelson first went to sea. In 1770 he took a post under his uncle in the guardship at Chatham. To gain more experience he went on a voyage in a merchant ship to the West Indies and at the age of nineteen became a lieutenant in the Navy.

From the picture by Robert Dodd *Rischgitz*

THE BATTLE OF CAMPERDOWN

In 1797 things were going decidedly the worse for England, Spain and Holland had allied themselves with France and the home fleet, moreover, was in a state of mutiny owing to bad treatment. Luckily, however, the mutineers were pacified and proceeded to defeat the Dutch at the Battle of Camperdown.

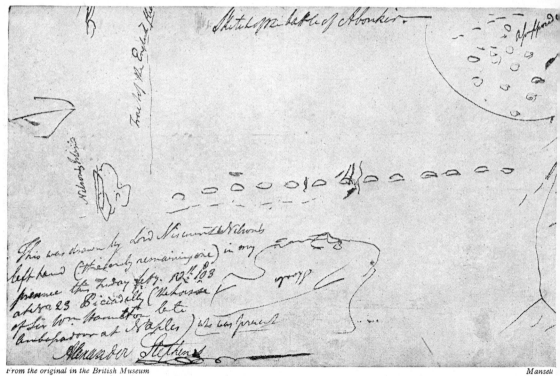

From the original in the British Museum *Mansell*

NELSON'S OWN PLAN OF THE BATTLE OF ABOUKIR

In 1798 Napoleon set out with the intention of capturing Egypt and attacking British India. He was, however, frustrated by Nelson's victory at the Battle of the Nile which regained for Britain control of the Mediterranean. The French Fleet was anchored in Aboukir Bay and Nelson's plan was to divide his squadron and sail up on both sides of the enemy. The French were short-handed and this plan proved brilliantly successful.

From the picture by Thomas Davidson   *Spencer Arnold*

NELSON CHASES THE FRENCH FLEET

Before the Battle of the Nile, Nelson's great difficulty was to locate the French Fleet. He followed it from Malta to Cape Passaro and on to Alexandria where he missed it and sailed on. By the time he returned there the French had succeeded in landing their army. But when Nelson won the Battle of the Nile he made it extremely difficult for Napoleon to bring back his troops from Egypt while the English Fleet was at large.

From a contemporary print Rischgitz

A RAFT FOR THE INVASION OF ENGLAND

Throughout the war England had to guard against a French invasion and had to keep the enemy fleet bottled up. Napoleon evolved a complicated scheme to draw the English away to the West Indies but even this failed. Here is a picture of one of the gigantic fortified rafts with which he hoped to convey his troops across the Channel. The failure of the invasion scheme was largely due to the brilliance of Admiral Nelson.

From the picture by F. Countz Rischgitz

THE KENSINGTON VOLUNTEERS

Great fear was felt at the possibility of a French invasion and the army was increased by half a million volunteers for home defence purposes. Forts, known as Martello Towers, which could be held by local troops until reinforcements arrived, were built all along the south coast. Here is one of the new volunteer regiments being presented with its colours, which may still be seen in Kensington Parish Church.

From a contemporary print   *Rischgitz*

PROCLAIMING PEACE WITH FRANCE

In 1802, the Treaty of Amiens was made between England, Holland, France and Spain. Here is a picture of the news being proclaimed at the Royal Exchange on April 29. The principal provisions of its terms were that Britain should restore all her conquests except Trinidad and Ceylon, and it was understood that Napoleon would withdraw the whole of his troops from Holland, Switzerland and Italy.

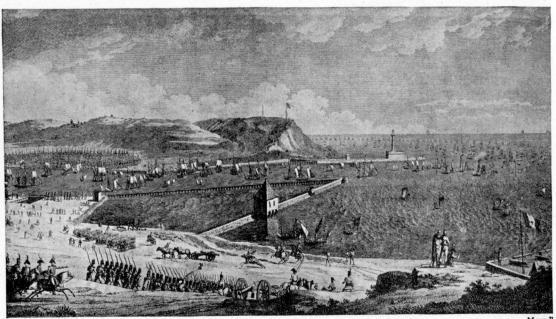

From a contemporary print   *Mansell*

THE PROJECTED INVASION OF ENGLAND

War broke out again the year after the Treaty of Amiens. Napoleon was again ready to invade England and he had his Grand Army of 100,000 men waiting at Boulogne for the moment when the English Fleet were off their guard and he would be able to cross the Channel. The English, however, kept control of the seas and since the French were blockaded in their ports, the invasion plan never matured.

From a contemporary print
Rischgitz

JOHN BULL STANDS UP TO NAPOLEON

Here is a political cartoon of the possible French invasion. John Bull, the universal Englishman, bars Napoleon's way into England, which is represented by the toy shop. It was Napoleon's ambition to conquer England, upon which, for many years, he had set covetous eyes. But the continued effective resistance of the English, terminating in the Battle of Waterloo, eventually brought about his downfall.

From an old print
Rischgitz

PITT AND NAPOLEON DIVIDE THE WORLD

Another political cartoon which shows Napoleon grabbing Europe and Pitt quietly taking possession of a very large slice of the rest of the world. Though Napoleon was the dominant personality in Europe, England had complete control of the seas and in spite of continual French aggression during these years managed to extend her Empire. England was fortunate in having a man like Pitt at such a critical time.

From an old print   *Rischgitz*

THE BATTLE OF TRAFALGAR

Nelson, after chasing the French to the West Indies and then back again, refitted at Portsmouth and blockaded Vileneuve's fleet at Cadiz. He knew that there were not enough supplies in the port and that the French Fleet was bound to come out. It did and Nelson inflicted a crushing defeat at Trafalgar. This victory, which finally established British supremacy at sea, was one of the turning points in the war.

From the picture by Benjamin West   *Mansell*

NELSON DIES AT TRAFALGAR

Nelson's ship, the *Victory*, was engaged with two French ships, the *Bucentaure* and the *Redoubtable*. Nelson himself and his flag captain Hardy were walking up and down the deck of the *Victory* when Nelson was struck by a musket shot from the *Redoubtable*. "They have done for me at last," he cried, and after lingering a few hours in great pain he died with the words: "I have done my duty, thank God for that."

From the picture by John Burnett   *Rischgitz*

CELEBRATING THE BATTLE OF TRAFALGAR

There was great national rejoicing at the Battle of Trafalgar which had put an end to any possibility of a French invasion and given England complete control of the sea. In the picture we see the Greenwich Pensioners, retired seamen from the hospital founded by William and Mary, celebrating the victory.

From a contemporary print   *Rischgitz*

LIVERPOOL AS IT WAS IN 1800

The importance of Liverpool as a commercial town dates from the Restoration. Before that time the population was not more than a thousand, but the development of the American and West Indian trade and the coming of the Industrial Revolution resulted in a steady increase in size and importance.

From an old print   *Mansell*

CARRYING GOODS IN THE EARLY NINETEENTH CENTURY

This type of stage wagon was the usual means of carrying goods in the days of Nelson. It had gradually replaced the pack horse of Tudor and Stuart times as a means of conveying goods. Sometimes it would carry passengers who could not afford to go by coach. The wide wheels prevented the wagon from sinking into the bad roads of the period which were usually mere tracks, impassable in bad weather.

From an old print   *Rischgitz*

THE MAIL-COACH AT THE GENERAL POST OFFICE IN 1806

A postal service has existed since earliest times in the form of king's messengers. In 1839 Sir Rowland Hill made great reforms in the postal service, amongst which was the introduction of the penny post.

From the picture by Rowlandson
Rischgitz

TOTTENHAM COURT ROAD IN 1813

Roads at this time were very bad and were rapidly becoming worse owing to the increasing use of coaches and large wagons. To improve matters the turnpike system was started. At intervals on their journey travellers had to pay a sum of money at the toll gate, this money going to the upkeep of the road.

From an old print
Rischgitz

GAS LIGHTING IN PALL MALL IN 1807

In 1799 a Frenchman named Philippe Lebon gave an exhibition in Paris of a new illuminating gas. This was seen by a German who brought the idea to England and gave a demonstration in the Lyceum Theatre in 1804. He then floated a company and the first street gas lighting was seen in Pall Mall in 1807. This cartoon shows the unpopularity with which the new invention was first received among the community.

From the picture by George Walker

OUR ANCESTORS GO BATHING

Rischgitz

This bathing scene makes a very amusing contrast to the present day. The machine for unrobing was drawn right down into the water so that a lady would not be seen walking down the beach, and the costumes are noticeably less scanty than they are to-day. There was much more modesty among the people than at court.

From the picture by Bunbury

A GAME OF BILLIARDS

Rischgitz

The origin of billiards is uncertain, but there can be no doubt that it was popular in Elizabethan times for there is a direct reference to it in Shakespeare's *Antony and Cleopatra*. From the seventeenth century onwards it was popular throughout Europe, being considered a " most gentile, cleanly and ingenious game." At one time billiards was played on a lawn like croquet, a form of the game which came back into popularity for a time in the nineteenth century. Apparently it was not so scientific as it is to-day !

From the picture by Rowlandson *Rischgitz*

A FASHIONABLE PLACE OF AMUSEMENT

In 1661 public gardens were laid out at Vauxhall and they quickly became the favourite fashionable pleasure resort of the town. In 1732 they were considerably improved by Jonathan Tyer, the manager, and in 1822 they were visited by George IV, and by his permission became the Royal Vauxhall Gardens. In 1859 they had ceased to be popular, and to-day there is nothing on the site to remind one of Vauxhall's former glory.

From an old print *Rischgitz*

MERRY-MAKING ON THE ICEBOUND THAMES

Fairs were originally associated with markets which were usually held on holidays and were accompanied by special facilities for amusements. A famous fair was held on the Thames when it was frozen over in 1814.

From the painting by Pugin and Rowlandson   *Rischgitz*

A PRISON YARD AS PLAYGROUND

The degree of comfort of life in prison depended on how much money the prisoner could afford to pay the gaolers. If he was well off he could do as he pleased ; if not he was left almost to starve. Here are some of the wealthy prisoners of Fleet Prison amusing themselves with a game of rackets. In the left foreground they are playing skittles. Rackets is still played to-day and had its origin in the impromptu game shown here.

From the picture by Jerry Barrett   *Rischgitz*

ELIZABETH FRY READING THE BIBLE IN A WOMEN'S PRISON

The indescribable beastliness of women's prisons in the early nineteenth century did not prevent Elizabeth Fry, the saintly member of the Society of Friends, from facing every kind of insult and degrading scene in her endeavour to compel a reform of these conditions. In 1817 she founded an association for the improvement of female prisoners in Newgate and devoted the rest of her life to prison reform,

From the picture by R. Caton Woodville   *By permission of the " Illustrated London News "*

COLONISING UNDER GREAT DIFFICULTIES

The coast of Guiana was sighted by Columbus in 1498 and settlements were made there as early as 1580 by the Dutch. English settlements came shortly after, but British Guiana did not really exist as a colony until 1814. Here are the British soldiers marching through the terrible swamps of the Essiquibo river to open up the land and to subdue the natives. This picture depicts the awful hardships they had to endure.

From the picture by A. Forestier   *Copyright : Fine Arts Publishing Company*

THE PRELUDE TO A CENTURY OF PEACE

The United States waged its first war with Great Britain to gain an independent national existence ; in 1812 it declared a second war to secure its rights upon the sea. Britain claimed the right to search American ships and this was naturally bitterly resented. Peace was signed in 1814, and since then the two great English-speaking democracies have been at peace with each other. Let us hope that it may endure.

From the picture by Meissonier   *Mansell*

NAPOLEON'S RETREAT FROM MOSCOW

In 1812 Napoleon marched into Russia. The Russians retreated before him until he had almost reached Moscow, when he fought and defeated them at the Battle of Borondino, but not without great losses.

From the painting by E. Crofts in the Mappin Art Gallery, Sheffield   *Rischgitz*

WELLINGTON'S MARCH FROM QUATRE BRAS TO WATERLOO

In 1815 Napoleon escaped from his exile in Elba and within six weeks had raised an army of 200,000 men against the allies, Russia, Prussia, Austria and Britain. The Prussians under Blücher were defeated at Ligny, and the British, after fighting a section of the French army, moved back to Waterloo, where the Duke of Wellington took up his position preparatory to fighting one of the vital battles in history

From the picture by E. Crofts   *By permission of the Corporation of Liverpool*

THE BATTLE OF WATERLOO

The Duke of Wellington took up his position on the main Charleroi-Brussels road on the crest of a low hill. Napoleon attacked continually throughout the day but Wellington never wavered. His line was badly shaken in the centre, his troops were exhausted, but he calmly readjusted his forces and continued to fight. Eventually the Prussians appeared. Napoleon flung his famous guards into the battle in a final desperate attempt at victory, but they were repulsed and the French army, with the exception of the two battalions of guards, fled from the field. Since that time Wellington has been known as the Iron Duke.

From the picture by D. Maclise

Rischgitz

MEETING BETWEEN THE TWO GENERALS

At 9.15 in the evening, after one of the greatest battles in history, the two allied generals, Wellington and Blücher, met. It was arranged that the Prussians should follow up the French army and this they did very effectively allowing the enemy no time to recover from their defeat. Napoleon had fought desperately but not even his famous " Guard " had been able to shake the invincible courage of the Duke and his army.

From the picture by Orchardson in the Tate Gallery

Mansell

THE FALLEN EMPEROR

Napoleon was now finally defeated and forced to abdicate. He tried to escape to America but finding the way barred, he surrendered to the British and he is seen here on Captain Maitland's ship the *Bellerophon*. The rest of his life was spent in exile on the island of St. Helena where he eventually died in 1821.

From the picture by R. Havell   *Rischgitz*

BEFORE THE BOMBARDMENT OF ALGIERS

From the middle of the sixteenth century Algiers was the centre of the Barbary pirates who were a continual menace to Mediterranean traders. In spite of the repeated efforts to exterminate them they all failed, but in 1816 Lord Exmouth, assisted by the Dutch, bombarded the town and wiped out the pirate fleet. Piracy, however, still continued in spite of another action three years later. In 1827 the French occupied the town and under their administration piracy was exterminated. Algiers is now a modern French town.

From the drawing by J. Sackhouse   *Rischgitz*

EXPLORATION IN THE ARCTIC

Sir John Ross, a naval captain, and later a Rear-Admiral, led three expeditions to explore the Arctic. This picture shows him on his first expedition in 1818, holding communication for the first time with the Esquimaux. He was honoured at home and by several foreign countries for his scientific discoveries.

From the picture by Paul Hardy   *By permission of " Pictorial Education"*

THE FIRST SAFETY LAMP FOR MINERS

Sir Hugh Davey is seen here demonstrating his safety lamp to a group of miners.   Before its invention it was impossible to light a coal mine properly as a naked flame was liable to cause an explosion in the mine. The boy on the right is carrying a lighting apparatus which was sometimes used.   It set up a stream of sparks which gave a poor light but was less dangerous than an ordinary flame.   Sir Hugh Davey's lamp was a great boon to the miners and did much to improve the terrible conditions under which they worked.

From an old print   *Rischgitz*

THE PETERLOO MASSACRE

At the beginning of the nineteenth century there was a great demand for Parliamentary reform. When nothing was done the country began to get restive and the Government used repressive measures to keep it quiet. When a vast but orderly crowd assembled in St. Peter's Field, Manchester, the magistrate ordered out the yeomanry to disperse the mob. In the ensuing conflict some people were killed and many injured.

From an old print   *Rischgitz*

THE CATO STREET CONSPIRACY

The Government upheld the magistrate's action at " Peterloo " but the majority of the nation was furious at the bloodshed that had been caused. In 1820, however, an event occurred which caused a reaction in favour of the Government. A number of violent Radicals, under a man named Thistlewood, conspired to murder the Cabinet while the members were at dinner. This cartoon shows the capture of the conspirators in Cato Street, Edgware Road. So ended a conspiracy quite as barbarous as the Gunpowder Plot itself.

GEORGE IV

1820-1830

GEORGE IV came to the throne in 1820 after having been Prince Regent for nearly ten years during his father's madness. He could speak French, Italian and German fluently; he had some taste for the arts and was extremely handsome. His tutor said of him at the age of fifteen that he would be " either the most polished gentleman or the most accomplished blackguard in Europe—possibly both." Unfortunately, he turned out to be the latter. With his natural accomplishments he reacted against the dull, economical life of his father, and at an early age, plunged into the dissipations of London Society, which flatteringly referred to him as " the first gentleman in Europe."

DOMESTIC TROUBLES

When quite young, George fell passionately in love with Mrs. Fitzherbert, and in spite of his later brutality towards her, she contrived to be his greatest friend throughout her life. Legally, George was not allowed to marry her, but in 1785 they went through a form of marriage in the Church of England, though the union could not be recognised by the State. Meanwhile George was terribly burdened by debts, and in 1794 he was legally married to Caroline of Brunswick, a German princess, because this was the only condition on which his father would pay off his debts. The two were very badly suited and, after years of trouble between them, George started divorce proceedings against Caroline. The Bill of Divorce only just got through Parliament at the third reading, but was eventually dropped. The matter, however, was finally settled by the queen's death in 1821.

When Prince of Wales, George, like most of the Hanoverians, had quarrelled with his father and lent his support to the opposite political party—the Whigs. Now George III had brought back to the crown a lot of its old power and his son might have continued this unfortunate policy and changed the Tory ministry when he became Prince Regent, but he did not do so. He deserted his old political friends—the Whigs— and allowed the Tories to continue in office. It is fortunate that he took this attitude as the country was not in the mood for a return to personal government by the sovereign.

TORY REPRESSION

England was in need of many reforms. For nearly twenty-five years the country had been at war and the return of soldiers and sailors resulted in widespread unemployment ; social conditions were very bad and there was still a danger that the revolutionary ideas of the French might spread among the distressed people; the Catholics and Dissenters from the Church of England were agitating for reform. The country had not adapted itself to peace nor to the new conditions brought about by the industrial revolution.

The Tory policy at this time was to avoid tackling these problems and to keep the people suppressed in order to avoid a revolution. The government put a tax on corn which had the effect of putting the price of bread beyond the reach of the working classes but protecting the country gentleman who would consequently support the government against the people ; moreover, it refused to reform the method of electing its members, fearful lest the constitution of the country should be upset. When the people could not afford bread, when a decayed village sent a member to Parliament and an industrial town like Manchester did not, it is no wonder that riots and agitations were common in the country. The Prince Regent had stones thrown into his carriage as he was going to open Parliament ; Wellington, the hero of Waterloo, had his windows broken by the mob ; an orderly meeting in Manchester asking for reform resulted in the soldiers attacking the crowd and many people being killed and injured ; there was even a plot to kill the whole Cabinet as it sat at dinner. The government, seeing how dangerous the situation was, made things worse by forbidding public meetings and free speech.

Throughout this period Castlereagh had worked hard and honestly, but he had worked, not for the future but for the present—not for reform but to subdue the troubles rising out of the need for reform. In 1822, worn out by hard work, he committed suicide, and his place was taken by Canning. Canning was a brilliant man, a scholar, a successful sailor and a great orator who gave to the government the inspiration which had been lacking under the hard-working, clear-headed Castlereagh.

CANNING'S FOREIGN POLICY

Canning and his supporters were in favour of the Emancipation of the Catholics, but, strangely enough, opposed to Parliamentary reform. Though some excellent measures, such as the abolition of many of the harsh laws against criminals, and the formation of a new police force by Sir Robert Peel, were passed during his period of office, his chief work was abroad.

The essence of Canning's foreign policy was to support the liberties of other countries. When Naples and Spain rebelled against their rulers, and Prussia and France started interfering for their own ends, Canning cried, " Hands off revolutions unless they are in your own country," but he was too late to stop France conquering Spain, or the Prussian army defeating the Neapolitan rebels. On the other hand, he dealt very effectively with the South American situation. The South American states revolted against control by Spain, and Portugal, France and Russia were watching for an opportunity of seizing some new possessions there. Meanwhile, Monroe, President of the United States, issued his famous doctrine of " Hands off America," which meant that, without interference from Europe, he would gradually absorb these states and all the wealth they contained. Canning now stepped in between the two parties. He declared that any interference with South America would mean war with the British Navy. This firm policy put an end to any danger either from the Monroe Doctrine, or from intervention from Europe. Before his death in 1827 Canning was to secure the liberty of yet another country. The Greeks rose in rebellion against their Turkish rulers, and Canning, only too pleased to lessen the power of the Turks, supported the Greeks, and the Turkish fleet was destroyed at the Battle of Navarino.

Just before this happened Canning died and his place was taken by Wellington. The Duke was not so successful as a statesman as he had been as a general, and his strong Tory ideas soon lost him his old popularity.

There was, at this time, much unrest in Ireland, which was clamouring for Catholic emancipation. An Irish barrister named Daniel O'Connell started the Catholic Association which stirred up agitation in favour of religious toleration for the Catholics. Wellington was opposed to this, but, seeing that the country was on the verge of civil war, changed his front, and a Bill was passed in 1729 which allowed Catholics to sit in Parliament and to hold official positions under the crown. Meanwhile the Test Act had been repealed in England, and dissenters from the Church of England gained similar advantages.

A CHANGING COUNTRY

George IV died in 1830. The most important aspects of his reign are the struggles for reform, the foreign policy of Canning and the development of the industrial revolution. Canals had been developed all over the country, roads were improved by the inventions of Macadam, and the first railways were opened and steamships came into use.

These inventions were not altogether popular. Men who had been accustomed all their lives to wooden sailing ships shook their heads over the newfangled steamship which started to appear ; country squires hated the idea of railways because they would interfere with their hunting. The country had not yet adjusted itself to these new conditions which were brought about by the great speeding up of transport and increase in machinery. Large manufacturing towns were in existence yet they had no representative in Parliament, which was still chiefly composed of the aristocracy. The country was still controlled by the landed gentry who could afford to buy their seats in Parliament, and not by the mass of the people. Conditions in the manufacturing areas were terrible ; no legislation had yet been introduced to protect the workers from long hours and poor pay, which put fortunes into the hands of their employers.

At the death of George IV England was an aristocratic country on the verge of democracy. The people had no say in the government of the country, but for the first time they were demanding that they should have. Enormous changes were bound to come and there was a great danger, so great was the general unrest, that they would come not through Parliamentary reform but through bloodshed and revolution. The future of the country was hanging in the balance.

From an old print   *Rischgitz*

THE CORONATION BANQUET OF GEORGE IV

George IV came to the throne in 1820. He had already acted as the Prince Regent for some years during his father's madness. He was an idle, pleasure-loving man who, like all the early Hanoverians, had quarrelled with the Court party and given his support to the opposite political party, in this case the Whigs.

Rischgitz

KING GEORGE IN IRELAND

The scandals of King George's private life made him extremely unpopular in England, but when he visited Ireland in 1821, where he was not so well known, he received a great reception from the whole of the nation. After a short stay there he was encouraged by the friendliness of the people to visit Scotland.

From the picture by Sir David Wilkie   *Rischgitz*

KING GEORGE AT HOLYROOD

King George arrived in Edinburgh in 1822 where he was greeted with as much enthusiasm as had been his experience when visiting Dublin. His official reception was arranged by Sir Walter Scott. This was in a sense an historic visit. George was the first English king to set foot in Scotland since Charles II

From an old print   *Rischgitz*

GEORGE IV AT BRIGHTON

In 1686 Brighton was merely a fishing town but within the next hundred years it had become a fashionable resort. Its popularity was further increased by George IV who, when Prince Regent, built the pavilion which he used as his chief residence. Moreover, Brighton's associations with Mrs. Fitzherbert, the king's favourite, ensured that it would be fashionable as well as popular. Since that time Brighton has become less fashionable but more popular, and it now ranks as one of the best known watering places in England.

THE TRIAL OF A QUEEN

In 1806 a commission enquired into Queen Caroline's conduct, about which stories were being circulated, but she was acquitted of any serious fault. After this she went abroad, but returned to England some years later to face a further trial, when she was again acquitted. Her premature death occurred a year later.

JOINING THE ARMY

This is a typical scene in a village inn in the early days of the nineteenth century. The villagers are all sitting round when up comes the recruiting sergeant with a fine story of the advantages of a soldier's life.

From the aquatint by Freeman after C. B. Newhouse   *Rischgitz*

ELECTIONEERING IN SCOTLAND

The difficulties of holding meetings or canvassing for votes in the outlying districts of Scotland were very great. The chief means of transport was, as yet, the coach, and here we see one travelling at full speed through a turnpike, with canvassing banners waving, on its way to the next town to impress the voters.

From the picture by James Scott   *Rischgitz*

THE HOUSE OF COMMONS IN 1821

The Houses of Parliament were burned down in 1834. Here is Parliament sitting in St. Stephen's Chapel which was used before the fire as the House of Commons. The Speaker is seated in the big chair under the light, and in modern times the Government would be on the left and the Opposition on the right.

From the picture by R. Caton Woodville *By permission of "The Illustrated London News"*

COLONISING IN SOUTH AFRICA

Natal was first discovered by Vasco da Gama on his voyage to India in 1497. Occasional traders visited it but apart from one settlement by the Dutch, which lasted only a short time, no real effort was made to colonise it until the British formed a company in 1823 for carrying on trade with the natives. This was the private venture of a man named Farewell. In 1835 Durban was founded by the settlers.

From a contemporary print *Rischgitz*

A CURIOUS STEAM CARRIAGE

The first practical steam carriage had been made by Richard Trevethick in 1802. Here is one of 1828, the invention of Mr. James of Birmingham. Its weight was two tons, its horse power about 15–20 with an estimated speed of 8–12 m.p.h. It carried six inside passengers and twelve outside. To avoid smoke only charcoal and coke were burned. As a safety measure its boiler was tested to ten times its working pressure

From an old print *Rischgitz*

A RAILWAY OF A HUNDRED YEARS AGO

For many years steam engines had been used for stationary work such as pumping and occasional haulage experiments, but it was not until 1825 that George Stephenson's engines pulled loaded wagons along the Stockton and Darlington Railway. In 1830 the Liverpool–Manchester Railway was started. Here is Parkside Station where Mr. Huskisson, a Member of Parliament, was killed by Stephenson's "Rocket."

From the picture by C. B. Newhouse   *Rischgitz*

A POSTMAN OF OTHER DAYS

Although in 1784 the first mail coaches with armed guards had been established, the mails were still some-times carried by riders on horseback.   Here is a post boy blowing his horn to awaken the turnpike that he might be let through the toll gate.   It is estimated that during twenty-five years mails were conveyed over seventy million miles, not a single robbery took place, and a million pounds was added to the annual revenue.

From an old print   *Rischgitz*

LONDON'S FIRST OMNIBUS

In 1662 public coaches, going on definite routes at stated times, were introduced in Paris.   In England there had been hackney carriages for hire since 1625 but it was not until 1829 that an enterprising gentleman named Mr. Shillibeer, introduced the omnibus into London.   The first omnibuses, carrying twenty-two passengers, were too large for the roads, consequently their size was reduced to carry twelve passengers.

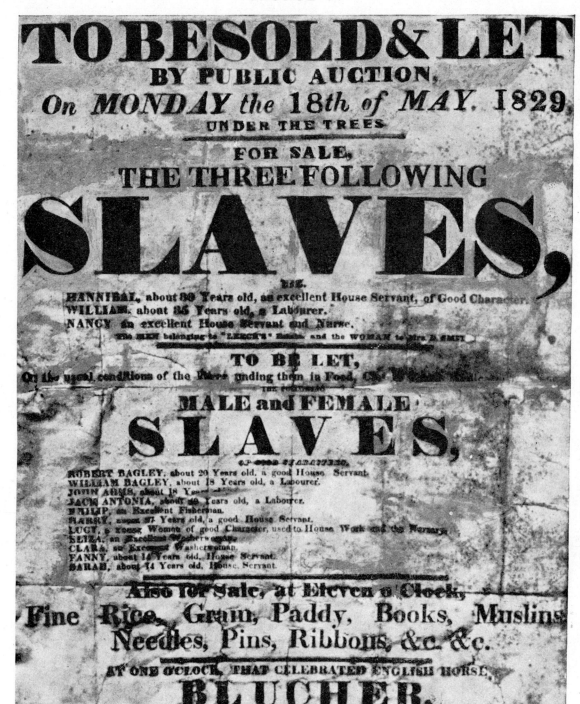

By permission of the Wilberforce Museum, Hull

SLAVES FOR SALE

The British first took part in the slave trade when colonies were founded in America and by 1702 there were 200,000 negroes in Virginia alone. In 1713 the Asiento Treaty with Spain allowed England to transport 4,800 slaves every year. Although the slave trade was declared illegal by an Act of Parliament in 1807, it was not until the Act of 1833 that slavery was successfully abolished in Great Britain's Colonies and Dominions. Other countries followed the example, but even to-day slavery still exists in some parts of the world.

WILLIAM IV
1830-1837

GEORGE IV had died without a son, and his brother William came to the throne. He was a bluff hearty sailor who was popular without being respected. At the time of his accession the country was nearer to civil war than it had been since 1688. The people, oppressed by the Corn Laws which raised the price of bread to a prohibitive rate, angry at having no say in the government of the country, and clamouring against the conditions under which they had to work, were demanding reform. The Government, on the other hand, frightened that the constitution of the country would be upset, steadily opposed reform and did its best to suppress the masses who were demanding it. In 1830 there were but two alternatives—civil war or parliamentary reform.

NEED FOR REFORM

The system of franchise and election in operation at this time was nothing short of a scandal. Rutland was represented in Parliament equally with Yorkshire ; a borough which had once been a village and no longer had any population sent a member to Parliament, while great industrial towns like Manchester and Leeds were not represented at all ; the only people who had a vote were the landowners. This situation had arisen owing to the shifting of the population from country districts to the large towns. Originally, England was an agricultural country and it was right that the people should be ruled by their landlords, but now it was industrial and the workers in the industrial centres were not represented in Parliament.

Wellington was Prime Minister at this time, and he was opposed to any idea of reform ; but feeling was running so high that he was driven from office and the Whigs under Lord Grey came into power. Grey was an ardent reformer, but his first Bill was thrown out by the Lords after it had gone through the Commons. Riots broke out and the king promised to create enough new peers to see it through the House of Lords, but at the last moment he broke his word and Grey resigned. For a week there was chaos, but the opposition, seeing the dangerous state of the country, gave way, and Grey came back to office on condition that the peers would not vote against the Bill, which became law in 1832.

THE FIRST REFORM BILL

The two main clauses of the 1832 Reform Bill were the abolition of the rotten boroughs whose seats were given to the large towns, and the giving of a vote to anyone living in a house rented at £10 a year. The effect of these two changes was to widen the class of people who had any influence in Parliament. Previously, both those who voted and those who sat in Parliament had been the landed proprietors. After 1832, the working classes in the industrial areas were represented and the middle classes got a vote. It must be noted, however, that the working classes only had a member of Parliament sent from their particular district, they had as yet no say in his election. The Reform Bill of 1832 gave political status to the middle class, but the social revolution had as yet only gone half way—it had not catered for the working class.

The Whig party continued in power for the rest of William IV's reign, not under the leadership of Grey—who had resigned—but under Lord Melbourne. It put through a number of other reforms : the Municipal Corporations Act which ensured that every town was governed by a mayor and a locally chosen town council ; a new Poor Law in 1834 ; the abolition of slavery in British Colonies in 1833 ; and the Factory Act of the same year.

FACTORY ACTS AND POOR LAWS

Factory Acts to improve working conditions had been passed at intervals for some years, but none of them proved to be of any value because there was no method of enforcing them. The Act of 1833, however, not only set a limit to the working hours of children and young persons generally, but it started a system of government inspection which made the new regulations reasonably effective for the first time.

With the change from agriculture to industry,

From the picture by Havell — Kischgitz

THE KING AND QUEEN OPEN NEW LONDON BRIDGE

The original London Bridge was built in the early thirteenth century, and on it was a row of houses with a chapel in the centre. The existing bridge, designed by Sir John Rennie and his son, was opened by William IV and Queen Adelaide in 1831. There was no bridge below it until 1894 when the Tower Bridge was opened.

a system had grown up of supplementing the miserable wages of the workers. This led to many abuses. Employers paid low wages, knowing that they would be increased out of public money and honest men who asked a living wage could not get work. This state of affairs was remedied by the Poor Law of 1834. Districts were organised throughout the country, and each district had its board of guardians who had to see that a workhouse was built and that no one received relief except in the workhouse. Yet this Poor Law had its disadvantages and was extremely unpopular among the people. It meant that a man who was out of work was virtually shut up in a prison and was incapable of helping himself; he simply had to wait until he was told there was work for him to do.

SLAVE TRADE

The development of colonies in the New World had led to the importation of large numbers of slaves from Africa. Slavery was a lucrative trade. The planters got cheap labour; the slave owners got good prices for the men they sold, and the African natives themselves gained by selling the men they captured in war to the Europeans. The only people who did not gain were the slaves, whose hardships upon the slave ships it is difficult for anyone to-day to understand. With so many financial interests at stake it was not easy for the Government to pass any laws against slavery.

Public feeling against the slave trade began to grow in the middle of the seventeenth century. Amongst those who were opposed to it were Pope, Dr. Johnson, John Wesley, Adam Smith the economist, and many others. In 1776, the first step against it was taken by a certain David Hartley who moved in the House of Commons that " the slave trade was contrary to the Laws of God and the rights of men," but the motion failed. In 1783, the Quakers formed a society to discourage it, following the example of the American Quakers who had done the same thing some years previously. Four years after the English Quakers founded their society, a committee was formed for the abolition of the slave trade. From 1788-1806 the question was frequently before Parliament, but in spite of the efforts by Wilberforce nothing was done. In 1807 a Bill was passed abolishing the slave trade, which however continued to exist as the penalties against it were not severe enough. In 1811, however, it was made a crime punishable by transportation and this year really marks the end of the slave trade in British Dominions. But it was not until 1833 that slaves were actually freed.

After Haghe *Rischgitz*

THE BRISTOL RIOTS

The riots and disturbances, like the Peterloo Massacre, which preceded the Reform Bill of 1832 were probably more violent in Bristol, where conditions were very bad, than anywhere else. It was unfortunate that the new police started by Sir Robert Peel were not in operation there when the terrible riot of 1831 broke out.

From the picture by Benjamin Robert Haydon *Spencer Arnold*

RETURN OF THE CONQUEROR

A picture of the Duke of Wellington surveying the scene of his former victory at Waterloo. Wellington's opposition to the reform of the franchise made him extremely unpopular and the scene when he was hooted by the mob on the anniversary of Waterloo must have been one of the most bitter in his life.

From the picture by F. W. Reynolds

Kischgttz

AN IMPORTANT STEP TOWARDS VOTES FOR ALL

William IV is here seen in the House of Lords giving his assent to the Reform Bill of 1832. By this Bill, which had caused so much strife, contention and bloodshed, all householders occupying houses rented at £10 a year and over were given a vote; seats were taken from small towns and villages and were at last given to the large manufacturing towns. This Bill paved the way to the fair representation and universal suffrage which exists to-day for it was followed by other Bills which further extended the franchise.

THE END OF THE "ROTTEN BOROUGH"

Sometimes a Member of Parliament would represent just a mound of earth where a village had once existed. The Reform Bill of 1832 did away with these "RottenBoroughs." This cartoon shows the reformers heaving away at the tree representing the Rotten Boroughs, while the die-hard Tories are endeavouring to prop it up. The Tories thought that reform would upset the constitution of the country, and continued to oppose it in spite of demonstrations in favour of it. The introduction of further and more drastic bills showed them to be wrong.

From a contemporary cartoon. Rischgitz

From the picture by Sir George Hayter Rischgitz

THE FIRST REFORMED PARLIAMENT

The result of the 1832 Reform Bill was that large numbers of the middle class, respectable tradesmen and small merchants, became a political force, while the power of the landed proprietors and aristocracy was considerably lessened. Parliamentarians thought that this Bill was, if anything, too radical, but the events of the next few years were to prove that the majority of the country thought differently from them.

From a contemporary cartoon   *Rischgitz*

EARLY DAYS OF THE TRADE UNIONS

By an Act of 1800 it was made illegal for workers to combine together for the purpose of demanding improved conditions, but in 1825 this law was relaxed so that it only concerned those who contemplated violence—and a rapid spread of the Trades Union movement resulted. This cartoon is a satire on the trade unionists of the time. Pouring ridicule on the Trade Union movement was one of many attempts to crush it.

From the picture by Havell   *Rischgitz*

THE OLD HOUSES OF PARLIAMENT

In 1834 the Houses of Parliament were burned down and all that remains to-day of the old buildings is the magnificent Westminster Hall where the big trials used to be held. This is a view of the old buildings from outside Westminster Abbey. It can be seen that they are without the famous clock known as Big Ben and the impressive spires which rise above the modern buildings. Westminster looked very different then.

From the picture by Pollard   *Rischgitz*

THE NEW GENERAL POST OFFICE

The old Post Office had been in Lombard Street, but during the years 1825–1829 a large new building was put up in St. Martins-le-Grand. Here is a view of the new Post Office with the mail coaches ready to start. The end of the eighteenth and the beginning of the nineteenth centuries saw great developments in the postal service, though obviously with horse drawn traffic they could not be nearly so efficient as they are to-day.

From the picture by Pollard   *Rischgitz*

MAILS HELD UP BY A SNOWSTORM

About this time England underwent some very hard winters and the Thames was frozen over several times. Here is a view of the great snow storm of 1836 which made the roads, never very good at the best of times, impassable for heavy traffic. The mails are being transferred from the heavy mail coaches which are stuck in a snow drift to the lighter and more easily managed post-chaise, to take them to their destination.

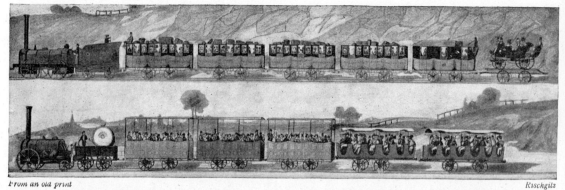

From an old print   *Rischgitz*

PASSENGER TRAINS ON THE LIVERPOOL-MANCHESTER RAILWAY

This picture shows the first- and second-class railway carriages in use in 1830. The second-class passengers had to sit on hard seats and were exposed to the wet and cold, but the first class had "good glass windows and cushions on the seats." Eventually the third class were improved and the second class abolished.

From an old print   *Rischgitz*

GOODS TRAINS ON THE LIVERPOOL-MANCHESTER RAILWAY

The Liverpool-Manchester Railway proved an enormous success—far greater than even its most ardent supporter imagined. People who had at first looked on railways with suspicion and alarm now went railway mad and enormous sums were invested in new ventures which were commenced all over the country.

From an old print   *Rischgitz*

ANOTHER EARLY RAILWAY

One of the new ventures was the Glasgow–Ganskirk Railway which was started in 1831. By 1840 there were as many as 1,331 miles of line laid down, and in 1845 there was such a mad speculation in railways that a financial crisis, reminiscent of the very disastrous South Sea Bubble, followed two years later.

From an old print
Rischgitz

A STRANGE CONTRAPTION

Here is a steam carriage which ran between London and Birmingham in 1832 and was capable of taking fifty passengers. There was much prejudice, however, against steam carriages, particularly from those who were financially interested in horse-haulage, and they were nearly driven off the roads by adverse legislation.

From an old print
Rischgitz

A STEAM OMNIBUS

Steam carriages still managed to survive and here is an "omnibus" which started running in 1833. Laws against them, however, became more and more strict and the death blow really came in 1865 when it was laid down that there should be three persons in charge of the machine ; a man should walk in front with a red flag to warn the populace of its approach ; and that the speed limit should be four miles per hour.

After Rowlandson and Pugin　　　　　　　　　　　　　　　　　　　　　　*Rischgitz*

BILLINGSGATE FISH MARKET

Billingsgate on the Thames, which formerly had an anchorage for small boats, has for centuries been London's fish market. When the fish arrives in the early morning remarkable scenes of activity used to—and still do—take place before the fish is finally distributed to all parts of the metropolis and outlying districts.

From an old print　　　　　　　　　　　　　　　　　　　　　　　　　*Rischgitz*

A NINETEENTH CENTURY BAZAAR

A picture of a bazaar held by the ladies of London in aid of the Charing Cross Hospital at the home of a John Penn, Esq., in St. James's Park. It is interesting to note the fashions of the period—particularly the men who are wearing darker clothes, and top hats which would have been impossible in the days of wigs. Hospitals a hundred years ago were supported by much the same methods as are used to-day.

Australian National Travel Association

THE BEGINNINGS OF A GREAT CITY

In 1836 Melbourne, named after the English Prime Minister, consisted of thirteen dwellings, eight of which were mud huts. Due to a constant stream of settlers its population by 1841 had grown to 11,000, and the discovery of gold at Ballarat ten years later brought the population up to the neighbourhood of 100,000.

Australian National Travel Association

MELBOURNE TO-DAY

Melbourne, the capital of Victoria, a prosperous commercial centre with a busy port, is the most populous city in Australia. This picture, showing the modern city with its tramways, motor cars and impressive buildings, forms a very remarkable contrast with the one above showing Melbourne in the nineteenth century.

From the picture by R. Caton Woodville   By permission of "The Illustrated London News"

THE GATEWAY TO INDIA

Aden, situated in a country with very little rain, has been a port since earliest times and possessed water tanks said to date from 1,700 B.C. In 1839 the British took Aden from the Arabs and built a system of aqueducts leading from wells inland to replace the old water supply. This picture shows the new irrigation system being inspected by the native and British soldiers. The building of these aqueducts was a brilliant engineering feat.

QUEEN VICTORIA

1837-1901

WILLIAM IV died on June 20, 1837, and he was succeeded by his niece Victoria, a girl of seventeen.

The young queen kept in office the existing ministry under Lord Melbourne, whom she chose as her adviser. Melbourne, with his tact, experience and charm, had a great influence over the queen's early life. It was unsafe, however, to rely exclusively on a purely party leader, since there was no guarantee that he would remain in office. Consequently, it was an excellent thing when, in 1840, she married Albert of Coburg, whose advice and help were quite independent of any party prejudice. The Prince Consort, as he was called, was at first unpopular owing to his stiff German ways, but his hard work, his sincerity, his loyalty to the queen and the country made him liked more and more as time went on.

TROUBLE AT HOME

In 1839 an unfortunate situation had arisen. Melbourne's ministry had been defeated and Sir Robert Peel, when asked to take office, refused to do so unless Victoria dismissed her Whig ladies-in-waiting. The queen refused to do so and Melbourne had to be recalled. It was felt that the Crown had gone against the country's wishes by making it impossible for Peel to take office after he had been successful at a general election, and the tense situation was further aggravated by the Chartist riots. The Chartists were the radical reformers who, not content with the Reform Bill of 1832, wanted universal franchise for men. Mass meetings were held all over the country ; great excitement prevailed and finally a monster petition, supposed to contain five million names, was presented to Parliament. On a closer scrutiny, however, this petition was found to contain only two million names, many of which were forgeries. The ridicule which was heaped upon Chartism after this fiasco killed it as a movement, though many of its ideas were later incorporated in the second and third Reform Bills.

Meanwhile, Peel had come into power in 1841.

There had been much agitation against the Corn Laws which imposed a duty on foreign corn. This helped the farmers who said that if the Corn Laws were repealed they would be ruined ; but it did not help the people who were unable to buy bread at a reasonable price. Under the leadership of John Bright and Richard Cobden, the Anti-Corn Law League was started and there were many demonstrations against this law which protected a small section of the community at the expense of the rest. The potato famine in Ireland brought matters to a crisis. The Irish, unable to get their staple food of potatoes and unable to buy bread because of its high price, were in a state of starvation. Peel, once a supporter of the Corn Laws, now saw that it was ridiculous to put a tax on food when people were starving and he reduced the tax on corn to a nominal sum in spite of great opposition from Parliament.

FOREIGN AFFAIRS

Europe was, at this time, in a very troubled state. The Congress of Vienna in 1815 had taken no thought for the national feeling of small countries or for growing democratic ideas, but had simply aimed at settling Europe as it had been before the Napoleonic wars. In 1848, Europe flared up and there were revolutions in Paris, Vienna, Berlin, and Rome.

The policy of Palmerston, now Foreign Minister, with regard to these revolutions was the same as Canning's had been in the reign of George IV—namely, intervention against any other nation which intervened in the affairs of another country. This policy, however, had its dangers. Canning, by joining with Russia to help the Greeks against the Turks, had greatly increased Russian power and great fear was felt that Russia wished to expand her sphere of influence not only in Europe but in the East.

Russia, her northern coast being icebound and useless in winter, wanted an outlet into the Mediterranean, and when she seized two Turkish provinces at the mouth of the Danube, England joined with France to resist the Russian advance and the Crimean War ensued in 1854.

England had been so long at peace that she had forgotten how to carry on a war. The troops in the Crimea fought magnificently, but owing to the inefficiency of the higher command they were not properly armed, fed, or clothed. There was a great outcry at home and Palmerston was made Prime Minister in the hope that he would remedy matters. This he did, and in 1856 Sebastopol, the key position in the war, was captured and peace was made.

Through the incompetence of the generals and the heroism of the troops in the Crimean War shines one figure who has had a profound influence on English life. Florence Nightingale, a young Englishwoman who went to the Crimea in 1854 and organised hospitals, raised money at home to carry on an efficient nursing organisation and did a great deal to improve the terrible hospital conditions she found there. Florence Nightingale was not only the founder of modern nursing organisation, but she has had a great influence on the opening of men's minds to the possibilities of what a trained and educated woman is able to do.

INDIAN MUTINY

The year following the end of the Crimean War occurred an event which alarmed the nation far more than that had done—the Indian Mutiny. Though the mutiny was confined to the army, its causes were really indicative of the feeling of the whole country. For some time western institutions had been introduced more and more into India, and when Dalhousie became Governor-General he accelerated this practice and developed British possessions by annexing native states when the ruler died without an heir. Though Dalhousie's object was to benefit the natives, it was felt that Britain was seeking to undermine the whole of Indian culture and life. The chief danger of the mutiny was that if British influence were lessened to any great extent, the way would be thrown open to Russia to usurp British authority in India. The defeat of Russia in the Crimean War and the final suppression of the mutiny, however, put an end to any fears about Russia's aggression either in Europe or in the East.

THREE GREAT STATESMEN

Palmerston had become Prime Minister during the Crimean War and for nine years he was the dominant figure in English politics. At his death he was succeeded by Gladstone, who had been his great political opponent but who he knew would follow him in office. During the period when these two men were in power, great changes took place throughout Europe. Italy, formerly a collection of different states, became united into one nation and Prussia, under the leadership of Bismarck, dominated the rest of the German States, absorbed Austria, and Germany as well as Italy became for the first time a united nation.

At home, Gladstone effected many reforms. In 1887 he put through the second Reform Bill which gave votes to an even wider section of the community than the 1832 Bill had done; he endeavoured to settle the Irish troubles, though his refusal to grant Home Rule left the main problem unsolved. In 1870 the Elementary Education Act was passed which gave to every child the opportunity of learning to read and write.

Gladstone had to give way to Disraeli in 1874 and the latter ministry is marked by trouble with Ireland stirred up by the Irish Home Rule leader, Parnell, and by a renewal of the conflict between Russia and Turkey. Turkey had been treating her Christian subjects with extreme barbarity and they had called in the Russians to help them. Feeling in England was against the Turks on account of their atrocities, but there was also considerable fear of Russian aggression and Disraeli sent an English fleet to help the Turks. Before war broke out, however, a settlement was reached by which Bulgaria was freed from Turkish rule and the Sultan gave an undertaking not to persecute his Christian subjects.

Gladstone came back to power in 1880 and he had to deal with risings in Egypt, now important to England since Disraeli had purchased shares in the Suez Canal, and the Irish question of Home Rule which eventually led to his fall. Before this, however, he had passed the third Reform Bill, which meant that every householder in town and country now had a vote.

THE BOER WAR

The chief event of the latter part of Victoria's reign was the Boer War. Repeated quarrels between the Dutch and English in South Africa led to war with the two Dutch colonies, Transvaal and the Orange Free State. The English at first underestimated the strength of the Boers, but Lord Roberts and then Lord Kitchener gradually turned the tide and the Boers surrendered in 1902. Meanwhile Victoria had died in 1901.

From the picture by Wells

Rischgttz

VICTORIA, QUEEN OF ENGLAND

William IV died in 1837 and he was succeeded by his niece, Victoria, a girl of only eighteen years of age. Here is a picture of the Archbishop of Canterbury and the Marquess of Cunningham announcing to Victoria the news of her accession. They had arrived while the princess was asleep. She was aroused and came down to see them in her dressing gown with her hair flowing over her shoulders. This young girl was to rule England from 1837-1901—the longest and in some ways the greatest reign that this country has ever known.

From the drawing by Campion *Rischgitz*

QUEEN VICTORIA'S CORONATION PROCESSION

Amid scenes of great rejoicing, the Coronation of Queen Victoria took place on June 28, 1838. This event not only ushered in a new reign, but a new era in British history. The Victorian era stands for decency in public life in contrast to the looseness of the Hanoverians. It was a period of imperial and industrial expansion.

From the picture by Parris *Rischgitz*

THE CROWNING OF VICTORIA

Not only did a very large number of visitors come to London for the Coronation but three important foreign ambassadors, Marshal Soult, the Napoleonic general, who received a great welcome ; the magnificently attired Prince Esterhazy of Austria ; and Savvim Effendi of Turkey who was so surprised at the whole proceedings that he could only mutter, "All this for a Woman!" This picture shows the actual coronation.

THE QUEEN AT HER FIRST COUNCIL MEETING

The queen wisely kept the ministers who were in office when she came to the throne. Lord Melbourne acted as her adviser on matters appertaining to government, and by his courtesy and fatherliness he soon earned her devotion. These early contacts influenced her outlook on politics for the whole of her long reign.

THE MARRIAGE OF THE QUEEN

In 1840, Victoria married Prince Albert of Coburg, afterwards known as the Prince Consort. At first he was unpopular, but his devotion to the queen and his hard work made him liked as time went on. It was advantageous that the young queen should be advised, not by a party politician, but by an independent helper.

EUSTON STATION IN 1837

Throughout the nineteenth century railways continued to develop rapidly, and it is about this time that the beginnings of trunk lines made their appearance. Here is an early picture of Euston Station with a first-class carriage in the foreground and a number of third-class carriages can be seen at the far platform.

THE STEAMSHIP REPLACES THE SAILING BOAT

The first practical steamship, the *Charlotte Dundas*, was tried on the Clyde in 1802. This was quickly followed by others, and from 1815 onwards, steamship companies started to run coastal services to Scotland. Here is the *Sirius*, a 700 ton ship which in 1838 sailed from Cork to New York in seventeen days. The early steamships were built of wood and had paddles instead of screws, their engines being supplemented by sails.

From the picture by Paul Haray   *By permission of "Pictorial Education"*

TRADING WITH NATIVES IN NEW ZEALAND

New Zealand was first mapped by Captain Cook who annexed the country in the name of the British Government. The Government, however, refused to have anything to do with the annexation, and it was not until 1840 that Hobson landed in northern New Zealand with official permission to buy the country from the natives. This action was just in time to forestall the French who had a similar project. Hobson founded Auckland and bands of settlers arrived, but owing to the procrastination of the government at home and wars with the natives New Zealand passed a very unhappy time until a strong government was instituted.

From the picture by R. Caton Woodville

By permission of "The Illustrated London News"

MAKING A TREATY WITH A SULTAN

The British made their first important settlement in Borneo in 1609. The usual collision with the Dutch followed, and British influence almost disappeared until, in 1847, Sir James Brooke made a treaty with the Sultan of Borneo who, on his part, agreed to part with none of his territory without British permission. Thus did Britain prevent the interference of any other country which might have led to foreign control.

From the picture by Paul Hardy   *By permission of "Pictorial Education"*

SOUTH AFRICAN SETTLERS ATTACKED BY KAFFIRS

For one hundred and forty-three years prior to 1795, the Cape was under the administration of the Dutch East India Company. In 1806, it was handed over to the British who were at war with France and Holland. Both the Dutch and English were in continual conflict with the natives who attempted to bar their progress.

From a contemporary print   *Rischgitz*

SORTING THE NEW PENNY POST

In 1839, a Bill was passed establishing a penny post. At the same time, Parliamentary franking was abolished, and stamps were introduced. These reforms were brought about by Sir Rowland Hill.

From a contemporary print   *Rischgitz*

WATERLOO BRIDGE IN EARLY VICTORIAN DAYS

Here is a steam carriage of 1840 approaching the toll gate on Waterloo Bridge. The invention of the petrol engine, and the subsequent development of the modern motor car, eventually spelt the death-knell of steam carriages. Even more rapid progress would have been made if it had not been for the antagonism of certain sections of the community. Strict laws limited their use, and heavy tolls made their running uneconomical.

From a contemporary print   *Rischgitz*

AN ATTEMPT ON THE QUEEN'S LIFE

In 1840, an attempt was made on the queen's life by a young man named Edward Oxford, who fired two shots as the queen was driving up Constitution Hill with the Prince Consort. In view of this attack, a Bill was hurried through Parliament enacting that if the queen died before the heir to the throne came of age, Prince Albert should become sole Regent. Fortunately the queen was to live for more than sixty years.

From a contemporary picture ᴋᴉschgtz

THE BAPTISM OF EDWARD VII

In 1841, the queen gave birth to her second child, a son, and this event "filled the measure of the queen's domestic happiness" as she herself said in her speech at the opening of Parliament in 1842. The following year, the young Prince Edward was baptised, the King of Prussia, who was visiting England at the time, attending the ceremony. It was sixty years before the young prince came to the throne and during this time he fitted himself for the high office he was destined for by travelling abroad and in performing public duties.

From an old print   *Rischgitz*

FACTORY LIFE IN THE EARLY NINETEENTH CENTURY

Conditions in the industrial centres were appalling. Factories were insanitary, and coal mines dangerous. But women and little children had to work in them for incredibly long hours and almost no pay. There was no education, and the men, women and children were treated almost worse than animals. This picture contrasts strikingly—the rich man, his son (in the foreground) and the poorly-clad, wretched factory workers.

From the picture by Baxter   *Rischgitz*

THE CHIMNEY SWEEP

In the nineteenth century the method of sweeping chimneys was very different to that of to-day. The chimneys were much larger and small boys were employed to climb up them and brush the soot off instead of using long brushes as they do now. Those who have read Charles Kingsley's *Water Babies* will have some idea of the miserable life those poor chimney sweeps used to lead and of the treatment they received. It was not until the year 1870 that laws were passed ensuring that all children should go to school.

CHILDREN AT WORK IN A ROPE FACTORY
Children were employed in factories because of cheapness. Here are two small boys looking after machines.

TERRIBLE CONDITIONS IN A COAL MINE
A young child pulling 2-5 cwts. of coal, in a truck attached to the waist, along a passage 16-20 inches high.

THE END OF THE DAY
The long hours of work and the dreadful factory conditions made it impossible for children to keep healthy.

From the portrait by Frith   *Mansell*

A GREAT NOVELIST AND REFORMER

Charles Dickens is recognised as being one of England's greatest writers. Few other men have been able to portray English life—both humorous and serious—as well as he has done. He not only makes us laugh at our own follies, but weep at the miseries of others. He draws our attention to the evils of the schools, workhouses and other institutions of his time, but he never forgets that he is a storyteller and not a moralist. Dickens was well qualified to speak of these evils because, when a youngster, he underwent many of them himself.

From the picture by G. Dawe in the National Library of Wales, Aberystwyth   *Rischgitz*

THE REBECCA RIOTS

In 1843, serious riots broke out in South Wales against the excessive charges at toll-gates. The rioters took their name from the Biblical quotation concerning Rebecca : "Let thy seed possess the gate of those which hate them." Many of the rioters were dressed as women, and they became so violent that numbers of soldiers and police had to be sent from London to quell them. This picture shows what these rioters looked like.

From an old print   *Rischgitz*

AN EARLY FLYING MACHINE

For some years balloon flights had been common, but in spite of many experiments with models, no one had yet succeeded in building a practical flying machine. In 1843, Mr. Henson made "the greatest attempt hitherto to construct an aerial ship. A trial, however, soon showed its defects, though it drew the attention and commendation of the scientists of both Europe and America." The first successful aeroplane flew in 1903.

Rischgitz

MANGLING THE CORN BILL

The Corn Laws were hated by the people because they made the price of bread so high. The landowners, on the other hand, benefited by them because they kept foreign corn out of the country. Consequently the aristocracy, who were landowners, attempted to "mangle" any Bill for their repeal which was put forward.

After Herbert
Rischgitz

THE ANTI-CORN LAW LEAGUE

In 1838, two men, Cobden and Bright, formed a league to get the Corn Laws repealed. Here is Cobden addressing one of his numerous meetings. In the end, Peel was persuaded by Cobden and the necessity of dealing with the famine in Ireland, to repeal the Corn Laws, and in 1846, the Bill went through Parliament in spite of great opposition from the small section of the community which gained by their existence.

A CHARTIST DEMONSTRATION

A certain section of the country, known as Chartists, not content with the reforms of 1832, and being in favour of universal suffrage for men, held demonstrations and eventually started riots all over the country. The movement ended when their petition to Parliament of five million names turned out to be largely a collection of forgeries. The reforms demanded by the Chartists were, however, destined to be eventually passed.

RIOTS IN IRELAND

Three questions have always troubled Ireland—Religion, Land and Home Rule. Wellington had partly settled the first by his Catholic Emancipation Act, but after the famine of 1845, the second two gave much trouble. In 1848, O'Brien started a rising in an endeavour to obtain Home Rule, but this was quickly put down, and although he was sentenced to death he was eventually pardoned. Further troubles were to come.

From a contemporary print   *Rischgitz*

KENT v. SUSSEX AT BRIGHTON, 1849

The first recorded county cricket match was played between Surrey and Middlesex as early as 1730, but it was not until 1872 that any effort was made to start systematic county cricket, the M.C.C. offering a cup to the winner of a county competition. The scheme fell through, however, and county cricket did not formally start until 1890. It is interesting to note the top hats which these early cricketers wore when playing.

From the picture by Frith   *Rischgitz*

HOLIDAY TIME ON RAMSGATE SANDS

Ramsgate has for long been a popular watering place. Here is the beach about 1854. It is interesting to note the change in fashions since the Georgian period; clothes had lost their elegance, they tended to be rather drab in colour and were usually unsuitable for anything but a formal occasion. Certainly the fashions of that time form a contrast to those of to-day! The people, however, seem to be thoroughly enjoying themselves.

From an old print Rischgitz

EDWARD VII'S FIRST PUBLIC FUNCTION

Prince Edward, the eldest son and second child of Queen Victoria, was born in 1841. Here he is, a small boy of eight, with his elder sister, performing his first public duty of opening the Coal Exchange. He went to both Oxford and Cambridge; was made a colonel in the army; travelled extensively abroad; and in 1863 first took his seat in the House of Lords. The same year he was married to Princess Alexandra of Denmark.

From the picture by Lieutenant Jones Rischgitz

THE FLEET CHEER THE QUEEN IN CORK HARBOUR

In 1849 the queen, her husband and two children paid a visit to Ireland, landing at Cork Harbour, which afterwards became known as Queenstown, now Cobh. *The Times* wrote of this visit : "Such a night of rejoicing has never been beheld in the ancient capital of Ireland since it first arose on the banks of the Liffey."

From the picture by F. C. Lewis   *Rischgitz*

A MESSAGE FROM THE QUEEN

Though Queen Victoria did not become Empress of India until 1876, she always kept in close contact with the Indian rulers. Here we see a Maharajah receiving a communication from the queen on the occasion of his Durbar on November 27, 1851. There was, at this time, much unrest in India which eventually came to a climax in the form of the Indian Mutiny. This impressive ceremony gives no indication of the state of unrest.

From the picture by S. Reynolds   *Rischgitz*

THE QUEEN VISITS THE GREAT EXHIBITION

A number of exhibitions were held in the earlier part of the nineteenth century, but the Great Exhibition held in London in 1851 was the first which was definitely international in character. It was held in a building, covering twenty acres, in Hyde Park and the Prince Consort acted as President. The main structure, known as the Crystal Palace, was afterwards re-built in South London. It was destroyed by fire in December, 1936.

Photo J. E. Bulloz   Musée Carnavalet

THE FIRST ENGLISH SOVEREIGN TO TRAVEL BY RAIL

The queen first travelled by rail in 1842 and she enjoyed the sensation so much that she continued to make frequent use of railway travel. She may be seen here in her special coach in 1843 chatting to Louis Philippe of France who visited England in an endeavour to cement the *entente cordiale* with this country.

After M. Alophe   Rischgitz

A ROYAL GROUP

Queen Victoria was always on good terms with foreign sovereigns. In 1842, she and the Prince Consort paid a visit to Louis Philippe of France, and the following year he returned the compliment and was presented with the Order of the Garter. Here we see Napoleon III, Queen Victoria, Empress Eugenie and the Prince Consort on a state visit to the opera in 1855. Louis Philippe was deposed and Napoleon III took his place.

From the picture by Jerry Barrett   *Rischgitz*

THE ROYAL FAMILY AT BROMPTON HOSPITAL

The queen and the Prince Consort took great interest in the affairs of the Crimean War, and they may be seen here, with their family, talking to one of the wounded soldiers, home from his campaigns in the Crimea, in the Brompton Hospital at Chatham. Such work gained the queen and her husband the love of the country.

From the picture by R. Caton Woodville   *By permission of Henry Graves & Co. Ltd.*

THE CHARGE OF THE LIGHT BRIGADE

The Crimean War is notable for the bravery of the soldiers against overwhelming odds. During the operations at Balaclava, a confused order led to the Light Brigade charging magnificently straight at the enemy guns, and in the face of a deadly fire they reached the guns, killed the gunners and even attacked the cavalry behind, but the position was hopeless and only a third of the original squadron returned to their lines.

After W. Simpson   *Rischgitz*

THE LADY WITH THE LAMP

Florence Nightingale, hearing of the terrible state of the hospitals in the Crimea, set out with thirty-seven assistants to look after the nursing there. She did marvellous work, largely reducing the number of casualties by her skill. Her influence was responsible for bringing about many much needed hospital reforms at home.

From an old print   *Rischgitz*

PROCLAIMING PEACE AT CHARING CROSS

The Crimean War came to an end with the defeat of Russia in 1856, and by the Treaty of Paris, the Black Sea was made neutral and all warships excluded from it; Sebastopol ceased to be a naval base, and Turkey was admitted as a European power. The Turks, however, continued to misgovern their Christian subjects who applied to Russia for help. The Russo-Turkish War ensued. England then made ready in support of the Turks to prevent Russian aggrandizement, but the quarrel was settled before we entered the war.

From the picture by Sir J. Gilbert   *Rischgitz*

THE ROYAL FAMILY RECEIVE THE GUARDS

Throughout the Crimean War Queen Victoria and the Prince Consort followed the operations with the keenest attention. Here is the queen, with her family, showing a very keen interest in the soldiers and her gratitude to them for their victory by receiving a company of the Guards on their return to England.

From the picture by Phillips   *Rischgitz*

MARRIAGE OF THE PRINCESS ROYAL

Queen Victoria and the Prince Consort led a very happy domestic life amid their growing family. A year after the birth in 1853 of their youngest child, Princess Beatrice, the Princess Royal married Prince Frederick, later the King of Prussia, and was granted a dowry of £40,000 and £8,000 a year for life by Parliament.

From the picture by Henry O'Neill Rischgitz

OUTWARD BOUND FOR THE EAST

Troops saying farewell to their wives and families before sailing for India. The Mutiny, which broke out in 1857, was caused by the introduction of western ideas which were looked upon with suspicion, and by the British policy of annexing native territories. The first outbreak occurred when the native soldiers were required to grease their rifles with what they thought was pig's fat, which by their religion they were forbidden to touch. The Mutiny was confined to the Ganges valley, and many of the native princes remained loyal.

From the picture by Sir J. Noel Paton   *By permission of Mr. Alexander Whitelaw*

THEIR FATE IN THE BALANCE

At Delhi, the mutineers were besieged until the city was eventually captured by Nicholson. At Cawnpore, a British garrison with some five hundred women and children were brutally massacred, and at Lucknow a small garrison maintained a magnificent resistance. Here is a group of unhappy people at Lucknow not knowing what their fate will be. The relieving troops, however, can just be seen coming through the doorway on the left. These troops were under the command of Sir Colin Campbell who evacuated the women and children.

After Barker *Rischgitz*

THE RELIEF OF LUCKNOW

General Havelock, in spite of marching 126 miles and fighting four battles in nine days, reached Cawnpore too late to save the garrison there; but with the help of Sir James Outram he took Lucknow after desperate fighting and was himself besieged there. On the day he was relieved, more than two months later, he died of hunger and exhaustion. The picture on the previous page shows the arrival of the relieving troops.

From the picture by J. Phillip *Rischgitz*

PALMERSTON SPEAKING IN THE HOUSE OF COMMONS

Palmerston entered politics as a young man and for many years held a subordinate position as Secretary-at-War. In 1830, he became Minister for Foreign Affairs, and for over twenty years exercised a dominant influence on the foreign policy of this country. It was not until 1855 that he became Prime Minister during the Crimean War, which he saw to a successful conclusion. He died in 1865 after over fifty years' service to his country.

From the picture by Collier   *Mansell*

A GREAT SCIENTIST OF VICTORIAN DAYS

In 1859, Charles Darwin produced a book, *The Origin of Species*. His theory was that man's evolution could be traced from animals and that the fittest species have survived, aroused tremendous conflict among educated people. Many considered it an attack on religion, but the theory of evolution gained ground, and with some modifications, it is accepted to-day. Though while at Cambridge "disbelief crept over him at a very slow rate, but was at last complete," yet he was never antagonistic to the Church and supported it in its social services.

From an old print   Rischgitz

PAST AND PRESENT IN 1859

By the middle of the nineteenth century railways had come to stay. Here is the old world typified by a broken-down coach and a ramshackle farm house contrasted with the railway and modern buildings of that time. It is very interesting indeed to compare the "present" of 1855 with the "present" of to-day.

From an early photograph   Rischgitz

A NINETEENTH CENTURY 'BUS

The steam car had proved impractical, and it was not until 1885 that Gottlieb Daimler invented the internal combustion engine. Horse carriages, however, continued to hold their own as public conveyances on the roads. This vehicle which was in use in 1868 is obviously the forerunner of the modern motor omnibus.

From an old print   *Rischgitz*

THE FIRST LONDON TRAM

The first tramway was laid down in New York as early as 1832, but it was not introduced into England until 1860. The advantage of these horse-drawn trams over the horse buses was not one of speed but of comfort because by running on rails they were not subject to the roughness of the roads which at that time were very bad. Here is the first tram which ran from Marble Arch to Notting Hill Gate in 1861.

From an old print   *Rischgitz*

THE FIRST UNDERGROUND RAILWAY

The first underground train ran from Edgware Road to King's Cross in 1853. Steam was used for many years, but in 1886, the first line was run under the Thames, and steam being unsuitable, it was intended that it should be worked by a cable. However, electric power, which had been developed by that time, was used instead. Since that time the Underground has steadily advanced in speed, efficiency and comfort.

After J. Barrett   *Rischgitz*

THE PRINCE CONSORT ATTENDS HIS LAST RECEPTION

The Prince Consort died at Windsor in 1861, and the queen, who had been devoted to him, was heartbroken.
The prince had gained the increasing respect of the people and monuments were erected to him all over the
country, the most famous of which are the imposing Albert Hall and the Albert Memorial in Kensington.

From the picture by R. Dudley   *Rischgitz*

RECOVERING THE ATLANTIC CABLE FROM THE OCEAN BED

The work of laying an Atlantic Telegraph Cable was started in 1857, and after great difficulties completed,
but unfortunately, after a short period, it did not prove a success. The next attempt came in 1865, but when
the *Great Eastern*, the ship which was chartered for the work, had laid 1,200 miles, the cable snapped, and
it was not until the following year that it was recovered and an enormous engineering feat accomplished.

After Gilbert   *Rischgitz*

THE CABINET DECIDE TO SEND AN EXPEDITION TO ABYSSINIA

A quarrel had arisen with Abyssinia over the murder of the British Consul in 1860, and the subsequent imprisonment of a party of Britons who were treated with extreme barbarity. In 1867, it was decided to send a punitive expedition which eventually released the prisoners who had undergone terrible sufferings.

After Louis Dickinson   *Rischgitz*

GLADSTONE BECOMES PRIME MINISTER

Palmerston, who was opposed to any violent reform, had foreseen the rise of Gladstone and had prophesied that when he came into power there would be "strange doings" in the country. Gladstone's first administration lasted from 1868-1874, and during it many reforms were put through, the chief of which was the Education Act of 1870 which set up school boards and gave elementary education to every child.

"NEW CROWNS FOR OLD"

In 1876, Disraeli, now Lord Beaconsfield, suggested that the queen should assume the title of Empress of India, but the Bill which he introduced into Parliament, though it was passed, met with much opposition because it was felt that he was simply satisfying a whim of the queen. Disraeli had in fact a very sound reason for his suggestion: he wished to increase the loyalty of the Indians by bringing them into closer contact with the Crown. Disraeli first took office in 1874 after leading the Conservatives for thirty years.

THE LION'S SHARE

The Suez Canal was completed in 1869, its success being largely due to the efforts and ability of a Frenchman, de Lesseps. Though the canal was built by a French company, the Khedive of Egypt held the majority of shares. These, Disraeli bought in 1875 and thereby gained for England the controlling interest in the canal and the key to the route to India. England has since had control of both the eastern and western entrances to the Mediterranean.

Reproduced by permission of the proprietors of "Punch"   *Rischgitz*

From the picture by S. C. Hall   *Rischgitz*

THE PRINCE OF WALES IN INDIA

The visit of the Prince of Wales to India—the first visit by a member of the English royal family—was calculated to bring the Indian Princes into closer contact with the Crown. Here is the Prince of Wales investing the Maharajah of Jaipur with the Order of the Star of India at Calcutta in 1876.

From the picture by C. D. Giles *Rischgitz*

SAVING THE GUNS IN AFGHANISTAN

British policy was to keep Afghanistan as a friendly independent power which would act as a barrier between British India and the Russians in the north. In 1877, however, negotiations with the Afghans broke down and as they made overtures to the Russians, British interests were endangered and war was declared in 1878.

From the picture by Louis Desanger *Rischgitz*

FROM CABUL TO KANDAHAR

During the Afghan War two settlements were made, but after each, hostilities broke out again. After the second outbreak, a British force was hopelessly defeated at Maiwand and was besieged in Kandahar. The nearest relieving troops were at Cabul, and General Roberts, with 10,000 men, marched 313 miles across mountainous country—illustrated in this picture—to rout the besieging army and relieve Kandahar.

Courtesy, *Agent-General for British Columbia*

THE BEGINNINGS OF CANADA'S FAIR CITY OF VANCOUVER

Here is Vancouver as it was in 1876 when it was first visited by the Earl of Dufferin and Ava, Governor-General of Canada. Vancouver has the finest natural harbour in the world and is now the western terminus of the Canadian Pacific Railway, and the centre of the lumbering trade in British Columbia and the west.

Courtesy of *Canadian Pacific Railway*

LAYING THE CANADIAN PACIFIC RAILWAY

In 1885, the Hon. D. A. Smith, later Lord Strathcona, drove in a golden spike to mark the completion of the building of the Canadian Pacific Railway from coast to coast. The work had been completed five years before the time contracted, and the existence of such a railway greatly increased the prosperity of the country.

GLADSTONE SPEAKING IN THE HOUSE OF COMMONS IN 1882

Gladstone's second administration lasted from 1880-1885. He was now an old man and his ministers were divided in their opinions as to his fitness, but he managed to pass two important Acts—the Married Woman's Property Act and the Third Reform Bill in 1881 which gave a vote to every man who owned his own house.

FOUR FAMOUS VICTORIAN POLITICIANS

Here is a picture of Devonshire, Dilke, Chamberlain and Gladstone. The last years of Gladstone's career are marked by his great struggle to get Home Rule for Ireland, and when his second Bill failed to pass the Lords in 1894, he retired from politics for ever. Gladstone's great opponent over the Home Rule question was the rising young statesman, Joseph Chamberlain who was later to be a great supporter of Tariff Reform.

DEATH OF GENERAL GORDON

Revolts in the Sudan led to the British Government deciding that it should be abandoned by its military and civil population. The evacuation was entrusted to Gordon who arrived in Khartoum in 1884. Eventually the rebel forces closed in round the town, relief came too late, and Gordon met his death two days before help came. In 1898 the Sudan was reconquered and, much to the dissatisfaction of France, put under British rule.

Rischgitz

QUEEN VICTORIA'S JUBILEE

June 20, 1887, was the fiftieth anniversary of the queen's accession to the throne, and a great Jubilee celebration was held to commemorate the event. The country threw itself wholeheartedly into the celebrations and every town and village in the realm did something to show its affection and loyalty to the queen.

Rischgitz

QUEEN VICTORIA'S DIAMOND JUBILEE

In 1896, the queen had reigned longer than any other English sovereign, and in 1897, when she had been sixty years on the throne, it was decided to hold a diamond jubilee celebration. At the suggestion of Chamberlain, Secretary for the Colonies, every part of the British Empire was represented by statesmen and soldiers. Here is shown the queen in her carriage surrounded by a cheering multitude outside St. Paul's.

Topical

QUEEN VICTORIA AND THREE FUTURE KINGS

Here is Queen Victoria with her son, Edward VII, her grandson, George V, and her great-grandson, King Edward VIII. Queen Victoria and her family have been ruling England for one hundred years and never has a line of sovereigns been so popular as Queen Victoria and the great kings who have followed her.

From the picture by C. D. Giles   *Rischgitz*

WAR IN SOUTH AFRICA

Quarrels between English and Dutch settlers led to a war in 1899 between the British and two independent Dutch States, the Transvaal and the Orange Free State. At first England underestimated the strength of the Boers and her troops were besieged in Ladysmith, in Mafeking and in Kimberley. Attempts to relieve these towns resulted in defeat, and Christmas, 1899, was a black period for England. The sending out of reinforcements, however, and the energy, first of Lord Roberts, and then of Lord Kitchener as commander-in-chief of the British forces, eventually turned the scales in favour of this country. Peace was made in 1902.

Rischgitz

LORD ROBERTS AT PRETORIA

Shortly after the disasters of December, 1899, Lord Roberts arrived in South Africa to take command. He had previously served in the Indian Mutiny and the Afghan Wars with great distinction, and under his brilliant leadership, in South Africa, the English troops soon reversed their former defeats. Under him, Pretoria and Bloemfontein, the capitals of the two Dutch republics, were captured and the strength of the Boer army broken.

From the picture by Frank Dodd, R.S.   *Rischgitz*

COLONEL PLUMER HELPS TO RELIEVE MAFEKING

Early in the war the British were besieged in Mafeking, but under Colonel Baden-Powell they held out until May, 1900. This picture shows Col. Plumer's attack from the north which was one of the subordinate actions leading to the relief of the town. Tremendous enthusiasm was aroused in England over its successful defence.

Rischgitz

THE QUEEN'S LAST JOURNEY

Though the queen was an old lady, and her health had been failing for some time, nevertheless her death on January 22, 1901, came as a shock to the country. She had ruled for so long, and been so much in the hearts of her subjects that it seemed impossible she should be no more. Her funeral, attended by five kings, was one of the saddest and most solemn events in our country's history. Among the chief mourners were King Edward VII, the King of Greece, the King of the Belgians, the King of Portugal and the German Emperor.

EDWARD VII

1901-1910

WHEN King Edward came to the throne in 1901, on the death of his mother, Queen Victoria, he was already sixty years of age and had gained much experience of public life. The queen, during the latter part of her reign, had been in virtual retirement and Edward had undertaken many of the duties which in the ordinary way would have fallen to her. Moreover, both before and after his accession he travelled extensively to India, Portugal, Germany, and Italy amongst other places, and consequently it is not surprising that the nation placed considerable trust in his ability to handle affairs both at home and abroad. His unceasing efforts to promote a friendly feeling between this country and other European powers earned him the title of " Edward the Peacemaker."

HOME POLITICS

At home his reign was marked by the rise to power of David Lloyd George, who was first elected to Parliament in 1890 and who was becoming more and more prominent on account of his attacks on the policy of Chamberlain. This policy was to develop and support the Empire and had been the real cause of the Boer War. Lloyd George by attacking it made himself extremely unpopular ; he earned the epithet of " pro-Boer " and on one occasion was forced to escape from a public meeting in disguise. Nevertheless, he continued in opposition against the Government, attacking the Empire tariffs, proposed by Chamberlain and supported by Balfour who was then Prime Minister.

At the general election in 1905 the Liberal party gained a large majority and Lloyd George took his first Cabinet post as President of the Board of Trade. In this capacity he acted in an efficient businesslike way, without over emphasising his own personality, until in 1908 he became Chancellor of the Exchequer under Asquith, when he showed himself to be the most vigorous politician of the time. His policy was one of social reform—to tax the rich to benefit the poor. In 1908 he put through an Old Age Pension Act by which the aged poor were given 5s. a week

pension. The following year he brought out his famous budget increasing the income-tax on the rich, putting a tax on public-houses, on the sale of spirits, and on the private ownership of land. This budget was rejected by the Lords, who thought it was endangering all private property, and a general election ensued in 1910. The Liberals were brought back with a diminished majority and the Lords were forced to sanction the budget. The quarrel with the Lords resulted in the Parliament Act of 1911 by which the Lords were only allowed to delay an Act and not veto it altogether. If it passed the Commons three times it automatically became law. A Bill was also passed by this Parliament which started a system of National Insurance. All lower-paid employees were to be helped by their employers to insure themselves against sickness. This proved to be an extremely beneficial measure and one of the most successful ever passed by Parliament.

King Edward had died the year before the quarrel with the House of Lords became acute. In 1910 Asquith had announced that if the Lords did not pass the budget he would appeal to the crown for help. This put the king, who did not wish to become mixed up in party politics, in a very difficult position and it is noteworthy that when making his speech at the opening of Parliament he used the phrase " in the opinion of my advisers " when speaking of the House of Lords. This phrase is very significant. It shows that the king, far from seeking to gain any personal power over Parliament, as many of the earlier kings of England had done, was only too anxious to step aside and let Parliament decide about its own affairs.

FOREIGN AFFAIRS

The majority of the country during Edward's reign was too absorbed in the excitement of home affairs to pay much attention to what was going on abroad. In spite of the king's efforts to establish friendly relations with foreign powers, and in spite of the work of Sir Edward Grey at the Foreign Office, storm clouds were already gathering over Europe which were to result in war.

Topical

THE SPORTING KING

By the time he came to the throne, Edward VII had gained much experience of public life and had travelled extensively. He was able to enter into close contact with all sections of the community and because of this, and his great interest in sport—his horses won the Derby twice—he was tremendously popular throughout the country. His efforts to promote European peace earned him the name of "Edward the Peacemaker." He was the first British monarch to take the title of "King of the British Dominions beyond the seas."

Through the tangle of European affairs up to 1914 it is possible to see one fundamental cause of the many troubles which were in progress. The rapid development of machinery, the increased production of goods, the growth of populations and the improvement of transport all brought the nations of the world into closer contact with one another, not in a spirit of friendliness, but of rivalry. The interests of European nations were no longer confined to Europe, but had spread all over the world. The necessity for foreign markets and the snatching of colonies to counterbalance the increased populations resulted in a state of friction throughout Europe and the world. For a long time Russia had been menacing the Indian frontier ; France hated Germany for seizing Alsace and Lorraine after the Franco-Prussian War ; Germany was jealous of France because of her activities in Morocco, and the Balkan States were seething with trouble.

GERMANY

This chaotic state of affairs was further aggravated by the situation in Germany. The German States had been united into one nation at a comparatively recent date by a combination of Prussian militarism and the genius of Bismarck, and being a new nation had not the outlets for trade and colonial expansion she would have liked. Moreover, the Kaiser's position was being weakened by a socialist element in the country, and to regain his diminishing power it was necessary for him to adopt a policy of force by stimulating the idea of militant imperialism. This policy was entirely in agreement with the Kaiser's own aggressive character and a rapidly arming Germany on the look out for colonies was not exactly conducive to peace.

In 1882 Germany had made a triple alliance with Austria and Italy, and the following year France made a dual alliance with Russia, so that even before the end of the century there were two antagonistic camps in Europe. For some years Britain kept entirely aloof, but between 1904-1907 she made an entente with Russia and France. Nevertheless, Britain still wished to keep on good terms with Germany, but when that country set about building a navy which rivalled that of Britain, whose existence depended on supremacy at sea, there began a race for armaments. Britain started increasing her navy ; Germany continued to arm, and the more she did so the closer did the liaison between England, France, and Russia become.

Though Britain had made no definite alliances, and though Germany was still angling after a promise of British neutrality in the event of war, it was always certain that a conflict between France and Germany would mean British support for the former as it was necessary for her to secure French co-operation in controlling the channel ports to safeguard her shipping.

RELATIONS WITH GERMANY

There was a strong feeling in Germany, however, that by making the triple entente Britain was pursuing a policy of encirclement ; that is to say, she was allying herself with the countries on German frontiers to weaken her position in any crisis which might arise. King Edward's visit to Germany did much to allay this suspicion, but nevertheless the general European situation remained the same. By the end of King Edward's reign there were two armed camps in Europe which, like a powder magazine, were ready to burst at any moment.

The death of King Edward in 1910 came as a profound shock to the nation. It was felt that his wisdom and his ability as a statesman would help to solve the serious Parliamentary troubles at home and to calm the troubled waters abroad.

THE WORK OF THE KING

Few men have been so popular. He brought the crown into closer contact with the nation by attending public functions, by his love for sport, and by his ability to enter into the life of the time. Even the radicals with socialist tendencies were prepared to grant him increased political power, and at his death he was universally mourned— not only at home where he had endeared himself to the hearts of his people, but also abroad. This is shown by his funeral which was attended by no less than eight crowned heads, many important ambassadors and by the representative of the United States. Never before has any man been so respected during his life and so honoured at his death. He had striven so hard for peace that perhaps it was fortunate he did not live to see the failure of his work in the world catastrophe of 1914.

In spite of the gravity of the political situation, few men realised—and, indeed, how could they have realised?—the full extent of the world calamity which was on the verge of taking place. Up till that time wars had been fought mainly by the soldiers themselves; science had not yet produced its death-dealing inventions for the mass slaughter of humanity.

Q

Rischgitz

AWAITING NEWS OF THE KING

King Edward's coronation was fixed for June 26, but two days before he was struck down with a serious illness and had to undergo an operation. He made a magnificent recovery, however, and in a fortnight was out of danger. The Coronation eventually took place on August 9 amid the great enthusiasm of the people.

Rischgitz

THE QUEEN REVIEWING THE TROOPS

During the king's illness, Queen Alexandra carried out some of the public duties which would have fallen to her husband. Here she is reviewing the Colonial troops on July 1, 1902. The beauty and grace which she brought to these functions soon won the hearts of the people. Queen Alexandra, the daughter of Christian IX of Denmark, had been married in 1863 to King Edward who received a grant of £40,000 a year from Parliament, exclusive of the revenues of the Duchy of Cornwall, now held by King George VI.

Rischgitz

PEACE DAY AT THE ROYAL EXCHANGE

Peace with the South Africans was signed on May 31, 1902. Its terms were very favourable to the Boers who agreed to accept British sovereignty, and who, in the Great War, fought side by side with their old enemies. It is interesting to note that Louis Botha, a Boer general, became the first Prime Minister of United South Africa.

Rischgitz

DEMONSTRATIONS AGAINST THE EDUCATION BILL

In 1902, a Bill was passed handing over the control of popular education to the County Councils and proposing to give grants out of the local rates to schools founded by religious bodies. This measure was very unpopular. Nonconformists, for example, objected to money being paid from the rates to help a Church of England school, and members of the Church of England objected to public money being used to help the Nonconformists. The passive resistance with which this Bill was met was overcome by a second Bill being passed two years later.

Rischgitz

OFFICERS OF THE FRENCH FLEET IN LONDON
King Edward VII is renowned for his activities in fostering friendly relations with other nations. In 1905, the officers of the French Fleet were entertained in London and this is a view of the procession on its way.

Rischgitz

EMPEROR OF GERMANY IN LONDON
Early in his reign Edward VII became known as Edward the Peacemaker. He concluded treaties with France, Spain, Italy, Germany and Portugal. In 1904 he paid a visit to Germany, and in 1907 this visit was returned by the German Emperor. About this time there was talk of antagonism between England and Germany, so in 1908, Edward paid another state visit to Germany, where he was well received, and which dispersed the cloud of distrust which had arisen, but the political situation was still very complicated.

Topical

FIRST FLIGHT ACROSS THE CHANNEL

The first men to fly in a power-driven machine were two brothers named Wright who made their first flight on December 17, 1903. They were followed by other pioneers, the most notable being Farman and Bleriot, two Frenchmen. In 1909, the latter won a thousand pound prize for the first man to fly across the Channel.

Topical

THE FIRST RACE MEETING AT BROOKLANDS

Brooklands motor racing track near Weybridge, Surrey, was first opened in 1907. Motor races had, however, taken place some years before this. In 1895, a race from Paris to Bordeaux and back again was won at an average speed of 15 m.p.h., and in 1900 the international Gordon-Bennett race was inaugurated. Brooklands is still the home of British motor racing, though the track is unsuitable for the highest speeds.

Rischgitz

FLEET STREET AND LUDGATE HILL THIRTY YEARS AGO

An interesting view looking down Fleet Street towards Ludgate Circus and St. Paul's at the beginning of the century. Horse traffic was still in general use, and though motor cars were known at this time, it was not until some years later that motor 'buses, taxis and private cars came into general use. Many of the advertisements are familiar to-day and the engine passing over the bridge at Ludgate Circus is noticeably modern in design. Clothes were smarter in those days and many of the men can be seen wearing silk hats and morning coats—a fashion which went out with the war. Fleet Street has for long been the home of journalism, and many relics of the past may still be seen round the interesting old courts and alleyways.

Rischgitz

DISTRIBUTING NEWSPAPERS IN PRE-WAR DAYS

Modern daily papers have complicated and highly efficient methods of distribution, with fast vans and organised sellers at the most advantageous points on the streets, as well as deliveries to newsagents, etc. In the early days of this century, distribution was necessarily much slower owing to the use of horse vehicles instead of motor traffic. Our newspaper organisation is to-day probably the most efficient in the world.

Rischgitz

WHEN TRAMS WERE DRAWN BY HORSES

Tramways had developed considerably since an Act was passed in 1870 facilitating the promotion of new companies. Horse trams were still in use, however, since electricity which had been tried in Birmingham as far back as 1890, had as yet proved unsatisfactory. In 1900, electricity was applied to an underground line in London and from then on it made rapid strides, both above and below ground, for many purposes.

Copyright, Russell & Sons, Southsea   Topical

A ROYAL FAMILY GROUP

This picture shows King Edward with members of his family during a visit which the Czar and Czarina of Russia paid to this country towards the end of King Edward's reign. The late King George and Queen Mary can be seen, together with the recent king, who is in naval uniform, and others of their children.

Topical

THE KING IS LAID TO REST

King Edward VII's brief reign came to a close with his death in 1910. Though he had been king for so short a while, his subjects had known him for many years as the Prince of Wales during his mother's long reign, and his passing was deeply mourned not only by his own people but also by other nations.

GEORGE V
1910-1936

THE early years of King George's reign were troubled by the serious state of affairs on the Continent and by the usual difficulties with the Irish. We have seen how, in Edward VII's reign, Europe became divided into two armed camps and how only a small spark was needed to set alight a blaze of international conflict. In Ireland the trouble arose out of Asquith's Home Rule Bill. This Bill would probably have been passed as the Lords, who had opposed previous Bills, were now, by the Parliament Act, only able to hold up a measure and not veto it altogether; but Ulster was very antagonistic to Home Rule and threatened civil war if they were in any way brought under the domination of the south—the Protestant Ulsterman hating the southern Catholics.

THE OUTBREAK OF WAR

Germany thought that England would never embark on a war when threatened with an Irish rebellion, but in 1914 both the Irish parties rallied to the English cause—with the exception of a minority of republicans known as Sinn Feiners, who caused a rebellion in Dublin in 1916 which had to be firmly suppressed.

The war into which for years Europe had been drifting was started by the murder at Sarajevo of the Archduke of Austria by two young Serbian students which led to the Austro-Serbian War.

THE COURSE OF THE WAR

First Russia and then France mobilized, and Germany declared war on each in turn. England asked Germany for a guarantee that Belgian territory would not be occupied and on receiving an ambiguous answer entered the war on the side of France and Russia.

The Germans invaded France, were checked by the heroic defence at Mons, but managed to get within twelve miles of Paris. At the critical moment they were defeated by a combined British and French force at the Battle of the Marne and forced to retire to the Aisne. Now began what is known as the race for the sea. The Germans hoped to capture the French ports and interfere with British trade, but they were stopped by the British after tremendous fighting round Ypres. Both sides now dug themselves in and a long period of trench warfare followed.

Meanwhile the Australian and New Zealand forces made a very gallant attack on Gallipoli—the object being to control the sea route up to the Black Sea so that supplies might be brought in to Russia. After desperate fighting on very unfavourable country, this attempt failed. In 1917 the Russians, who were badly organised, without food, clothing or amunition, revolted and went out of the war. Fortunately for the Allies, the United States came in, chiefly because of the sinking of the *Lusitania* in which many American lives were lost.

At sea Britain remained supreme in spite of German submarine attacks on her merchant vessels. Only one great battle was fought—at Jutland, where both sides suffered severe losses. The British fleet did not push home an initial advantage because Jellicoe quite rightly came to the conclusion that if he were defeated Britain would lose command of the sea and be forced to make peace. As it was, the German fleet never again came out to face the British.

In 1917, General Allenby captured Jerusalem and in 1918 Turkey surrendered to Britain, who took possession of Constantinople. The same year the Germans made a last desperate attack on the Western Front. At first they were successful, but on August 8th they were defeated and the Allies pushed them rapidly out of France. Austria capitulated on November 4, revolution broke out in Germany, the Kaiser abdicated, and the Armistice was signed on November 11.

THE PEACE TREATY

In January, 1919, the Peace Conference sat at Versailles, near Paris, and in June the Peace Treaty was signed. Small countries formerly included in the Austrian Empire—like Hungary and Czechoslovakia—received their independence; Alsace and Lorraine were returned to France, who had lost them in the Franco-Prussian War of 1870; German colonies in Africa and the Pacific, and territories which had been misgoverned by Turkey, were put under various powers to be trained in self-government and known as mandated territories; finally, Germany had to pay a huge sum in reparation for the damage caused by the war.

LEAGUE OF NATIONS

Largely due to the influence of President Wilson of the United States, the League of Nations was started. Powers signed a solemn covenant not to go to war without first submitting their dispute to the League; an international court of justice was set up at The Hague; the League of Nations was organised also for considerable social service; attacks on disease, the white slave trade and the use of drugs. The historian cannot foretell the future, but it may be that the success of the League of Nations will come through this social service more than through the difficult task of international arbitration.

England is still recovering from the effects of the Great War. Millions of men were thrown out of work, trade was crippled, and there was no work for the young men coming forward. By 1926 so little recovery had been made and wages were so poor that a general strike was declared by the workers. To the surprise of the world, this was settled without violence. In 1931 the world was swept by an economic depression, there was a crisis in England, the Government resigned, and a national party formed. Thanks, however, to the co-operation of the country, the crisis was surmounted and the work of recovery now progresses rapidly.

THE KING AND THE COUNTRY

Throughout the terrible times from 1914 to the present day, there has been one stable influence in the country and in the Empire. When crowned heads were falling all over the world, King George not only kept his popularity but increased it enormously. Never did he obtrude himself in party politics and his advice to his ministers came from a great fund of wisdom and experience untinged by any partisan feeling. In many countries the crown has been done away with and dictatorship substituted for democracy. Not so in England, where though in previous times the King was a despot he is now the bulwark against despotism. The monarchs of England, since the time of Victoria, have endeared themselves more and more to the hearts of the people, and although Edward VIII felt that he could not carry on this great tradition, it is quite safe to say that our present king, George VI, and his wife, Queen Elizabeth,

will preserve the bond of union between the Mother Country and the Dominions.

Let us consider some of the changes which have come about in the country since King George V came to the throne in 1910. At that time there was no wireless as we know it to-day—the B.B.C. did not start until 1922. There were few motor-cars and even those were very inefficient and uncomfortable. Flying was in its infancy—in 1910 Paulhan won a prize of £10,000 for the first flight from London to Manchester.

The development of all these things has made life much more hurried. News can be flashed round the world in a few seconds; even a small motor-car can travel at 50 m.p.h.; steamships have made sea travel infinitely speedier and more comfortable; mails are carried round the world in a few days by aeroplanes.

A FASTER WORLD

This development of transport has led not only to increased speed in social life, but to an increased speed in the commercial and political world. Quicker thought and quicker action is called for—and perhaps this is one of the chief reasons for the world being as unsettled as it is. Nations now know exactly what other nations at the other end of the world are doing; each is jostling up against each other, and it seems as if the world is too small to hold them all.

Fortunately, in spite of the difficulties which modern civilisation has engendered, we can look upon great improvements. Class snobbery is being broken down; living is cheaper; conditions are better; more people are educated and better educated; wealth is not now confined to the few.

Admittedly, there are troubles; admittedly, everything is not as it should be. But now we have seen the past we can also see that, in spite of all our present troubles, society is better off than it has ever been before, and that there is every hope that social welfare will continue to progress. Though there are still wars and rumours of wars there is nevertheless a rapidly growing feeling in favour of peace—particularly among the English-speaking countries which cover a very large part of the world.

During the reign of King George V we survived great dangers; continued to develop the resources of our country and build up a happier nation. It is for us to see that this work goes on. If we keep the peace, if we work for each other and not only for ourselves, we have the opportunity of building a new world based on freedom and justice.

L.E.A.

KING GEORGE V AND QUEEN MARY IN THEIR CORONATION ROBES

Edward VII died suddenly in 1910, and he was succeeded by his younger son, George V, whose elder brother, Prince Albert Victor, Duke of Clarence, had died in 1892. King George, in 1893, had married Mary, daughter of the Duke of Teck, who had previously been engaged to the Duke of Clarence. King George's reign proved to be a triumph for the monarchy—while other kings were falling he became more and more popular.

Topical

SUFFRAGETTES MARCH THROUGH LONDON
The movement in favour of votes for women started in the second half of the nineteenth century and grew rapidly. About the time of George V's accession its members resorted to violence and outrage to advertise their cause. Success came after the Great War when a vote was given to all women over twenty-one years of age.

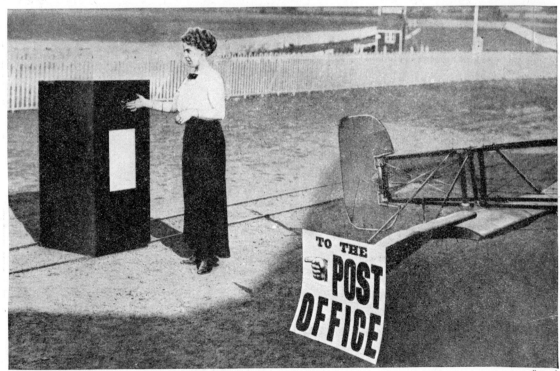

Topical

THE FIRST AIR MAIL
The air mail was first inaugurated in September, 1911. Here is a young lady posting a letter at Hendon to be delivered at Windsor. Air mail development was, of course, interrupted by the war, but since 1918 it has gone ahead at a great pace. It is now almost world-wide and every day sees great improvements—more frequent services, less time taken in transit and an increasing range of nations and towns served.

KING GEORGE V CROWNED EMPEROR OF INDIA

Topical

Shortly after his coronation in England, the king visited India where, at Delhi in September, 1911, he was crowned Emperor. Queen Victoria had been crowned Empress of India, but she did not visit India in person for the ceremony. At this ceremony the capital of India was transferred from Calcutta to Delhi.

London News Agency

THE KING AND THE KAISER

Edward VII had travelled extensively, and King George V followed his father's example. As a young man he had seen much of the world during a distinguished career in the navy. In 1913 he paid a visit to Germany where he is here seen driving in Berlin with the Kaiser. In 1914 he visited the French President in Paris but the Great War put an end to any further travels except for his visits to the front shown later.

THE SPARK THAT SET THE WORLD ABLAZE

In June, 1914, the heir to the Austrian Throne was murdered by a young Serbian fanatic named Princep, who is here seen being arrested immediately after the fatal shot was fired. Austria claimed that the murder was instigated by Serbia and war ensued. Russia prepared to help the Serbs and on her refusal to stop mobilizing, Germany came in against her. This was the signal for a general European conflagration.

ENGLAND DECLARES WAR

France was bound by treaty to help Russia and England, and had guaranteed to protect the neutrality of Belgium. Consequently when Germany marched through Belgium in an effort to catch France unprepared, Britain declared war on August 4. This picture shows the crowds round the Foreign Office awaiting news.

Sport and General

THE PRINCE OF WALES JOINS UP

Here is the Prince of Wales, and until Dec. 10, 1936, King Edward VIII, leading the Grenadier Guards on a route march. He was keen to see active service abroad and in spite of strong official opposition owing to the importance of his safety he succeeded in doing so, and was frequently under fire on the Western Front.

London News Agency

KING GEORGE V IN THE TRENCHES

Throughout the terrible years of the Great War the king not only did a tremendous amount of work at home, but he also took a personal interest in the soldiers themselves. He visited the Western Front and here he can be seen inspecting the trenches and the conditions in which the men had to live. These personal visits of King George did a great deal to keep up the morale of his soldiers which is so vitally important in war time.

Imperial War Museum

IN THE TRENCHES

The majority of the fighting on the Western Front took the form of trench warfare. Here is a typical scene, showing one of the soldiers on the look out, while his comrades are sleeping. Terrible weather often resulted in the trenches being half flooded—to the acute discomfort of the soldiers who had to live in them.

Imperial War Museum

BATTLE OF THE MARNE

During the first few weeks of the war the Germans advanced, driving the Allies before them, until they were within forty miles of Paris. In September the French mobilized all their available forces and with the help of the British defeated the Germans after desperate fighting at the Battle of the Marne, and so saved Paris.

Imperial War Museum

A HEROIC FAILURE

In the second year of the war forces were despatched to Gallipoli, one of the objects being to gain control over the Dardanelles and form a liaison with the Russians through the Black Sea. Landing on a barren coast in the face of enemy guns, and without cover, the troops fought magnificently, but the Turks had been forewarned and it was soon realised that a rapid advance was impossible. After nine months of fruitless endeavour, the British troops were successfully evacuated, leaving the enemy in occupation of Gallipoli.

Imperial War Museum

A GREAT NAVAL EXPLOIT

As the war proceeded, the German submarines became a definite menace to Britain's food supplies. Their main base was the Belgian ports, Ostend and Zeebrugge, and to block these ports the famous "Zeebrugge Raid" was undertaken, when an old battleship, the *Vindictive*, was deliberately sunk in the harbour. The blockade was further secured by the sinking of a German destroyer near the entrance.

Topical

THE END OF THE GREAT WAR
The Armistice was signed on November 11, 1918, and in May the following year, a conference was held at Versailles, near Paris, to decide on terms of peace. The difficulties of reaching a lasting settlement were tremendous and the results of the Versailles Treaty are still being anxiously watched in the world to-day.

Topical

A LEADING STATESMAN
One of England's chief representatives at the Versailles Conference was David Lloyd George who is seen here with the king and Prince of Wales at Victoria Station in June, 1919. Mr. Lloyd George, who is still a great orator, has been one of England's most prominent statesmen since the reign of Edward VII.

Topical

THE PRINCE VISITS AUSTRALIA

The Prince of Wales, following in the tradition of his father and grandfather, travelled widely, not only to all parts of the British Empire, but to other countries as well. In 1919 he visited Australia and here he is seen receiving an enthusiastic reception at Perth. On the front of the car are the three feathers—his crest.

Topical

STREET FIGHTING IN DUBLIN

At the beginning of the war, an extreme party called Sinn Fein arose in Ireland which demanded complete freedom. This quarrel was shelved as far as possible during the war, but it broke out again in 1920. Ireland was granted Dominion status, but De Valera and his followers were not satisfied, and there was fighting for another year. De Valera is to-day the dominant influence in the politics of the Irish Free State.

Topical

KING GEORGE V AT WEMBLEY

In 1924 a great exhibition was held at Wembley in which every part of the British Empire was represented. The object was to encourage Empire trade, and the king, always vitally interested in such matters, may be seen here inspecting a representation of a West African village which he examined during his visit.

Topical

THE LOCARNO TREATY

Quarrels between France and Germany over the Rhine frontier had been going on for generations and in 1925 an attempt was made to settle the trouble. By the Locarno Treaty, France, Belgium, Britain and Italy agreed to guarantee the Rhine frontier. That is to say, the powers which signed the Locarno Treaty would support either France or Germany against the aggression of the other. There has been much discussion about the Locarno Treaty in recent months and it is possible that some revision will have to be made.

Topical

MODERN TRAFFIC "ROUNDABOUTS"

London streets were never built to hold the tremendous traffic that exists to-day and new methods of controlling it had to be evolved. One of these methods was to do away with cross roads wherever possible and establish "roundabouts." Here is an example of the new system in successful operation in Piccadilly Circus.

Topical

THE GENERAL STRIKE

In 1926 the country was paralysed for ten days by a general strike, due to the greater part of the organised workers supporting the coal miners in their resistance to further reductions of their already low wage. To the amazement of the rest of the world, apart from a few incidents, there were no serious riots and no bloodshed. The proverbial good sense of the Englishman asserted itself both among the strikers and the temporary workers.

END OF A GREAT FLIGHT

One of the greatest pilots who has been preparing the way for regular overseas services is Sir Alan Cobham who in 1925 flew to Cape Town and back, and the following year to Australia and back. He is seen here alighting on the Thames in front of the Houses of Parliament at the successful end of the latter flight.

THE FASTEST MACHINE ON LAND

For many years Sir Malcolm Campbell has held the land speed record in his 2,500 h.p. "Bluebird" car. Since 1931 he has raised the world's record from 246 m.p.h. to 301 m.p.h., thus achieving his ambition to be the first man to travel at 300 m.p.h. Here is the record-breaking car which Sir Malcolm demonstrated at Brooklands before a large and enthusiastic crowd. One of the difficulties of high speed record breaking is to find a suitable place to do it. This last record was broken at Salt Lake in the United States of America.

Topical

AN INTREPID AIRWOMAN

Miss Amy Johnson, now Mrs. Mollison, is one of our most famous pilots. In May, 1930, she flew nearly ten thousand miles to Australia, and since then she has made many famous flights including one to the Cape of Good Hope in a little over four days. Here she is after landing from her recent two-way record to the Cape.

Topical

A FAMOUS RECORD-BREAKING TRAIN

Not only have there been great developments in the air and on the road, but the railways also have been going ahead rapidly. England now boasts the fastest long-distance steam train in the world, the L.N.E.R. "Silver Jubilee" which runs between Newcastle and King's Cross at an average speed of 67 m.p.h. Here is one of the most famous of the great L.N.E.R. engines, "The Cock o' the North" running at speed.

Sport and General

A GREAT SPORTSMAN

King George took a great interest in all sporting events, many of which he attended personally. He is seen here at Twickenham shaking hands with the Scottish team before a Rugby International against England.

Sport and General

A FAVOURITE SUMMER SPORT

The years following the Great War have seen a tremendous growth of interest in sport of all kinds. Football draws vast crowds through the winter, and in the summer tennis courts in parks and clubs are crowded with players and spectators. Here we see a match at Wimbledon between Germany and the U.S.A. The friendly rivalry of sport helps to cement international friendships. The Davis Cup for which these countries are competing is a world-wide international tennis championship started in 1900 by an American, Mr. Dwight Davis. Wimbledon is the Mecca of lawn tennis enthusiasts and here the world championships are held.

A SWIMMERS' PARADISE

Sport and General

Swimming is another healthy recreation of modern days, and here we see a crowded open-air swimming pool. The love of the open air is clearly shown, too, by the crowds of cyclists, hikers, and motorists, who set off every week-end to spend their leisure hours away from the noisy and crowded streets of the cities.

Courtesy Metro-Goldwyn-Mayer

ONE OF THE TWENTIETH CENTURY'S GREATEST INVENTIONS

Probably the most popular amusement which has developed during the twentieth century is the cinema which, with the recent introduction of sound and colour, becomes more and more realistic every day. Here we see the stars Ronald Colman, Elizabeth Allan and others at work in the studio on a picture taken from Dickens' great novel *A Tale of Two Cities*. The most recent invention is the introduction of television.

London News Agency

THE " NATIONAL " GOVERNMENT, 1931

Britain had been swept by an economic blizzard. In 1931 the Labour Government, the majority of whose members refused to accept the proposed economy " cuts," was driven from office, and Mr. Macdonald formed a " National " Government consisting of Conservatives, Liberals and a sprinkling of his Labour colleagues.

Topical

GANDHI IN ENGLAND

Gandhi, as an Indian political leader, aimed to secure the total independence of his country from British rule. From 1922-1924 and on other occasions he was imprisoned for non-violent Civil Disobedience. In 1931 he attended the Round Table Conference in London which met to discuss Indian affairs and administration. Gandhi was born in 1868, educated at London University and called to the Bar, returning to India in 1891.

Topical

KING GEORGE V AT TEMPLE BAR

The king, by ancient custom, must ask permission of the Lord Mayor before he can enter the City of London in state. Here he is seen, accompanied by Queen Mary, receiving the Pearl Sword at Temple Bar on the occasion of his Silver Jubilee while the procession was on its way to the service at St. Paul's Cathedral.

Topical

THE JUBILEE PROCESSION

The affection the people of the Empire had for King George V, was amply demonstrated at his Jubilee. Rarely has London witnessed such scenes of rejoicing as when the royal procession drove through London on its way to St. Paul's Cathedral and back to Buckingham Palace. Rarely has the world seen such a moving scene.

THE KING WHO WAS NEVER CROWNED

On January 20, 1936, King George V died, and on January 22 the Prince of Wales was proclaimed king as Edward VIII. It was no mean task to be called upon to follow his beloved father, but his early training had been such that the nation and the Empire looked forward to the reign of a man who had endeared himself so much to them. As Prince of Wales he had toured the whole Empire and his visits to the distressed areas at home brought new hope to those who, for many years, have suffered the terrible consequences of the economic depression. The whole world was waiting expectantly for May 12, 1937, the appointed date for the Coronation. But it was not to be. The king had informed the Prime Minister, Mr. Baldwin, that he intended to marry an American lady, and in doing so he had asked whether a morganatic marriage, excluding any issue of such a marriage from the succession, would be acceptable. The Prime Minister, on behalf of the nation and the Empire, replied that such a marriage would not be acceptable to the Cabinet. On receiving this reply, the king, unwilling to raise a constitutional crisis, or to give grounds for the raising of a ''king's party,'' abdicated on December 10, 1936, in favour of his brother, the Duke of York.

KING GEORGE VI AND QUEEN ELIZABETH

The Accession Council was held at St. James's Palace on December 12, 1936, to whom the new king made the following Declaration:

"Your Royal Highnesses, My Lords and Gentlemen—I meet you to-day in circumstances which are without parallel in the history of our country. Now that the duties of Sovereignty have fallen on Me I declare to you My adherence to the strict principles of Constitutional Government and My resolve to work before all else for the welfare of the British Commonwealth of Nations. With My Wife as helpmeet by My side, I take up the heavy task which lies before Me. In it I look for the support of all My peoples.

"Furthermore, My first act on succeeding My Brother will be to confer on Him a dukedom, and He will henceforth be known as His Royal Highness The Duke of Windsor."

The new King took the style of George VI. And so opens a new chapter in British history.

INDEX

INDEX

Made and Printed in Great Britain by Odhams (Watford) Limited Watford, Herts.

SHAKE